Chaos of disciplines

Chaos of disciplines

ANDREW ABBOTT

THE UNIVERSITY OF CHICAGO PRESS

CHICAGO AND LONDON

ANDREW ABBOTT is the Ralph Lewis Professor and
chair of the Department of Sociology at the University of
Chicago. He is author of *Department and Discipline:
Chicago Sociology at One Hundred* (1999) and *The System
of Professions: An Essay on the Division of Expert Labor*
(1988), both published by the University of Chicago Press.

The University of Chicago Press, Chicago 60637
The University of Chicago Press, Ltd., London
© 2001 by The University of Chicago
All rights reserved. Published 2001
Printed in the United States of America

10 09 08 07 06 05 04 03 02 01   1 2 3 4 5

ISBN: 0-226-00100-8 (cloth)
ISBN: 0-226-00101-6 (paper)

An earlier version of chapter 2 appeared as "Positivism
and Interpretation in Sociology," *Sociological Forum* 5 (1990):
435–58; reprinted by permission of *Sociological Forum*. An
earlier version of chapter 4 appeared as "History and
Sociology: The Lost Synthesis," *Social Science History* 15
(1991): 201–38; reprinted by permission of
Duke University Press.

Library of Congress Cataloging-in-Publication Data

Abbott, Andrew Delano.
   Chaos of disciplines / Andrew Abbott.
      p.   cm.
   Includes bibliographical references and index.
   ISBN 0-226-00100-8 (cloth : alk. paper)—ISBN 0-226-
00101-6 (pbk. : alk. paper)
   1. Sociology—Philosophy. 2. Social sciences—
Philosophy. I. Title.

HM585.A23   2000
301'.01—dc21
                                          00-055182

FOR SUE

Contents

Preface

WHEN I went to college, I majored in something called "History and Lit," with a special focus on England in the eighteenth and nineteenth centuries. Supposedly there was a History and Lit method, but I never figured it out. In my first year, I would go to tutorial with another student, named Jay. We would be talking about Fielding or Pitt or Walpole and he would say something insightfully psychological. So when our tutor Harold would turn to me with the next question, I would make some psychological remark. Harold's face would fall and he would turn to Jay, who would at once make some deft economic argument. Harold's face would light up. I would try economics on the next go-round, evoke the same resigned reaction, and watch Jay glide successfully on to a subtle political analysis. By the time I tried politics, he was back with psychology. I was always out of fashion, unable to see which analysis was right for which question.

I have always been a little too eclectic. Unable to make up my mind whether to be a scientist or a humanist, I learned what I could about both. I took most of my college courses outside my major (maybe that's why I never figured it out), drifting toward graduate school with no idea of what field to enter. I chose sociology because more than any other social science sociology would let me do what I pleased. If I went into sociology, I wouldn't have to make up my mind what to do. An accident helped. My one graduate school application outside sociology—to the University of Chicago's Committee on Social Thought—was rejected because I misunderstood the application instructions and sent some of the materials to sociology instead. As a result, I got admitted to (and attended and eventually became chairman of) the Chicago sociology department, a department to which, according to my own understanding of the admissions process, I had never applied.

An eclectic is always losing arguments. One lacks the closed-mindedness necessary to treat others' positions with the contempt they so easily display for one's own. Of course in interaction I fake this contempt as well as the next academic. But I usually rush off to bone up on what I have just been denying. And I have never managed that happy disregard of whole areas of intellectual life—mathematics, say, or history—that so simplifies the lives of some of my colleagues.

In pursuit of eclecticism, I have for the last fifteen years tried to eradicate some obnoxious intellectual boundaries, in particular that between interpretive and positivistic work in sociology and kindred fields. I girded myself in some theory and some methods and went a-tilting at this windmill in the name of a Dulcinea I called "narrative positivism." There resulted a lot of ill will from narrativists and positivists who, although deeply interested in interdisciplinarity, didn't want to be mentioned in the same breath. For each, I was the vanguard of the hated other. Indeed an eclectic is always being attacked for ignoring what he in fact takes for granted. Once after I had given a paper at Rutgers's interdisciplinary center about ten years ago, a graduate student in history pulled me aside and told me, with quiet confidence, "You know, you really ought to read this guy Goffman."

It was in fact an earlier paper presented at this center, in September of 1986, that contained my first discussion of the ideas undergirding this book. The book originated in my attempt to understand people's reactions to my eclecticism. Over the years that I have mulled over these questions, the chief institutional support for my work on them has been the Social Science History Association. My original reflections were presented at SSHA meetings, with the encouragement and support of people like Daniel Scott Smith and Eric Monkkonen. Two of the book's chapters—those on constructionism and historical sociology—had their first appearances at SSHA meetings (in 1991 and 1990 respectively). The chapter on historical sociology was published in an earlier version by the association's journal, *Social Science History*, in 1991. The construction chapter has circulated fairly widely in a photocopied version, under the more zingy (or more offensive, depending on how you look at it) title of "So Reality Is Socially Constructed: So What?" In any case, SSHA has been the only association in my experience where true eclecticism reigns amid intense personal commitments to particular paradigms and subject matters.

The two other chapters on "fractal distinctions," although sharing the intellectual program of the SSHA papers, first appeared elsewhere. Chapter 2 (on stress) was first presented to the Department of Sociology and Anthropology and the Hispanic Research Center at Fordham University in 1987, an invitation for which I have to thank Doyle McCarthy and John Huckle. It was in this empirical investigation of a single substantive scientific literature that I first began to imagine a general theoretical analysis for scholarly disagreements. An earlier version of this paper appeared in print, after much stress indeed, in *Sociological Forum* in 1990.

The general essay on fractal distinctions (chapter 1) came later. It was my inaugural lecture in the Social Science Division at Chicago in 1993. This was a great occasion, complete with friendly hecklers and frowning doubters—a rowdy but more or less receptive crowd. I have tamed the platform style a little (only a little) for this published version.

While I was elaborating this cultural analysis of disciplines and their antics, however, I had a related insight about social structures. It was an insight many others had had before, the first of them (as far as I can figure out) being the great anthropologist Evans-Pritchard. This insight was that many social structures look the same in large scale and in small scale. I first ran into a clear example of this phenomenon in the work of a Rutgers colleague, anthropologist Michael Moffatt. After a sufficient number of other examples built up in my files, I wrote (in 1988) the original draft of chapter 6, which has enjoyed a decade-long life in photocopy circulation under the title of "Self-Similar Social Structures." That draft contained a short speculation about fractal distinctions, derived from the 1987 stress paper, which gradually blew up into the four chapters that begin this book.

Chapters 5 and 7 were written for this book in 1997–99. All the earlier papers had long existed in draft or even published form by that point, but had been set aside during the grinding years (1993–96) that I held the Mastership of the Social Science Collegiate Division at Chicago. Chapter 5 aims to place the four preceding chapters in social structural and historical context. It obviously owes much to my earlier work on the professions. Less evidently but no less strongly, it is indebted to the practical experience I gained as a dean trying to facilitate (ameliorate?) the intellectual gyrations of one of the world's great collections of social scientists.

Chapter 7 emerged out of a long, friendly, and slightly tipsy argument with Paula England and others at a dinner after an ASA Publications Committee meeting in December 1994. I lost the argument, as usual, but the experience stimulated my theoretical thinking. An essay on morals, this chapter is very different from anything else I have published. My work contains fewer overt moral and political judgments than that of many of my peers. In part this is because I believe in keeping such judgments out of academic work (and indeed because I believe that exclusion to be possible) and in part because I am simply less committed to changing various aspects of the world than are many friends and colleagues. But I hope in this essay to extend the book's general argument into an understanding of the relation between moral-political and academic judgment, a topic that has disturbed me since I first read Kant's *Critique of Judgment* in my second year of graduate school. (Unlike many friends, I did not find either Weber's or Marx's views of this problem to be close to my own.)

While a principled defense of eclecticism and indeed of a certain form of relativism is the personal aim of the book, understanding recent developments in sociology is its substantive one. I have felt the tensions between eclecticism and single-minded dedication most clearly within my own career and have worked out my theory by reflecting on that issue of personal concern. So the book reacts directly to developments in sociology over the last thirty years: the deaths of Parsonianism and of labeling theory, the rise of Marxism and historical sociology and the new sociology of science, the dominance of a certain style of empiricism, the varying guises of social constructionism, and so on. Another way of reading this book, then, is as a rather cranky study of a discipline: opinionated, but nonetheless somewhat supported by evidence.

My intellectual debts remain as ever. My colleagues at Chicago have been supportive and exciting. In the files I find written comments on various of these papers from a wide variety of colleagues here and elsewhere: Harrison White, Joe Hopper, Raine Daston, Tom Gieryn, Bernice Pescosolido, Alan Sica, John Comaroff, and a whole host of students in the Indiana University Sociology Department, who commented en masse on chapter 1. The book also reflects the subtle reading of Susan Gal. But I should not list. I have talked about these ideas with so many people that it is impossible to list them. I simply acknowledge, as does the book's theory, that all my ideas ultimately come from others.

On the material side, I should note the kind support of the Warden and Fellows of Nuffield College in the University of Oxford. I redrafted chapter 6 and began chapter 7 while on a short stay at Nuffield in Hilary Term 1998 and completed final (well, almost final) revisions of the whole manuscript during another visit in Trinity Term of 1999. There is no greater gift to an overworked academic than quiet solitude in a well-supported environment away from his normal commitments. This Nuffield has repeatedly given me, and I am very grateful.

Setting out one's personal acknowledgments feels a little bit like writing to a college alumni bulletin. "Susie and I are still married and living in Scarsdale," etc. Corny, but true. As it happens, Sue and I are still married and happy in Chicago. Over the decade or more that this book has taken to develop, the degeneration of AT&T has wrought havoc in Susan's work life and Woody arrived to uproot us with new pleasures and pains. Sue and Woody have put up with more self-absorption and pettiness on my part than anyone should have to endure. Lest the reader make the mistake I sometimes do, let me be clear that by empirical indicators my son's arrival vastly improved my academic productivity.

I have dedicated the book as a whole to my wife, who has supported me so steadily through the long years this argument has taken to come into focus. Individual chapters I dedicate to individuals, following the practice of Ravel in "Le tombeau de Couperin." Chapter 1 to Colin Lucas, at whose kind invitation it was written and whose knowledge of life's complexities surpasses any attempt to theorize it. Chapter 2 to George Levine, who supported my original thinking on disciplines and who kept me going in dark intellectual times at Rutgers. Chapter 3 to Carolyn Williams in the hope that she might finally learn why I wasn't as excited as she about literary theory in the mid-1980s. Chapter 4 to Daniel Scott Smith, who published early work of mine on the history–social science border when nobody else would. Chapter 5 to the memory of Morris Janowitz, who forced me to think ecologically and structurally about social life. Chapter 6 to the memory of E. E. Evans-Pritchard, who stated many of its central ideas long ago, and whose honest, heartfelt, and humane anthropology has always seemed to me the very model of scholarly work. Chapter 7 to the memory of Harry Bredemeier, who helped me live through the alienating early years of my instructorship at Rutgers and who demanded that I give up my distanced position and take up moral questions. These are people I have learned from and argued with. The life of the mind gives nothing better.

Nuffield College, Oxford
June 1999

Prologue

EVERY SPRING the MCAT examinations select the medical elite from among the upper extreme of the college population in terms of scientific and rational abilities and attitudes. But three years later those selected will choose specialties ranging from psychiatry to family practice to cardiology, thereby replicating within the compass of medicine the entire humanistic-rationalistic scale that the MCAT defines on the college population as a whole.

On the other side of the world, the great hierarchy of the caste system relegates certain groups so firmly to the bottom as to exclude them from the four varnas altogether. Yet among these excluded harijans, an internal hierarchy exactly replicates the much larger one that places them beneath all the caste Hindus.

These two social structures have a peculiar property in common: the property of self-similarity. No matter what the level at which we inspect them, we find the same pattern repeated. Nor is this simply a matter of looking at a linear scale in progressively finer detail. The world of medicine covers much more than just those in the upper extreme of scientism, just as some harijans enjoy substantial authority and power in their daily existence. These are truly self-similar structures, in which fine detail recapitulates gross structure.

A similar pattern emerges in cultural systems. At any given time the avant-garde of art is itself broken up into a thousand little cells, each imagining itself to be the true avant-avant-garde, leading those who will lead the general art public. Similarly, just as psychiatric practice offers a category system explaining everyday life to the average denizens of modernity, so does psychoanalysis offer an explanatory system to the psychiatrists who treat everyman. Or, to come suddenly close to home, if we take any group of sociologists and lock them in a room, they will argue and at once differentiate themselves into positivists and interpretivists. But if we separate those two groups and lock *them* in separate rooms, *those* two groups will each in turn divide over exactly the same issue.

Thus cultural structures too may have the characteristic of self-similarity. In the book that follows, I apply this argument about cultural self-similarity to a particular example, holding that self-similarity provides a general account of how knowledge actually changes in social science. I begin with a theoretical and general analysis. This leads into three chapters of examples, one analyzing the stress literature of the 1970s and 1980s, one discussing the vagaries of arguments about "social construction," and one discussing the transitions of historical sociology. This section of the book closes with a chapter-length discussion of academic disciplines and their structure, a discussion that turns the book toward the theme of social structure.

The book's two final essays take the analysis to new venues. In chapter 6, I complete the turn from cultural to social systems, making the case that self-similarity is an important general form of social structure. A short chapter appendix examines self-similarity as a general mode for the perception of cultural and social structures. Chapter 7 makes the more extravagant move of applying a self-similar logic to the relation between thought and practice, and indeed to moral judgments themselves.

My general aim is to establish self-similarity as a fundamental modality of structure in human affairs. I regret that the social structural and moral arguments are as undeveloped as they are here, represented by only one chapter each. But the larger claim really rests on a comprehensive theory of the social process, and that must await another book.

I begin then with self-similarity in cultural structures.

SELF-SIMILARITY IN SOCIAL SCIENCE

1

The Chaos of
Disciplines

HOW DOES social science change? In its complex history some see immanent trajectories, others see local practices. Some see political determination, others see internal competition. I shall here set forth yet another theoretical account of changes both in social science in general and in sociology in particular. The mechanism proposed is a very general one, applying equally well to other kinds of interacting cultural systems—the plastic arts, music, perhaps even language. But it is best seen in a particular case, and so I shall analyze this very familiar example.

I write about sociology partly because it is my own discipline. But it is also the most general of the social sciences, or, to put it less politely, the least defined. So it provides within a single disciplinary compass examples of many of the processes I am discussing at the level of social science in general. As the reader will see, the idea that a subset of a larger unit can contain scaled-down versions of structures and processes in that larger unit—the idea of micro-cosm—is central to my argument. The immediate result here is that in this chapter I shall switch back and forth (or perhaps better, up

---

For those who happen to have read my book *Department and Discipline* (Abbott 1999a), let me point out that the first five chapters of the present book respond to the promise in the final sentence of that earlier one—they discuss how social science must work if we take the view that its cultural structure is comprehensively indexical. (Of course this book was in fact all but complete when the "earlier" one was finished.) As such, this book continues the program, hinted at in *Department and Discipline*, of creating a social theory of contexts (temporal and structural), a project that in turn derives (logically but not biographically) from yet another half-finished book entitled *Time and Social Structure*. From the reader's point of view then, chapter 1 of this book follows immediately from chapter 7 of *Department and Discipline*. I dedicate this chapter to Colin Lucas, Vice Chancellor of the University of Oxford.

and down) between talking about sociology and talking about social
science.[1]

The mechanism I propose is in the first instance purely cultural;
my account is, in that sense, internalist. By contrast, most current
views of intellectual succession are externalist; knowledge is somehow wed to power and power propels change.[2] But I shall treat both
sociology and social science as more or less autonomous bodies of
thought under their own rules. I do not challenge the foundational
uncertainties of modern epistemology; there is indeed not one sociology but many. But the way those many sociologies interact betrays
a common pattern, a universal knowledge upon whose terrain the
local knowledges wander. No one can deny the importance of local
knowledges and practices—what people call sectarian subdisciplines or alternative epistemologies depending on their academic
politics. But I am here more interested in the larger but implicit
framework such local knowledges end up making together.

---

1. A simple form of this notion of self-similarity—the idea that man is a microcosm of the macrocosmic universe—is a long-standing staple of philosophy, and in
particular was a commonplace of much of ancient Greek thought. I am unaware of a
version that saw microcosms as multiply nested in the manner of fractals, although
one could imagine such a view as implied by various versions of the "great chain of
being" (Lovejoy 1960).

2. As many people have remarked, there is an obvious "externalist" account for
the recent French revival of the idea (originally in Marx) of an intimate connection
between knowledge and power; in French, the two words rhyme.

This is as good a place as any to warn the reader not to expect a review of prior
writing in the sociology or philosophy of science. One might ask (both reviewers of
the manuscript did) how this book relates to Whitley 1984 or Fuchs 1992 or even
Collins 1998. The answer is easy; other than sharing some subject matter, it doesn't
relate to them much at all. Whitley referred complex contingencies in disciplinary
development to the outcome of a series of variables. Fuchs follows in the same tradition, attributing variety in scientific production to various antecedent organizational
variables. Both follow precisely the kind of approach that I have rejected in my work
on professions (1988a) and my various attacks on the variables paradigm (1988b; 1998;
1999a, chap. 7). Moreover, neither book has much of an account of the origin of ideas
(only of styles of ideas), whereas the present book does. Collins's book is a mass of
facts undigested by the sketchy theory he applies to them, whereas the present book
is mainly a book of theory, illustrated by some detailed and some not-so-detailed
examples.

More broadly, this is not a book about the sociology of academic disciplines, but
a book using the example of the sociology of academic disciplines to set forth an
argument that is much more general. The true intellectual sources of my views on
symbolic systems lie in the theory of culture as it was before it was overrun by the
textual glitterati. I grew up on the Cassirer-Langer-Mead philosophy of knowledge,
the Kuhnian sociology of science, the Marxist theory of ideology, and the classical
tradition of social and cultural anthropology from Malinowski to the early Geertz.
But as the book before you will argue, these are just my personal footnotes for what
are in fact generally available ideas. Part of the message of the book lies in its attempt
to step out of the metaphor of cumulation. So again, there will be no review of the
literature, whether in sociology of science or beyond it.

My interest in that larger implicit framework is both theoretical and practical. On the one hand, I feel that an understanding of it will clarify the relations between various subsets of social science and sociology. Knowing the framework simplifies—perhaps even explains—those relations. But on the other hand, I also feel that a focus on the larger framework is not merely intellectually useful as an idea, but also normatively proper as a commitment. That is, we should become explicit about what is implicit in our practices. For our debates within the social sciences about "universalism" and "local knowledge" have obscured the fact that the vast majority of social scientists share the moral project of knowing society in a way that everyone else in society thinks of as universalist. We can try to add "the voice of the unheard" to our work, but the unheard know very well that social science is something other than their world, that it is addressed to someone other than them. The project of social science as a definable enterprise is, in reality, the production of sharable, "universal" knowledge of society. We ought to stop kidding ourselves that it is not.[3]

But the larger, universal framework for social science is by no means the standard, often-parodied axiomatic structure. Rather it resembles what the Romans called the law of peoples (*ius gentium*), a law that they applied to diverse groups at the edges of the empire and that they distinguished from the formalized civil law (*ius civile*) that applied specifically to Roman citizens. There is no universal social scientific knowledge of the latter kind—systematic, axiomatic, universal in a contentless sense. There is only universal knowledge of the former kind, a universal knowledge emerging from accommodation and conflict rather than from axioms, a universal knowledge that provides tentative bridges between local knowledges rather than systematic maps that deny them, a universal knowledge that aims, like the *ius gentium*, at allowing interchange among people who differ fundamentally.[4]

1. The Interstitial Character of Sociology

I begin by noting a defining characteristic of sociology—the fact that the discipline is not very good at excluding things from itself.

---

3. As the argument will make clear and as I shall show in detail in chapter 7, the debate just summarized provides yet another example of a self-similar social structure. It re-creates within the academic community the larger opposition between various partisan groups in the "real world" and the universalists of academia.

4. On *ius gentium* and *ius civile*, see Paton 1964. An obvious implication of this view of "universal" knowledge, one that I shall sketch in chapter 7 and explore in a book tentatively entitled *Methods of Discovery*, is that social science methodology

Not that particular topic areas haven't been excluded; the study of women's lives, for example. But once such an area makes a claim for sociological attention, the discipline doesn't have any *intellectually* effective way of denying that claim. So sociology has become a discipline of many topics—always acquiring them, seldom losing them.

Styles of sociological thought have this character as much as do subject areas. The many sociologists who deny that sociology is a science have not persuaded their scientific colleagues that sociology is humanistic. Conversely, for every sociologist who thinks causal analysis important there is another who pursues narrative explanations. For every sociologist who believes in objective knowledge, another denies it. For every reflective interpretivist there is a rigorous positivist.[5]

Sociology, in short, is irremediably interstitial. In fact, this interstitiality is what undergirds sociology's claims as a general social science, claims not necessarily justified by its contributions in theory, method, or substance. Rather, sociology's claim as the most general social science rests on its implicit and fuddled claim that "no form of knowledge [about society] is alien to it."[6] The discipline is rather like a caravansary on the Silk Road, filled with all sorts and types of people and beset by bandit gangs of positivists, feminists, interactionists, and Marxists, and even by some larger, far-off states like Economics and the Humanities, all of whom are bent on reducing the place to vassalage. The inhabitants put up with occasional rule by these gangs and pay them tribute when necessary, but when somebody more interesting comes along, they throw off the current overlords with little regret.[7]

This interstitial quality of sociology recapitulates locally the rela-

---

ought to consist of a flexible series of "ways of changing what we are currently doing" rather than a fixed list of possible modes of analysis.

5. As a result, general sociological discourse consists of dire prophecies of disciplinary demise from one embattled oracle or another, even while the discipline muddles along ignoring the prophets' advice.

6. After all, the "classics" of sociology—Marx, Weber, Durkheim, et al.—were in fact general social scientists, not sociologists in the modern sense. The "no form . . . to it" is a paraphrase of Terence, *Heauton Timoroumenos*, 1.77.

7. This caravansary quality can be illustrated by sociology's sources of faculty; in my own department, less than half of the faculty were undergraduate majors in sociology. Most are people who stopped by sociology along the road and just settled down there.

The reader may well ask whether such generalism will not wither in competition with other, specialist disciplines, much as the towns of the Silk Road eventually died from the single-minded force of empires. I leave until later in the volume my full answer. For the moment let us recall that generalism may be an excellent strategy in an age of interdisciplinary study and university reorganization and shrinkage, an age when the caravansary seems like a better model for real-world organizations like firms, markets, and states than the model of formal organization so recently popular. An interesting set of review essays on sociology is Halliday and Janowitz 1992.

tion of the social sciences in general to the natural sciences and humanities. The social sciences stand uneasily between these other modes of knowledge, the mode of facts and the mode of values. In its modern version, this placing of social knowledge in the gap between facts and values derives from Kant. It is revealing to study the exact way in which Kant did this.

As is well known, Kant began his analysis of knowledge by splitting knowledge into pure and practical reason: the knowledge on the one hand of the natural and on the other of the moral world. The first of these was mediated by objective cognition, the second by the intuition of freedom. What Kant put asunder few indeed have reunited.[8]

Yet Kant himself repented. In his third *Critique*, he introduced the concept of "judgment" to cover the gap between facts and moralities, and it is in the opening pages of that book that we can see him deciding where in his system to place knowledge of social life. He tells us that when the will behaves in a routine way attributable to some "natural concept," rules describing the will's behavior are "technically practical principles" that lie under the pure (that is, the cognitive or scientific) reason.[9] Among the examples of such "precepts" is statesmanship (along with housekeeping, farming, the art of conversation, and the prescribing of diet!).[10] Since statesmanship here refers to rule-based knowledge of how people are likely to behave, it is plain that Kant considers some large portion of social science to consist of such "technically practical principles" under the pure reason.

But this means that Kant's dualism begins to collapse. The first two critiques make a chasm between the world of knowledge (pure reason) and that of action (practical reason). Yet here in the third critique certain kinds of rules of *action* are placed under the *pure* reason because they refer to "lawlike" regularities of action. Thus, Kant first makes an overall distinction between pure and practical reason, but then here within the pure reason, he again distinguishes a pure and a practical reason.

Kant made the same move within the practical reason, although not in the *Critique of Judgment*. In various works on politics, he defines the laws of human commonwealths as quasi-natural constraints on the moral individual's transcendentally free activity.[11]

8. Throughout this particular discussion, "practical" means "having to do with action" (*praxis*, in Greek), not "useful in an everyday way."

9. Kant 1968:8.

10. Kant 1968:9.

11. My general sources here are "Perpetual Peace," "Universal History" (both in Kant 1963), and "On the Old Saw: That May Be Right in Theory but It Won't Work in Practice" (Kant 1974).

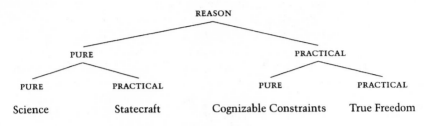

Figure 1.1

Thus, in the essay "On the Old Saw: That May Be Right in Theory but It Won't Work in Practice," he says, "Law is the limitation of each man's freedom to the condition of its consistency with everyone's freedom to the extent possible in accordance with a universal law."[12] Kant's aim in "The Old Saw" is to set aside worldly wisdom (the craftlike statesmanship that he identified as the *practical* part of *pure* reason in the third critique) in favor of these "duty-creating" constraints that keep transcendentally free individuals out of each other's way. Such constraints construct a quasi-natural, cognizable social world within the transcendental realm of free individuals, thus separating the world of *practical* reason into this pure (cognitive) part and the other, practical (transcendentally free) part.

But this last is precisely the same distinction that Kant made under the pure reason, a distinction that itself recapitulated the overall distinction of pure and practical reason. In summary, Kant has first split pure and practical reason and then, under *each* of those headings, has split pure and practical reason once again (see fig. 1.1).

I want to draw two morals from this philosophical excursus. First, the subject matter of social science has by this procedure been made sometimes subject to pure and sometimes to practical reason. It lies between knowledge and action, between facts and values. I shall return to this topic in chapter 7.

Second, Kant has produced this interstitiality via the tricky logical device of making a distinction and then repeating it within itself. This procedure is familiar, but not usually as a mode of reasoning. We usually use it in the concept of nested hierarchies. So we say, for example, that captains stand over lieutenants, lieutenants over squad leaders, and squad leaders over individual troops. Note, however, that such a hierarchy specifies no relation between people or units at a given level; one platoon is the same as another in terms

_____

12. Kant 1974:58.

of hierarchical standing, although there may be a division of labor differentiating them.

But Kant has made a *relational* judgment at one level and then repeated it at the next. We might write a normal hierarchy as follows:

> a is over b and c
> b is over d and e
> c is over f, g, and h

But under Kant's relational judgment here, we have:

> a is over b and c
> b is over d and e,   *and also* d is to e as b is to c
> c is over f, g, and h, *and also* f is to g as b is to c
>   *and also* g is to h as b is to c

That is, the relation of the general terms is recapitulated in the specific ones, as we see in figure 1.1. This is not a simple hierarchy.

Such a relationship takes a simple form only in one case—if the proliferating relations embody an ordered scale. Then the relational pattern simply picks up points on that ordered scale. So, we might divide 100 percent into the top 50 percent and the bottom 50 percent, then divide each half in half and so on. The result is an elaborate way of using dichotomies to represent linear order.

But Kant obviously does not think there is an infinite gradation from absolute pure reason through some proportionately mixed varieties of reason to absolute practical reason. He has done something else. He has created what I shall call a "fractal distinction." The name captures the fact that such a distinction repeats a pattern within itself, as geometric fractals do.[13]

---

13. There are, of course, dozens of general sources on fractals. For useful expositions, see Barnsley 1988 (somewhat mathematical), Lauwerier 1991 (general and straightforward), and Peitgen, Jürgens, and Saupe 1992 (monumental). Throughout the following exposition, and indeed throughout the book, I have tended to focus on fractals that are nested dichotomies. There is no necessary restriction to this case; it is simply the most familiar and hence makes for the easiest exposition. In chapter 6, I shall discuss some functional fractals that are obviously not dichotomous, and in chapter 7 I will return to the topic of changing the "shapes" of fractal with which we think. For the present, let the warning stand that my argument concerns something much broader than mere nested dichotomy.

I should note, for those interested in sources, that the Barnsley book was my first serious exposure to the concept of fractals. However, I had some inkling of them before reading it; my first paper mentioning fractal distinctions dates from 1986. A crucial paper in making me wonder about scale phenomena in social life was physicist Kenneth Wilson's "Problems in Physics with Many Scales of Length" (1979), which introduced me to the concept of renormalization.

2. Fractal Distinctions

The concept of fractal distinctions not only proves useful in understanding the external location of the social sciences generally. It also
provides an essential tool for understanding relations within them.
Indeed, as I shall show, both the external and the internal structures
are produced by the same mechanism.

We typically distinguish the various social sciences and various
positions within them using a set of dichotomies. Every graduate
student learns them. Some of these dichotomies concern the object
of study: a focus on social structure or on culture, emphasis on the
emergent versus the individual levels, beliefs about the constructed versus the real nature of social phenomena. Other dichotomies
involve the aspects of social phenomena taken as problematic—
choice versus constraint, conflict versus consensus. Still others differentiate methodological styles—narrative versus analysis, positivism versus interpretation. And some concern the nature of the
knowledge obtained: pure versus applied knowledge, situated versus
transcendent knowledge.

All of these dichotomies are, like Kant's pure versus practical reason, fractal distinctions. Synchronically, this means that if we use
any one of them to distinguish groups of social scientists, we will
then find these groups internally divided by the same distinction.
Diachronically, as I shall argue below, fractal distinctions cause a
perpetual slippage of the concepts and language of social science.

We begin with synchronics. Consider methodological approaches.
For about sixty years, sociology has been divided into two broad
methodological strands, usually called quantitative and qualitative.
Put starkly, the quantitative position recognizes only those social
phenomena measurable on univocal scales. The qualitative side attributes multivocality to all social phenomena and therefore denies
strong measurability. This sounds like a simple opposition. But
within each one of these strands can be distinguished "quantitative"
and "qualitative" positions. On the quantitative side, for example,
the admired "causal" methods like regression contrast with the den-
igrated "descriptive" methods like scaling and clustering. On the
qualitative side, there are relatively formalized measurement procedures that are used by some sociologists of culture and by most
practitioners of conversational analysis, while strongly interpretive
strategies characterize much of the new sociology of science (see
fig. 1.2).

Reflection reveals that all the dichotomies just mentioned behave
in this fractal manner. Consider "pure" versus "applied" sociology.

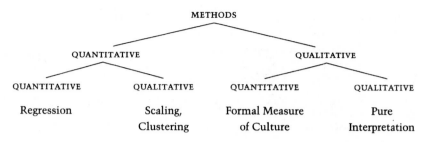

Figure 1.2

Within "pure sociology" we have general theory on the one hand and empirical research in areas like stratification or demography on the other. But within "applied sociology" there too is a theoretical strand, focusing on how application works, which stands over against the actual applications themselves. Or again, a long-standing wisecrack (usually attributed to James Duesenberry) holds that economics is about how people make choices and sociology is about how people have no choices to make. Yet within economics, constraints (e.g., budget constraints) play a major role, while much sociological theorizing in research areas like stratification relies heavily on theories about individuals' choices. The reader can no doubt supply the examples that fit the other dichotomies mentioned.

Such fractal distinctions are analogous to segmental kinship systems. A lineage starts, then splits, then splits again. Such systems have a number of important characteristics. For one thing, people know only their near kin well. I may be quite clear that my collaborator is more positivistic than I and that our research group as a whole takes a more complex, interpretive approach than do other groups working in the area. But I am likely to be hazy about matters further away. To a sociological theorist, OLS and LISREL amount to the same thing, just as ethnomethodology and symbolic interactionism are indistinguishable to a sociological empiricist.[14]

Second, like tribesmen sociologists get to know one another through long discussions about kinship that serve to establish their common ancestors. That is, two sociologists newly together will argue about the relative merits of positivism and interpretation until they know roughly where they stand relative to one another and relative to the principal methodological communities in the disci-

---

14. The classic work on such systems is Evans-Pritchard's *The Nuer* (1940). See chapter 5.

pline. The single dichotomy thus encapsulates a whole proliferating system of relations without requiring new labels for each "generation" and each position. In this lies the great power of these simple contrasts; they are, in Lévi-Strauss's celebrated phrase, good to think with.[15] Cheap and portable, yet immensely fruitful.

But simplicity has the price of indexicality. A simple contrast summarizes an entire structure only by becoming rootless. If I tell you I am a positivist, you in fact know only that in my usual domain of interaction most people I deal with are more interpretive than I. Unless you can already identify that usual domain of interaction, you don't really know anything more than you knew before I spoke. Relative to you, I might be strongly interpretive. Where people do not already know each other's positions, therefore, the indexical character of our most important terms guarantees cacophony. (Hence the futility of most seminars.)

This indexicality can of course be used instrumentally. In the first instance, it provides a general means for rejecting any assertion about a fractal dichotomy by changing the frame of reference. For example, it enables one to reduce an opponent's position to a version of one's own simply by changing that frame of reference. For example, in *Culture and Practical Reason* (1976), Marshall Sahlins is at pains to say that Marx ultimately agrees with him on certain fundamental matters. First, he shows that his and Marx's apparently opposed positions on culture and social structure can be found to have a common logical ancestor that is "cultural" by contrast with some "social structural" concept of equivalent generality. (In kinship terms, he and Marx have a common ancestor who had a sibling producing an entirely separate lineage.) But he also shows that Marx at times assumes a *cultural* position within his (Marx's) own local arena. That is, Marx has logical siblings relative to whom *he* seems cultural. Now these two demonstrations do not add up to a demonstration that Marx and Sahlins take fundamentally similar positions, as Sahlins implies. They simply show that indexicality allows one to find contexts that make the two positions *look* alike (see fig. 1.3).

This strategy fails only in the case of extremists who take the same side of a dichotomy at every level, a fact that explains why extremist positions prove so paradoxically defensible in intellectual life. An example is the work of certain economists, who at any level

---

15. Actually, the original phrase is "good to think" *(bonne à penser)*. Like "play it, Sam," this locution has been improved by the oral tradition into "good to think with." The original is in Lévi-Strauss 1963b:89.

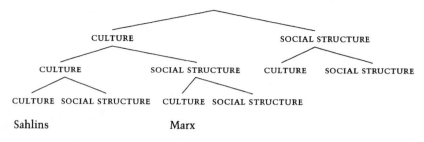

Figure 1.3

of argument unfailingly choose to think in terms of choice rather than constraint. Any constraint they deconstruct as an aggregated outcome of prior choices. The immense internal consistency of such a position renders it unassailable by context-changing fractal arguments.[16]

At any given time, then, a fractal distinction profoundly shapes our understanding of our own and others' social science. On the one hand, it measures our similarities and differences no matter how great or small those may be. On the other it generates endless misunderstanding and provides a disturbingly powerful tool for nonsubstantive argument. All of these characteristics arise from the relational character of fractal distinctions, which makes them generate a clear local structure that replicates a hazy larger one.

Note that none of this presupposes any external agendas. It is true, of course, that most remarks about fundamental principles in the social sciences have more to do with establishing the lineage and power of the speaker than with clarifying those principles. It is also true that general statements about the position of particular disciplines within this mesh of dichotomies are usually concerned with disciplinary hegemony and resources rather than with knowledge of the social world. But most of the actual effects of these di-

---

16. There are in fact only two avenues for attacking such fractal consistency. The first emphasizes its cumbersome character. So, for example, if we want to explain how people achieve Nobel Prizes in economics, constraint just offers a much simpler approach than choice. The most useful fact in predicting who gets the Nobel Prize is not knowing who made which career choices, but rather knowing that there is only one prize for perhaps every five thousand economists. The second attacking argument involves *reductio ad extremum*. Thus, one challenges a consistent choice position, for example, by asking whether all suffering necessarily reflects the choices of those who suffer. Or, one challenges an absolute denier of objective knowledge by asking whether there is no criterion for calling Nazi eugenics false science. Or one challenges a consistent narrativist position by asking the narrativist whether he believes in the absolute uniqueness of all events, and, if so, how he believes any form of general interpretation of society to be possible.

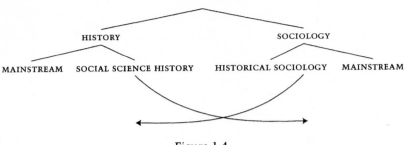

Figure 1.4

chotomies—both the complications created and the clarifications enabled—arise in the fractal character of their syntax rather than in the pragmatic uses to which they are put. External agendas invoke fractal distinctions for many purposes, but the distinctions' real power resides in their fractal, indexical nature, not in something outside.

This relational character makes fractal distinctions more general than linear scales, which seem superficially similar. For example, most of us would say that the distinction of history from sociology reflects the distinction of narrative from causal analysis. But within each discipline the fractal distinction is repeated, producing on the one hand mainstream history versus social science history and on the other historical sociology versus mainstream sociology. But social science history is closer to the mainstream of sociology than to that of history, and historical sociology to the mainstream of history than to that of sociology. That is, we cannot assume that the dichotomy of narrativism versus causalism simply produces a linear scale from pure narrativism to pure causalism, because the second-level distinctions produce in this case groups that have moved past each other on the scale (see fig. 1.4).

It is, however, wrong to emplot this particular example as a simple fractal distinction. For the two levels of the split reflect different kinds of structures. The first split—the disciplinary distinction of history and sociology—concerns how problems are posed. The subsequent distinction of social science history from other history, like that of historical sociology from other sociology, more concerns method.[17] Moreover, this structural pattern arose because fractal distinctions in fact work themselves out in time, not simply at a

---

17. The best definition of social science history is thus as a field where narratively posed problems are addressed with causalist methods, while historical sociology is a field where causal problems (that is, general questions like when does revolution occur) are answered by (somewhat) narrative analyses of cases.

single point. The general distinction between history and sociology originated in the structuring of academic and professional associations in the late nineteenth century, while the particular realization of social science history came in the 1960s and that of historical sociology in the 1970s. We must therefore turn to the temporal structure of fractal distinctions.

3. Fractal Distinctions in Time

Once again, we begin with the interstitiality of social science in general and of sociology in particular. How might ideas change in an interstitial social science, a social science unwilling to let go of pure *or* practical reason, of objectivity *or* subjectivity, of analysis *or* narrative, positivism *or* interpretation?

Under a Hegelian model, any unified version of social science would call its opposite into existence, and the two would then be synthesized into a new social science transcending the earlier versions. This new version would then itself call forth a new opposition, another synthetic transcendence and so on. Such a progressive, dialectical model was at the heart of Gouldner's (1970) concept of a crisis in sociology. Parsons was the thesis, Marx the antithesis, and the welfare-state apologetics of "Academic Sociology" the synthesis. To this, "Reflexive Sociology" would be the new antithesis.

In retrospect, Gouldner seems very much ahead of his time. He defined Reflexive Sociology as the recognition that "the search for knowledge about social worlds is also contingent upon the knower's self-awareness." This statement could be taken straight from any contemporary postmodernist text. The problem is that it could also be taken from the homespun prose of Evans-Pritchard writing more than thirty years *before* Gouldner:

> I wonder whether anthropologists always realize that they can be, and sometimes are, transformed by the people they are making a study of . . . I learnt from African "primitives" much more than they learnt from me, much that I had never been taught at school.

Such continuous revival sounds less like Hegelian dialectic than rediscovery or renaming. Every now and then, we might think, social scientists recall that their ideas are as contingent on themselves as on their objects of study.[18]

---

18. Gouldner 1970:493; Evans-Pritchard 1976:245. As it was put by K. Burridge, a student of Nadel and Evans-Pritchard, in his retirement address:

The history of anthropology, as I came to realize later, is not only a series of cycles, readdressing much the same problems under different names and idi-

The centrality of rediscovery is also evident in the litany of articles entitled "Bringing the Something-or-other Back In." Some ninety-one articles and books have brought something back in since George Homans first used the phrase in the title of his 1964 ASA presidential address, a virulent attack on Parsons for ignoring purposive action. And the things brought back in have included both sides of most of the important social scientific dichotomies. Some writers have brought people back in, others behavior. Some have brought social structure back in, others culture. Some have brought ourselves, others the context. Some circulation, others structure. Some capitalists, others workers. Some firms, others unions.[19]

---

oms . . . there was no question at the time of reinventing the wheel. It was a restatement in current idioms of discourse on what had, over time, become ritualized, opaque. Burridge 1989:92.

And lest we think that rediscovery itself has not been rediscovered many times, consider the celebrated lines of T. S. Eliot:

> And what there is to conquer
> By strength and submission, has already been discovered
> Once or twice, or several times, by men whom one cannot hope
> To emulate—but there is no competition—
> There is only the fight to recover what has been lost
> And found and lost again and again: and now, under conditions
> That seem unpropitious.
>   "East Coker," 182–88 (from Eliot 1943:31).

Gans 1992 discusses a number of works on rediscovery, especially Sorokin 1956.

19. It should not be thought that forgetting and reinvention happen only with respect to subject matters. Several colleagues have pointed out the reinvention of methodological techniques. Path analysis is the most famous of these (really more a rediscovery, of Wright's work by Wald and Simon), but one could also include the reinvention of AID (the automatic interaction detector) as CART (classification and regression trees). Game theory, the current vogue in economics and political science, had an earlier vogue (in the 1950s and 1960s) in social psychology.

It should also be noted that fractal divisions occur even deep within purely methodological communities. Much of the Bayesian versus frequentist debate in statistics actually encapsulates, within that highly technical field, much broader conflicts between subjective and objective approaches to social reality. When the frequentist Sir David Cox, in speaking of the work of Bayesian Adrian Raftery, concedes, "Integrating is more appealing than maximizing . . . that's the Bayesian point of view" or later "Bias is a relative term, is it not?," we are clearly replicating a debate in which most outsiders would see all statisticians as located absolutely on the positivist pole. (Both quotes from spoken remarks at a conference on Bayesian analysis at Nuffield College, Oxford University, 22 June 1999.) Also perpetually rediscoverable are theoretical paradigms. Think how many times "institutionalism" has been discovered, reinvented, or otherwise brought back in during this century, from Commons to Williamson in economics, from Selznick to Meyer in sociology, from Ely to Skowronek in political science, and so on.

A similar pattern of fractal cultural structure has been discussed by Gal and Irvine (1995). They are more concerned to see the fractal system as used pragmatically, with political intent, hence their process of "erasure." Although I mention the pragmatic use of fractals here (in the Sahlins and Marx example, above), I return to the topic at more length in chapter 7.

A glance at these articles makes one think that sociology, and indeed social science more generally, consists mainly of rediscovering the wheel. A generation triumphs over its elders, then calmly resurrects their ideas, pretending all the while to advance the cause of knowledge. Revolutionaries defeat reactionaries; each generation plays first the one role, then the other.

A similar rediscovery seems to underlie the history of "social construction." The insight that social reality is produced by practice rather than given ex ante has made at least four separate appearances in this century's social science: first in the pragmatism of Dewey and Mead, then in the relational Marxist epistemology of Mannheim, then in the strong constructionism of existentialism and phenomenology, and finally in recent theoretical work from France. There are different wrinkles to these appearances, and of course there is a new terminology in each case. But there is no real progress, no fundamentally new concept. We simply keep recalling a good idea.

But to see here the simple harmonic motion of a pendulum is to miss the importance of the history that does occur. For example, a quite different process appears in sociology's great dispute between "conflict" and "consensus." The "conflict theorists" of the 1960s and 1970s asked why there was so much social conflict. They took individuals as inherently orderly and attributed conflict to oppressive social institutions. They labeled their opponents of the older generation as "consensus theorists." The people so labeled did not see *themselves* as arguing a particular viewpoint, but rather thought themselves an eclectic mainstream. Yet most of their arguments did seem particular when viewed in the new context provided by conflict theory. For the mainstream had asked why there was not *more* social conflict. For them social life was a Hobbesian free-for-all precariously ordered by normative institutions of social control. This was indeed the reverse of the conflict position.

There is little question that conflict theory won the day, not only by sheer youth, but also in direct combat. So as the 1970s passed, the dichotomy really wasn't a dichotomy any more. Only the conflict lineage survived. Yet by the mid-1980s, the younger generation was rediscovering the centrifugal tendencies of individuals and the problem of order amid diversity, the same things that had obsessed the now-defunct consensus theorists. With this rediscovery came a renewed defense of normativism. But now the politics were reversed. Group norms (as a concept) were now being defended by the "conflict" school (now under the leadership of the baby boom Marxists) against a new opponent. This was rational choice theory—

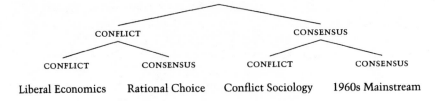

Figure 1.5

again a view that individuals make a good social world unless disor-
derly institutions somehow mislead them and thus itself a "conflict
theory" (see fig. 1.5).

This is a particularly nice example. The death of consensus theory in sociology left 1970s conflict sociology (broadly defined) as the
sole representative of a much larger lineage that was *consensualist*
by contrast with the conflict theory presumed by economics. More
generally, the triumph of a position in intellectual life usually guarantees that position's downfall by placing it in a new context of fractal comparison. Indexicality works through time.

This perpetual recontextualization forces each newly triumphant
position to recognize that it has omitted central matters of concern
or that, like sociological conflict theory, it is itself now representing
what it thought it had defeated. Another consequence of rediscovery
in real time is that there is an extraordinarily complex history of
terminologies. For the old ideas return under new names.

The term "social construction of reality" was created, for example, by the third of the four generations of constructionists. They
created the label to underscore what Mannheim had only implied
under his theory of relational knowledge. Moreover, the third generation (Berger and Luckmann) used the phrase "symbolic universes"
to refer to what would *now* be called "discourses," thus pointing
toward the philosophical literature (e.g., Mead and Cassirer) where
the present term points toward literary studies. The different con-
textualizations make the one concept look quite different.

But finally and perhaps most importantly, any temporarily victorious pole of a dichotomy must comprehend subject matters that
had been more comfortably comprehended by its erstwhile opponent. If sociology (or social science, for that matter) is not to relapse
into the pure humanities or the pure natural sciences—if it is not
to lose its interstitiality—then defeating one's enemies means taking up their burdens.[20] Thus, it has now been elegantly shown that

---

20. In fact the humanities and natural sciences are split like this as well. The
problem is simply particularly evident in the social sciences.

occupational categories are socially constructed by census makers, often with implicit political agendas—making women's work invisible, for example.[21] But since unemployment and job loss are still of burning scholarly and political interest, the victory of a constructionist approach to occupations does not mean that we can stop studying job mobility, but rather that we must now somehow restructure our realist analyses with the appropriate constructionist doubts. This is a difficult task indeed, but we must do it, lest the constructionist insight simply lead us away from any politically effective analysis of unemployment and job loss.

This necessity of ruling an alien turf places both long- and short-run constraints on the extent of victory in the contests that unfold in these fractally proliferating lineages. In the long run, it forbids complete victory by one side or the other. For a truly universal predicate is inherently uninteresting, even meaningless. If "everything is discourse, because everything is mediated through language," then language is neither interesting nor consequential. It cannot explain the differences that interest us in social life, for it does not explain where differences originate, but only the means by which preexisting differences cause later ones.

In the short run, the takeover of alien turf means a reshaping and restructuring of the victorious terminology itself. Calling mathematics rhetoric brings great insights as long as we actually think rhetoric denotes something quite different from our ordinary concept of mathematics. As long as we think rhetoric means artifice dominating substance, persuasion dominating logic, and so on, it is possible to say quite insightful things about the "rhetorical" nature of mathematical arguments—about the hidden persuasions in an apparently objective language, about the nature of the taken-for-granted, and so on. But once we believe mathematics really is rhetoric pure and simple, metaphor becomes denotation and its foundation crumbles.

The remapping of alien turf into one's own terminology can take several forms. The simplest is takeover; mathematics, in the example just given, can become recognized simply as one subdivision of rhetoric rather than as a subdivision of something different called, say, objective argument. But meaning is a two-way relation. Concept denotes content but at the same time contents define concept. So the ingestion on equal terms of a mass of alien material simply destroys an overarching concept that much the faster.[22]

---

21. Sources on occupational classification include Conk 1980, Szreter 1993, and Desrosières and Thévenot 1988.

22. Of course, this inference assumes that the contents under a concept have a certain stickiness (although not an "objective reality") that makes them resist re-

Therefore, far more likely is what I would like to call the "New York" form of ingestion, recalling the well-known "New Yorker's Map of the United States," half of which is taken up with Manhattan, another quarter with New Jersey, and then the remainder with America west of the Delaware. The New York ingestion is the diachronic analogue of what we noted above: the tendency to know one's close relatives well and one's distant relatives not at all. In it, an opponent's turf is absorbed but vastly reduced in relative size. The concept of attitude provides a good example. For W. I. Thomas and his school in the 1910s, "attitude" was a large and complex concept; interpreting the attitudes of Polish peasants took five volumes. But after positivism triumphed in postwar sociology, attitudes—now redefined as simple answers to certain kinds of questions—became merely one among many causal forces determining behavior. They became one more personal attribute alongside sex, race, religion, socioeconomic status, income, and so on. The positivists' Manhattan—the demographic variables—remained much the larger part of the map.

There are undoubtedly other modes of ingestion. All require bringing the conceptual and substantive knowledge of the defeated side of a dichotomy under the victorious one. All therefore tend to undermine the consistency and clarity of the victor; indeed all conduce to reproducing the old dichotomy under the new heading. The fact that sociology cannot effectively rule out forms or areas of social knowledge thus perpetually undermines hegemonic discourses within the discipline. Every triumphant discourse finds itself having to take up the problems, and implicitly the language, of the defeated.

This process continuously creates new terms for old things. As "culture" has become the dominant trope for discussion of social life, what used to be called solidarity (with distinct echoes of social structure) is now called identity (with equally distinct echoes of culture).

The consequences of this sliding for graduate education can easily be imagined. Faculty and students look to fundamentally different sources and assign different meanings to any given technical term. My generation footnotes the constructionist position to Berger and Luckmann. Our elders attribute it to Mannheim or, if students of Blumer, to pragmatists like Mead. But many of our current

---

definitions, of whatever kind or degree. I am quite willing to assume, on empirical grounds, that ideas about society (and indeed social reality itself) have that sticky quality, although they certainly do not have the immobility implied in the phrase "objective reality."

students are convinced that social constructionism was invented by Foucault and the feminists and that all of preexisting sociology from Mead and Thomas to Mannheim to Berger and Luckmann was an exercise in hegemonic objectivist discourse. They talk about construction with different labels, and when they do use words familiar to the middle generation, they use them in different senses.

The word "culture" shows this process with painful clarity. A generation ago the word received a clear and limited definition from Geertz ("culture is a system of symbols by means of which people communicate their knowledge of and attitudes towards life") that presupposed the opposition of culture and social structure or of culture and behavior. Today's students use the word in a much broader form, embracing most of what is called social structure by my generation. But of course Geertz's position itself changed the situation that preceded it. After all, the contentious history of the culture concept in the nineteenth and early twentieth centuries preoccupied Kroeber and Kluckhohn (in 1952) for an entire book.[23]

A fractal distinction thus produces both change and stability. Any given group is always splitting up over some fractal distinction. But dominance by one pole of the distinction requires that pole to carry on the analytic work of the other, so the endless subdivision that we label by the word differentiation does not seem possible. There results a continuous bending of terminologies that breaks down the original metaphors that produced dominance.

4. Mechanisms

This pattern of split, conflict, and ingestion needs more detailed analysis. As I just noted, the most familiar comparable temporal process is differentiation. Indeed, under the guise of "branching processes," differentiation is often taken as a general model for action in time.

When increasing size allows, differentiation does indeed sometimes occur in social sciences. For example, market research began within sociology as Lazarsfeld and others used their new variable-based methods to predict consumption behavior. But once established as a separate body of work and workers, market research itself then split (in the 1960s) into market research proper—the quasi-sociological analysis of consumption with formal methods—and a looser study of general strategies for distributing and "positioning"

---

23. See Geertz 1973:89.

consumption products, a study that eventually merged with marketing more generally.

In such a case, a social structural differentiation recapitulates or
parallels a cultural one. And this particular form of differentiation,
along the lines of "purity," is quite general to knowledge-based occupations. Specialists in knowledge tend to withdraw into pure work
because the complexity of the thing known eventually tends to get
in the way of the knowledge system itself. So the object of knowledge is gradually disregarded.[24] This process is familiar throughout
the professions, where applied work ranks below academic work
because the complexities of professional practice make practical
knowledge messy and "unprofessional." But we see the process in
academia itself; much of the very high-status discipline of economics is quite unconcerned with empirical reality. Similarly, it was the
gradual withdrawal of sociology and anthropology into inward, professional concerns that left the terrain of general social commentary
open to humanists, who have invaded it with vigor and insight, if
not always accuracy and intelligibility.

But differentiation survives within a fractal lineage only when
increasing size and resources permit it. To see exactly what this
means, we need to be more careful about definitions. Figure 1.6
shows three patterns I want to distinguish. The first is traditional
differentiation. At each generation, a lineage splits into subordinate
parts of increasing specificity. The second pattern is fractal differentiation, which is the simple version of the phenomenon discussed
here. In this pattern the fractal distinction repeats itself at each succeeding generation *within all lineages.*

The third pattern is that of "fractal cycles," in which only one
line divides per generation, because intense conflict exterminates
all but a particular hegemonic view. However, the concerns of the
"sterile" line are "remapped" onto a version of the fertile one; this
is the "taking up of the concerns of the defeated" discussed above.
The fractal cycles pattern is thus a subset of the fractal differentiation one.

We can see the difference between fractal differentiation and fractal cycles by looking at sociology itself. The great growth of sociology during the 1950s and 1960s allowed rapid fractal (and traditional) differentiation until the 1970s and 1980s. But while most
academic disciplines expanded greatly in the postwar period, they

---

24. I first made this argument in Abbott 1981, and have an enduring fondness for
it because it was my first major article. Luckily for me, it has recently been confirmed
in resolutely technical fashion by Sandefur (2000). I shall return to this mechanism
in chapter 5.

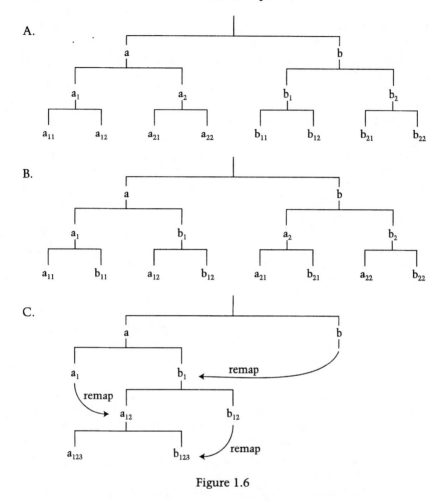

Figure 1.6

grew much more slowly in the periods before and since. Space is most clearly constrained in the elite cores of disciplines, where there is never much increase of crucial resources—of university positions, of space in elite journals, of visible venues at conferences, and so on.

It is therefore particularly at the center of disciplines that we see the ceaseless play of fractal distinctions that I outlined above. Its simplest form is the generational paradigm. By generational paradigm I mean a single step in the fractal cycle: an episode of conflict, defeat of one side, division of the winners, and remapping of the losers' concerns onto the equivalent descendant of the winners. The typical "victory" of a particular side of a fractal distinction seems to

last about twenty to thirty years. Social constructionism, as I noted
earlier, reappears at about twenty-five-year intervals: at the turn of
the century, in the 1930s, in the 1960s, and again in the 1980s. Academic Marxism first flowered in the early 1960s and was largely
moribund—done in less by the end of the Cold War than by the
rise of feminism and cultural studies—by the late 1980s. Labeling
theory—a radical constructionist paradigm in the sociological study
of deviance—was proposed in the late 1950s and dead by 1980.[25]

There is good reason to expect a cycle of about this length.
Twenty years is about the length of time it takes a group of academics to storm the ramparts, take the citadel, and settle down to the
fruits of victory. There is a common pattern. First come insightful
theoretical treatises and quirky but creative empirical work. Often,
as with labeling theory, it is the quirky empirical work—in that case
Erving Goffman's work on mental patients—that catches the disciplinary eye and imagination. And, as labeling theory also shows,
there is no need for personal association between members of the
new "school." It was really Howard Becker, writing after the fact,
who named and thereby created the labeling "school."

The five years or so of "exciting new work" are followed by systematic treatises setting out the new point of view. Theoretical
terms are temporarily stabilized in books with titles like *Keywords*
or *The New Sociology of X*. The stream of empirical work swells.
Now well into their assistant professorships, the new generation
holds counter-plenary sessions at meetings, drawing the multitude
from the elders' celebrations of old pieties. By the end of the first
decade the new [sic] view has invaded survey articles and the more
current of textbooks. Consolidation follows. By this point, the major
theoretical work is done. So students are directed to produce more
and more detailed empirical studies (complex comparisons, analyses
of subproblems), which help anchor the paradigm. Results are often
disappointing, however; somehow the excitement of *Asylums* or
The Making of the English Working Class is never recaptured.

To be sure, there are always incentives to oppose the new argument. Because the orthodox hold much patronage, some young
people defend orthodoxy. But the emphasis of the new school on one
side of the fractal distinction inevitably forces orthodoxy's paladins
into the other. Orthodoxy itself begins to seem the muddled eclecti-

---

25. Examples are endless and of course not limited to sociology. "Culture and
personality" and "neo-Freudianism" (McLaughlin 1998a,b) are good examples from
anthropology and psychology respectively.

cism of the middle-aged when compared with the clear logic of battle among the young. Thus the fractal reappears.

At this point, two directions are possible. The fractal debate can relapse into eclecticism as the combatants rise to disciplinary and university responsibility and slow their scholarly output. Alternatively, one or the other side of the fractal distinction can win. In that case, eclecticism arrives through the remapping mechanism noted above. Victory simply forces the victors to take over the turf of the losers, a seizure that in turn starts the victorious terminology sliding away from its one-sided purity.

My picture is of course oversimplified. The Young Turks often seek and often find allies among the elder generation. Yet even so the generational lines seem strong. In the 1970s and 1980s, Charles Tilly refused to become the sectarian historical sociologist the younger generation wanted him to be, taking a strong eclectic position that since all sociology was (or ought to be) historical, there was no point in developing a specific "historical sociology." This decision cost him the leadership of the new field, which went instead to the younger generation's Theda Skocpol. The core of most "new schools" usually does consist of a relatively narrow band of ages.

The fractal cycle indelibly marks careers that begin in its different phases. Students whose dissertations constitute the detailed empirical work of the later phases can find themselves advocating strong opposition when the cycle has already moved toward reconciliation and eclecticism. Leaders who articulated a fractal split as brilliant younger scholars are becalmed as the cycle's winds blow themselves out. The slide of meaning leaves little ground for the doctrinaire—or sometimes even for the consistent—although, to be sure, one way to survive is to put one's energy into staying continually abreast of the changing languages for the constant problems.

Generational paradigms are the simplest form of fractal cycle. Obviously, fractal cycles are sometimes longer than one generation. One mechanism lengthening them is what we might call fractionation. Marxism provides a useful example. Because the early voices of academic Marxism were utterly rejected by the academic mainstream, Marxists tended to speak more to themselves than to outsiders, with the inevitable consequence that fractal cycles began within the group rather than between it and the mainstream. The first American generation of academic Marxists—the corporate liberals of the early 1960s—was materialist, sometimes to the point of economic reductionism. But its successors were not. Some of them drew on the mixed materialism of Althusser and Poulantzas, where

historical changes in "determination in the last instance" allowed
one to occasionally escape economic reductionism for other forms
of material determination. Others turned to the more explicitly cultural Marxism of the English school, which at times escaped material determination altogether. Fractal squabbles among themselves
in an explicitly Marxist arena thus stalled the larger fractal dynamic
between the Marxists and the mainstream until academicization
brought Marxism into that mainstream. Once the serious academicization of Marxism began, the larger dynamic took over again and
Marxists joined, indeed often led, the large-scale social scientific
swing toward the cultural and the immaterial that we observe today.
But during the earlier period, fractionation reigned triumphant and
the Marxists spent most of their time attacking themselves. Note
that intense issues within fractionalized battles can seem incompre-
hensible to outsiders; most non-Marxists never took the position of
extreme economic reductionism and hence had no particular need
for Althusser's great insight, which took the form of "bringing the
non-economic back in." The "discovery" of the problem of structure
and agency is the same. Those who never believed in absolute structural determination wonder what all the fuss is about.

Fractionation thus produces fractal cycles of several generations.
Other mechanisms lengthening the cycle usually involve interaction between multiple fractal distinctions, a topic I shall take up
shortly.[26]

The fractal cycle is at heart a profoundly traditional mechanism.
Like any good ritual, it unites opposites. On the one hand, it generates perpetual change. Old ideas are always being thrown out. Intellectual autocracy is perpetually overthrown. On the other, it produces perpetual stability. The new ideas are always the old ideas
under new labels. The new people are the old people in new roles.
This last is of course the price of having our cake and eating it too.
The wine of youthful revolution is usually followed by the hangover
of rejection or stagnation in middle-age. But on the whole, the ritual
is profoundly useful. We get to keep our best concepts forever and

---

26. An interesting example of a fractionation that failed is the neo-Freudianism
of Sullivan, Horney, and Fromm, discussed by McLaughlin (1998b). The case of neo-
Freudianism makes clear (by its counterexample) that one of the crucial foundations
of the kind of fractal system I describe here is the underlying substrate of tenured
positions, which ensure that no broad type of thought is ever completely lost. Fromm
fell from grace not only because his ideas became more and more heretical, but because he lacked an institutional base of any kind. Most academic groups can always
preserve some kind of minimal institutional base. For an interesting example of ongoing fractionation on a methodological basis, consider Leontief's (1982) remarks about
mathematicization in economics.

yet can retain our belief in perpetual intellectual progress. We get the best of traditionalism with the best of modernity. Because our basic concepts are perpetually burnished by the complexities of re-mapping, the fractal cycle undermines the familiarity that breeds contempt or, worse yet, indifference.[27]

Before going on to the question of interaction between fractal dis-tinctions, I would like to underline the general power of the concept of fractal distinctions. The concept makes sense of many incompre-hensible things about social science and its development. First of all, it explains the persistence of terms that appear to be undefinable despite their central importance to our disciplines. They survive be-cause they are indexical terms that facilitate our discourse by their very indexicality. They give us a common if slippery language to establish relations between one another. They provide an extraordi-narily powerful element for both offense and defense in academic discourse.

Moreover, the motion of fractal distinctions in time accounts well for the perpetual sliding of conceptual definitions in social sci-ence, as it does for the steady waxing and waning of new paradigms. It gives us a model for the perpetual rediscovery that seems so cen-tral to social science and shows us elegantly how groups can, through changing contexts of fractal comparison, find themselves defined publicly in ways precisely opposed to their self-images. Above all, it accounts for the ways in which the surface revolutions of social science articulate with an extraordinary constancy in basic concerns and shows us indeed how those emergent-level phenomena articulate, in ways not always pleasant, with individual lives.

---

27. There are, of course, other important mechanisms involved in the replication of academic knowledge over time. I defer a more general discussion until chapter 5. For example, a centrally important mechanism in creating drift in academic knowl-edge is the fact that academics generally do not try to teach what they learned, but what they wish they had learned. They most often forget to teach what they take for granted. Graduate students are left to learn that taken-for-granted from pure example.

I should also note, more broadly, that there are many types of cultural change not considered here. Probably the most important, given my emphasis on the change of meaning in terminologies, is the situation where we *don't* think a terminology has changed in meaning when in fact it has done so radically. In my own work, the most familiar example of this is the word "profession," which meant something almost completely different in the nineteenth century than it does today. Again, Eliot puts it best:

> For last year's words belong to last year's language
> And next year's words await another voice.
> "Little Gidding," 118–19 (from Eliot 1943:54).

The reader will have noticed that the underlying mechanism I propose here has much to do with academic careers and their structure. I will return to this topic in more detail in chapter 5.

5. Multiple Fractal Distinctions

I have so far pretended that the fractal distinctions that undergird
social science exist independently. But of course, they do not. Indeed
there are strong elective affinities between them. Thus, work on
choice usually focuses on the individual level, while constraint is
often seen as emergent. To be sure, these affiliations can be broken.
When Gouldner wrote *The Coming Crisis*, Marxism had no positivist
version, soon to be provided by Erik Wright, nor yet a choice version,
soon to be provided by John Roemer. But in general affiliations among
various poles of my fractal distinctions are strong and enduring.

Perhaps the strongest of these affinities is what we might call
the methodological manifold: an affiliation of four or five separate
distinctions generally labeled by the distinction of qualitative versus
quantitative. At the heart of this manifold is the nearly absolute association of positivism with analysis and of narrative with interpretation. So strongly linked are these two dichotomies that the other
way of lining them up—narrative with positivism and analysis with
interpretation—is nearly nonsensical to most sociologists.[28] Beyond this initial identity, the affiliation of the two sides of the methodological manifold with particular dichotomies remains clear,
if not so rigid. Analytic positivism is nearly always realist rather
than constructionist in its epistemology, generally concerns social
structure rather than culture, and usually has a strongly individual
rather than emergent cast. Most of its proponents are strong believers in transcendent social knowledge. By contrast, narrative interpretation usually invokes culture (perhaps social structure as well),
is willingly emergent, and nearly always follows a constructionist
epistemology. Most members of this school—from Blumer to Foucault—believe social knowledge ultimately to be situated, not
transcendent.

Quantitative	versus	*Qualitative*
POSITIVISM		INTERPRETATION
ANALYSIS		NARRATIVE
REALISM		CONSTRUCTIONISM
SOCIAL STRUCTURE		CULTURE
INDIVIDUAL LEVEL		EMERGENT LEVEL
TRANSCENDENT KNOWLEDGE		SITUATED KNOWLEDGE

---

28. That the associations of positivism with analysis and interpretation with narration are nearly absolute was made very clear by the reaction to my own 1992 paper
"From Causes to Events," subtitled "Notes on Narrative Positivism." Within a short

Breaking these affinities is the most powerful mechanism for knowledge change in social science. Interesting new social science can always be produced by trying a combination hitherto unknown. Hence the appeal of positivist and choice-based Marxist theories, and indeed of the quasi-positivist studies of culture now emerging (e.g., the work of John Mohr). But these, however interesting in themselves, are merely static variety—filling in the holes of a cross-tabulation. Changing these affinities provides a far more powerful mechanism of intellectual change when taken in the context of the fractal cycle. To argue this and to move toward a more general formulation of the argument, let me develop an extended metaphor.

Imagine that we are tourists in a rectangular-grid city. The bus leaves us at a big park in the middle of town. Imagine that one fractal distinction is east versus west. Suppose we choose one of these directions, walk a mile, then stop and choose again, walk half a mile, then stop and choose again, walk a quarter of a mile, and so on. At each choice, half of us go one way and half the other. The first four moves in the procedure are shown in figure 1. 7. Eventually, we will end up uniformly spread out on an east-west axis four miles long. By this procedure, that is, our group can discover what is happening anywhere on this axis. The fractal distinction fills the (one-dimensional) space well. Note too the important fact that this rule of motion enables us to achieve that coverage without any initial specification of who goes where. That is, the rule works *precisely because* it is an indexical rule embedded in time.

But now suppose that north versus south is a fractal distinction as well. Now people must walk north or south after walking east or west. Suppose we say that whoever walks east must next walk south, and whoever walks west must next walk north. (This constitutes "affiliating the dichotomies," as in the methodological manifolds discussed above.) We start out choosing east or west, walk a mile, then walk a mile south if we came east, and north if we came west; then we stop and choose east or west, walk half a mile, then walk half a mile south if we came east, and north if we came west, and so on. Again, at each choice point half go one way and half the other. As figure 1.8 shows, this rule spreads us out along the line of the southeast-northwest diagonal. If people started north or south with the same east-west affiliates, they would end up on the same diagonal by a different route. By affiliating the dichotomies, that is, we still know only a one-dimensional fragment of a two-

___

time of its publication I was being shelled accurately by both positivists and narrativists. See Hanagan and Tilly 1996 and Abbott 1996.

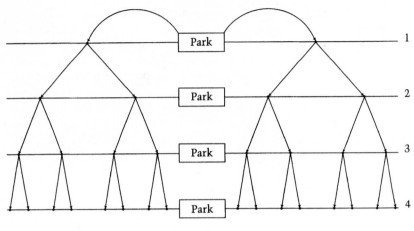

Figure 1.7

dimensional space. We have two fractal distinctions, but they don't help us fill the whole space with investigators. Only by *dissociating* the two distinctions can we actually fill the whole space.

Let me translate the example back into sociology. If positivists are always opposing interpretivists, and positivists always choose realist epistemologies and interpretivists constructionist ones, then even the fact that positivists are themselves internally split into positivists and interpretivists, as are the interpretivists as well, and so on and on, even that fact will not allow us to explore very many of the possible knowledges of society.

This analogy gives us a way of theorizing social science knowledge that is not progressive in the strict sense, but that nonetheless provides a model for disciplined knowledge change as well as for Kuhnian "revolutions." Social science aims to send investigators down most of the streets of the city. That is, we want to fill the space of possible inquiry. I'm not interested here in whether we think of the city as the universe of things to know about society (in which case the metaphor evokes a correspondence theory of truth) or as the universe of *ways* to know things about society (in which case we avoid that theory but are concerned with saturating the space of possible epistemologies). Either way, we are trying to fill up this multidimensional space with the unidimensional paths taken by our investigators. We establish sets of rules for how to proceed so that we don't have to remain in continuous communication with one another, but can remain on our separate paths—as disciplines, subdisciplines, research groups. By establishing these rules, we not only have tools for understanding each other when we meet on the

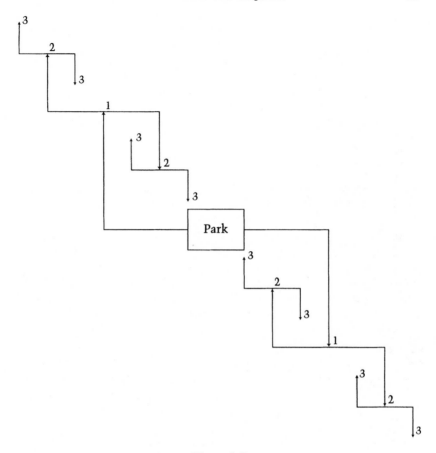

Figure 1.8

street—the "fractal distinctions are good to think with" argument that I gave above. More important, we can also independently fill up the space so that when we return to the bus we will have the fullest possible knowledge of the city. (It goes without saying that the city has as many dimensions as there are fractal distinctions.)

What determines how much we know of the city is thus the set of rules for compounding the fractal distinctions with one another. Profound changes in those rules will lead to profound changes in where we go. New compounding rules may take us to areas never before visited. But note that at the same time this model allows us to *lose* knowledge. New rules may fill more of the space but still systematically ignore places visited under simpler rules. Moreover, any one level of total knowledge (any one proportion of the space filled) can be achieved by a multitude of quite different sets of rules, nor is there any guarantee that equal amounts of knowledge will be knowledge of the same things. That is, there are many different ways to fill 50 percent of the space. We might fill all the right-hand half, or the right half of every quadrant, etc. Note that these different ways would differ *vastly* in the degree to which all parts of the space were "nearly known," that is, within a certain distance of a known area.[29]

This model of social scientific knowledge is thus not progressive in the usual sense, although it does admit the loose criterion that "better" knowledge is knowledge that fills the space more completely, knowledge of higher fractal dimension. But at the same time, in the concept of "changing the rules for compounding fractal distinctions" we have a clear model for "scientific revolutions," which often have the properties just noted. They make us know the same things in different ways, and their new knowledge seems to be in some way incommensurable with the old, precisely because it is achieved by a different route. Thus I argue that the major changes in sociology, as in other social sciences and among the social sciences in general, arise through the reshuffling of these affiliations between the fractal distinctions, within the context of individual fractal cycles. And I note that this is not only a descriptive statement; this is not only how social science works in practice. It is also a prescriptive one urging us to recast the compounding rules and giving us at least a conceptual criterion for how to judge the results of that recasting.

It should now be clearer what I meant at the outset by a form of universal knowledge that emerges from accommodation and conflict rather than from axioms. When there are many different epistemological routes to one place, people who have taken them will "see" a different thing when they arrive. What is universal about social science knowledge is the project of getting there and of mutually decoding our routes. This project is all the more complicated once we recognize that, as the concept of fractal cycles implies, most of us have been wandering in the city for long enough to have

---

29. Readers with knowledge of fractals will recognize that this question of "rules for compounding distinctions" is the question of changing the shape of the fractal with which we try to fill a space. A fractal is always of some lower dimensionality than the space it is trying to fill. But different fractals fill different proportions of the full dimensional space. There are various criteria for thinking about this "filling." In the current example, we might want to think a set of rules for compounding fractal distinctions better if it enabled us to guarantee that the maximum distance from any point in the "city" to an existing form of social scientific knowledge was minimized. I return to this problem in the closing pages of the book.

lost any sense of where we started. Axiomatic retracing of our routes from the central square is impossible; none of us knows where it is. We run into each other on some street corner, our disciplines and subdisciplines having brought us there by varying routes, and we try to locate one another's past and present by discussing our rules for traversing the labyrinth of our fundamental conceptual structure. All the worse, the endless fractal cycles are perpetually changing the meanings of our very languages. But once in a while something remarkable occurs. Somebody learns enough from somebody else to wander into a whole new area of the city.

The next three essays elaborate this argument through a detailed analysis of historical examples of fractal patterns in sociology and in related social sciences.

2

The Duality
of Stress

AMONG THE central processes discussed in the preceding chapter
was remapping, the comprehension of formerly alien matter under
the victorious pole of a dichotomy. When one side of a fractal distinction becomes dominant, it is forced to extend its type of analysis into territories that turn out to be ill suited to it. It also ingests
terminologies and conceptualizations largely alien to its own logic.
There results a destructive sliding of the core concepts on which
victory was built.

In this chapter I consider in detail an example of this process of
ingestion—the fate of the concept and image of stress in the heyday
of empiricist sociology from 1965 to 1985. The case illustrates many
of the basic arguments of the preceding chapter. We see clearly the
problems of comprehending alien matter under a victorious paradigm and the ways that the fractal distinction ends up restarting
itself, in new language, within a cohesive research community. Quantitative and qualitative prove not to be opposed ends of a spectrum,
but different poles of a fractal process.

I begin by examining the history of the stress concept used by the
general culture. The cultural stress concept was the combined leg-
acy of several different scientific literatures. This heritage gave a
deep duality to stress as a concept; cases of stress are always infused
with multiple and ambiguous meanings.

I then consider what became of these multiple meanings when
they were handled within the quantitative methodological manifold

I must thank the libraries of Lehigh University for facilitating the periodical survey
reported in this chapter. I dedicate this chapter to George Levine, the Kenneth Burke
Professor of English at Rutgers University.

that has dominated sociology for the last forty years. Since that manifold normally assumes that multiple meanings do not exist, we do indeed have a case of "comprehending the opposite"; an emergent, triumphant paradigm must take over the language and concepts of an area unsuited to it. A phenomenon defined by its earlier heritage as having multiple meanings must be analyzed within the single meaning framework of an explicit "science" of stress.

To show how this "comprehension" works, I begin by establishing what major complaints quantitative students of stress had about their own literature. I then show that a surprising number of these "problems" arose from the handling of a multivocal, syncretic concept within the quantitative methodological framework.

The closing section reverses my earlier argument. If problems arise through compounding or mixing of fractal distinctions—in this case the analysis of multivocal "realities" within univocal methods—can we retrace our path through the fractal choices to discover some "new routes" to take in the study of stress? I consider the implications of my analysis for future quantitative studies of stress, comparing the predictions and suggestions I made when this paper was originally researched in 1986–87 with the results that had emerged in the stress literature by the mid-1990s.

It is useful to restate the theoretical argument. The process of ingestion, as I have called it, results from the fact (taken here as a premise) that social scientists do not want to let anything go, do not want problems or subject matters or even conceptualizations of the world to become alien to them. This should not necessarily be construed as a drive to intellectual hegemony. Rather it is an urge to comprehensiveness that always ends up taking in more than it can digest. Just as in large the social sciences can never decide whether they are disciplines of facts or values and so vacillate between the two, so individual research traditions can never stay within limits, spending their energy on defeating local opponents who embody some antithetical fractal position. Once victorious, they always end up trying to ingest their opponents' turf.

Opponents' turf—both of concepts and problems—is likely to be ill suited to the victors' forms of knowledge for two principal reasons. First, there are elective affinities between objects of empirical research on the one hand and methods and theories on the other. While there isn't any one right way to study most topics in social science, objects of research often favor or invite certain kinds of analysis. Things that are already measured by money are tempting targets for mathematicization, for example, because the task of defining them numerically has already been done, albeit in ways that may be erroneous, unreflective, politically motivated, arbitrary, and so on. Similarly, social entities that have good archives are tempting targets for historical analysis, even if they don't have any real historical continuity at all.[1]

The presence of elective affinities means that when an area is ingested by researchers whose choices fall outside those affinities, the temptation to reintroduce defeated distinctions and methods is extreme. We see this particularly in cases of fractally extreme arguments. So the attempt of economics to extend price-based analysis to areas like family life has now ended up with the questioning of purely economic approaches, even as the attempt of Marxism to give purely economic accounts of political and cultural life in the 1960s and 1970s gradually crumbled under the reintroduction of noneconomic social structures like the state and the later reintroduction of cultural structures beyond the material realm altogether.

It is also true that in everyday social scientific life elective affinities conceal the extraordinary difficulty of truly general social analysis, analysis that transcends these affinities. It is easy to attack opponents because their accounts of their turf seem less effective than one's account of one's own. But when they have been finally routed, one must suddenly extend one's own account to *their* turf. Then the power of the affinities becomes suddenly manifest. It was easy for the various historicist views of social science to attack the static theories characteristic of the 1950s for their inability to explain social change. But when those theories were defeated and change was implicitly taken to be the primitive state of social life, suddenly the newer view had to explain the stability of much of social life, a stability that used to be "handled," as it were, by the stability theorists with their "norms." In fact, this task has been quietly and completely ignored by historical sociologists.

The other, and more important, reason for the indigestibility of alien turfs is the fact that disciplines shape or construct their objects of investigation very much to their own tastes. What is taken over, when conflict theory defeats consensus theory, or when the constructionist sociology of science ousts the Mertonians, includes much that has already been carefully constructed by those who were defeated. Empirical social reality has no given shape to be liberated from the stupid concepts of predecessors. Rather it has been shaped—by data collection, by theoretical concepts, by the very making of things to measure and discuss—into something in the

---

1. On the reification of historical realities based on merely apparent continuity, see my history of the *American Journal of Sociology,* in Abbott 1999a, chaps. 3–6.

image of predecessor's paradigms. When this something is taken over, it proves recalcitrant indeed.

It is this problem that we study in the present chapter. The stress concept as it was received by quantitative sociology and related literatures in the mid-1960s had a long history. It had inherited a long series of intellectual and research lineages. Having been mostly an "applied" rather than a "pure" concept, it had a multiple character that proved extraordinarily indigestible in the mouth of univocal, positivistic stress science.

1. Where Did Stress Come From?

Although the word "stress" was used to denote a general anxiety rooted in the cares of life as early as 1914, the term was not general in popular literature until the early 1950s, when it was popularized by Hans Selye. But the *concept* of stress—that is, the idea that life places difficult demands on individuals, who then succumb under the strain to psychological or biological disease—first appeared long before, originating in the Romantic critique of modernity.[2] That the stresses and strains of modern life could cause mental disease was "an almost ritualistic belief" of the nineteenth century.[3] Benjamin Rush had attributed outbreaks of mental disease to the American revolution. The Jacksonian reform movement that built America's mental hospitals based its etiological theories on stress and its "moral therapy" on stress removal. Grob tells us, "The moral causes of mental disease included—to cite only a few examples—intemperance, overwork, domestic difficulties, excessive ambitions, faulty education, personal disappointments, marital problems, jealousy, pride, and, above all, the pressures of an urban, industrial, and commercial civilization, which was considered to be unnatural to the human organism."[4]

What the Jacksonians saw as causes of *mental* disease, the later nineteenth century saw as causes of *nervous* disease. In his 1880 best-seller on *American Nervousness*, George Beard argued that the pressures of modern life often led to "neurasthenia," which is quite recognizable as modern psychiatrists' "anxious depression." A syn-

---

2. My discussion of stress theories of mental disease in the early and mid–nineteenth century relies heavily on Rosen 1959 and Dain 1964. For the later period, discussed in following paragraphs, illustrative sources are: on neurasthenia, Rosenberg 1962 and Gosling 1976; on traumatic neurosis, Schivelbusch 1979. See also Abbott 1982, pt. 4, for a discussion of social control and psychiatry in the period 1880–1930. The original reference to the term is in Cannon 1914.

3. Rosenberg 1962:254.

4. Grob 1973:156.

drome of vague anxieties, fears, and fatigue, neurasthenia was usually accompanied by minor, nonspecific pains in heart and gut, as
well as by headache and other "nervous" symptoms. As Rosenberg
puts it, "The human body, like the dynamo, could produce only a
limited amount of nervous force, while the stress of nineteenth century life acted upon the human nervous system as so many added
lamps would upon an electrical circuit."[5]

Other stress-disease concepts emerged as well. Doctors described
a variety of "occupational neuroses"—telegrapher's spasm, writer's
cramp, and so on. (These were the old names for carpal tunnel syndrome.) Like neurasthenia, these were "functional neuroses," in
which a chronic stress produced painful symptoms without visible
pathology. There were also "traumatic neuroses," in which a single
acute trauma produced similarly mysterious symptoms.

By the Progressive Era, the notion that chronic and acute stress
could cause nervous and mental disease was a popular truism. To
discover the dimensions of that truism, we can turn to the popular
literature.

My search covers the first twenty volumes of the *Readers'
Guide*—from 1900 to 1957, by which time the quantitative stress
literature had taken its modern form. We can begin with the heading
"stress, psychological" in volume twenty, then search backward to
find its ancestors. For example, "stress, psychological" first appears
simply as a heading with the caption "see tension." "Tension" has
itself various ancestors, and so on. In addition, at some points the
Guide has several active headings for a single concept or for a concept and its subparts, and we can follow these lines as well. By working backward and forward in this fashion, one uncovers a universe of
indexing headings that captures all the basic literatures eventually
related to stress.[6]

---

5. Rosenberg 1962:250.

6. For all these headings, I have reviewed the titles, and in dozens of cases the
texts, of the articles involved. I have not searched the earlier period because of the
switch to other indexing systems. Of course there are major changes in the *Readers'
Guide* throughout its publication, but since I am seeking popular concepts, and since
the *Guide* generally dropped journals that became esoteric, I can assume that the
Guide covered roughly the same region of interest throughout.

I have tried to make the analysis as reliable as possible. All headings "ancestrally
connected" to the original one were searched, without exception, and all articles
within them counted to yield the figures that appear below. The grouping of categories was essentially interpretive, based on reading the titles and, in many cases, the
complete texts of the articles involved. (Since there were thousands of articles involved, of course I could not read them all.) This reading also supports my discussion
of the contents of the various fields. It should be noted that the *Guide's* classifications
themselves introduce another distinctively interpretive element.

Within this genealogy, several somewhat separate lines lead to the current stress concept. One can give general names to these lines and group under them the relevant indexing heads from the *Guide:*

General Label	Headings from the *Readers' Guide*
1. anxiety	anxiety, fear, stress (physiological), stress (psychological), tension, worry
2. mind/body	medicine (psychosomatic), mental healing, mind and body
3. performance	fatigue, rest
4. hygiene	adjustment (social), mental hygiene
5. nervous disease	nervous disease, neurosis
6. mental disease	mental disease
7. nervous system	nervous system

For each volume of the guide, figure 2.1 shows the percentage of all stress articles provided by each of the first four of these seven themes, these four being the major topics; the full data for the figure appear in table 2.1.

The first theme here is anxiety. "Anxiety" meant problems of "fear" and "worry" that were perennial, cyclical concerns. The fears were of many things—economic crisis, war, darkness, certain kinds of animals. The worries concerned the same things, along with the lesser worries of everyday life. Often, such fears and worries were labeled by effect rather than cause. They might, for example, be called "nerves"; "the 'liver' of the last century has become, we are told, the 'nerves' of today."[7] After World War II the more modern terms "tension" and "anxiety" made their first appearance as index headings, although neither became a substantial index entry until the 1950s.

Closely related to anxiety is a second literature, which specified these ties of psyche and soma, what I shall call the mind/body literature. This literature usually thought in terms of mind's *control* of the body. The numerical dominance of this theme in 1900 reflects the waxing of Christian Science, New Thought, and other mind cure movements, as well as the slightly later mainline psychotherapies of the Emmanuel Movement and psychoanalysis. All these movements combined beliefs about the psychological etiology of physical problems, psychophysical monism, and psychological, often hypnotic, treatment. After its turn-of-the-century peak, the mind/body theme largely disappeared until the 1940s brought the first fruits of

---

7. Repplier 1910:199.

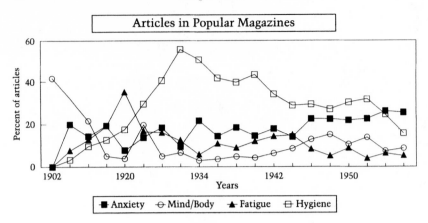

Figure 2.1

Table 2.1

	Anxiety	Mind/Body	Fatigue	Hygiene	Nervous System	Nervous Disease	Mental Disease
1900–1904	0.0	41.7	0.0	0.0	58.3	0.0	0.0
1905–1909	19.8	32.1	7.6	3.1	12.2	22.1	3.1
1910–1914	14.2	21.6	12.8	9.5	11.5	23.6	6.8
1915–1918	19.2	4.8	19.2	12.5	7.7	25.0	11.5
1919–1921	7.5	3.8	35.0	17.5	7.5	17.5	11.3
1922–1924	13.7	19.6	16.7	29.4	9.8	4.9	5.9
1925–1929	18.2	4.7	16.2	40.5	3.4	5.4	11.5
1929–1932	9.5	6.7	12.3	55.3	4.5	6.7	5.0
1932–1935	21.5	2.5	5.8	50.4	9.1	4.1	6.6
1935–1937	14.2	3.3	10.8	41.7	5.8	10.8	13.3
1937–1939	18.4	4.4	8.8	39.7	3.7	8.1	16.9
1939–1941	14.4	4.0	12.0	43.2	9.6	4.8	12.0
1941–1943	17.7	6.1	14.3	34.0	2.0	13.6	12.2
1943–1945	13.9	8.2	14.8	28.7	3.3	23.8	7.4
1945–1947	22.5	12.5	8.3	29.2	4.2	14.2	9.2
1947–1949	22.3	14.9	4.7	27.0	4.7	6.1	20.3
1949–1951	22.1	10.3	8.8	30.1	2.9	10.3	15.4
1951–1953	22.6	13.5	3.8	31.6	2.3	10.5	15.8
1953–1955	25.9	7.0	6.3	24.5	1.4	9.8	25.2
1955–1957	25.4	8.3	5.2	15.5	3.1	6.7	35.8

formal psychosomatic medicine: the endocrinological connection of stomach ulcers with personality around 1940, the analysis of asthma, colitis, hypertension, and similar diseases later on.[8]

These first two literatures—the literatures of anxiety and mind/body—conceived of problems of living (what the quantitative stress

8. On the Emmanuel Movement, see Gifford 1978.

literature would later call life events) as *interfering* with the individual's physical or mental health. By contrast, the two other literatures central to the culture's stress concept—what I shall call the performance and hygiene literatures—saw them the other way around, as signs of an individual's failure to successfully *adjust* to modern life. In the first pair of literatures, the individual was taken as given and society was the problem. In the second, society was given and the individual was the problem.

The turn-of-the-century performance literature originated in scientific management's concern for work performance and peaked, as did that concern generally, shortly after the First World War. These articles mostly concerned fatigue at work. Fatigue had become a general cultural metaphor by the 1920s, when "that tired, run-down feeling" made its debut as a popular culture concept and popular magazines debated the "real meaning of fatigue." During and after World War II, studies of performance under combat stress revisited this long-standing area of interest.[9]

Of much broader impact than the performance literature was the enormous literature on hygiene of the mind. The mental hygiene movement had begun when psychiatrists wearied by insoluble chronic psychoses turned to acute psychosis and prevention. This move made mental hygiene the dominant approach to questions of stress and disease, particularly mental disease, by the early 1920s. It remained dominant for decades. The mental hygiene movement believed that untreated life problems led to nervous and ultimately mental disease. Prevention was accomplished by adjusting the individual and society to each other. Since social change was seldom possible, the adjustments were perforce made by individuals. One could only adjust to stress, not protest it or fight it off, as the literatures of anxiety and mind/body implicitly suggested.[10]

There were, then, four major themes involved in the popular literature on stress and disease up to midcentury: a concern about anxiety, an ambivalence about mind and body, an image of performance under pressure, and a general theory of adjustment. In their views of the stressed individual, the four themes present two antithetical sides of one problem: the relation between individual and society in modern life.[11]

---

9. The "real meaning of fatigue" is a quote from Johnson 1929.

10. Basic sources on the mental hygiene movement are Dain 1980; Abbott 1982; Grob 1983.

11. These four major ancestors of stress are complemented by three minor themes: nervous system, nervous disease, and mental disease. "Nervous system" is chiefly important as the original, general heading from which nearly all the others later separated. "Nervous disease" covers a variety of topics, some of which are stress

On the one side, there was the notion of individual role performance under pressure, a notion whose echoes of efficiency and optimality tied it directly to scientific management and to rationalization. On a larger scale, but still on this "social" side, was the notion of the "efficient use" of the individual in society, the idea of adjustment through (mental) hygiene. Both these literatures (performance and hygiene) defined job loss, marital difficulties, and other personal problems as signs of or occasions for individual maladjustment.

On the other, "individual" side, the literature of anxiety viewed the very same events not in terms of their potential disutility to society, but in terms of their actual damage to the individual. The anxiety literature told of the direct impact of the modern social structure on the individual, an impact deriving not only from modern rootlessness, but also from the disappearance of old definitions for anxiety-provoking events.[12] Similarly, the mind/body literature's first subject was the defense of the individual against external threats, those of the social structure as much as those of microorganisms. The later, psychosomatic version of this theme expressed even more clearly the social, and specifically modern, origins of ailments like ulcers, colitis, and hypertension.

The cultural concept of stress, then, was itself a dual concept. It assembled four related themes into the single image of the stressed individual, an individual at once damaged by society and maladjusted to it. This image had (and has) its great meaning for us precisely *because* it binds anxiety and mind cure with social adjustment and performance, linking these with the larger antithesis between romanticism and individualism on the one hand and rationalization and mechanization on the other. By binding together these opposed figures of damage and maladjustment, the dual image of the stressed individual gives us one of our only common and legitimate ways of talking about central problems of modern existence. The public will not read Spencer, Durkheim, or Freud. But it will eagerly consume articles and talk shows that discuss the central concerns of such writers via the question of stress. In such popular venues, the image of stress is expanded or reduced to fit any situation. The duality of damage and maladjustment can comprehend a nation, a business firm, a marriage, a moment. At all these levels,

---

related, others not. Finally, "mental disease," although central to the nineteenth-century approach to stress, became less so in the twentieth. The sudden resurgence of popular interest in mental illness in the 1950s signaled not a return to the question of stress and disease but the discovery of new ataractic drugs.

12. See, e.g., Abbott 1980; Lears 1982.

the notion of stress makes life comprehensible. It explains unfortunate events.[13]

Note that the stress concept's duality of damage and maladjustment is *not* a fractal distinction, despite its "flexible size." Rather, it is what I shall call a "syncresis," using the Greek word for putting together things that are normally opposed. A syncresis has the property of constitutive ambiguity; a given episode of stress—at whatever level—involves both damage and maladjustment at the same time. It might seem that there is damage from the individual's point of view and maladjustment from the society's. But the individual is always worrying that "maybe it's me who is to blame," while few if any societies completely ignore the burdens they place on individuals. Thus, a syncresis involves both points of view at once. We might then argue that the individual (or the society) "is of two minds about the matter." But we should not allow such a phrasing to hypostatize the distinction into a pair of separate inner emotions. A syncresis is constituted of ambiguity; to separate its parts is to destroy it. Syncreses thus do have the fractal character that they reappear irrespective of levels of reduction. But unlike fractal distinctions they are not oppositions that subdivide, but oppositions that unify.[14]

2. Problems in the Scientific Study of Stress

The stress symbol helps define difficult events precisely because it captures our own ambiguities and ambivalences about them. It might seem that the proper methods to study such a phenomenon are by definition qualitative. For a syncretic symbol is necessarily multivocal, and the assumption of multivocality is the defining characteristic of interpretation as opposed to positivism. Therefore, since interpretation is one of the fractal choices made by the qualitative methodological manifold (see chapter 1), it seems to follow that the proper study of stress must be qualitative. Indeed, throughout much of the period before 1965, most professional study of stress was qualitative and interpretive. Psychiatrists and psychologists discussed stress by discussing individual cases in detail. But as fractal

---

13. This sentence is a paraphrase of Evans-Pritchard's deadpan title for chapter 4 in his Azande book: "the notion of witchcraft explains unfortunate events" (Evans-Pritchard 1976).

14. I must apologize for burdening the reader with yet another new concept; one of the reviewers of the book complained of its profusion of mechanisms and concepts. The reader will find in the index a complete list of them, with page references for their first introduction, under the index heading "concept of. . . ."

cycles in academia brought survey analysis and other "scientific" methods to hegemony in the behavioral sciences, it became necessary for them to analyze even phenomena to which they were ill suited, like stress. It was necessary to comprehend the opposite. As a result, the stress area began to support a large quantitative literature.

What do we expect when a syncresis or any other inherently multivocal concept is studied under a methodological manifold presuming univocality? Of course we expect disorder and misunderstanding. One scholar might view divorce as a maladjustment problem originating in the personalities of feuding couples, while another might view it as a damage problem originating in excessive societal demands on the individuals involved. The first would reply that strong personalities could prioritize and thereby handle demands, the second that personality problems would themselves arise from the excessive demands. And so on. Damage and maladjustment are chicken and egg. We can see these chicken-and-egg problems easily by studying the "problems" the scientific stress literature has seen in itself. Many of these can be shown to arise from the struggles of the syncretic stress concept within the restrictions of the quantitative methodological manifold.

Before looking at these problems, however, it is helpful to understand the quantitative stress literature's terminology. Some definitions, then. The literature views the individual as subject to a number of pressures, which are called "stressors." These can be chronic forces like loneliness or long-lasting diseases (e.g., arthritis), or they can be acute forces like divorce or bereavement. Acute stressors are usually called "life events."[15]

The result of stressors on the individual is called "distress." (The *popular* literature usually calls stressors "stresses" and distress "stress.") Distress is measured in various ways, but most often by self-reports of feelings. Between the force of stressors and the outcome of distress lie what are called mediating factors. Most of these are resources that "buffer" the effects of stress—friends ("social support"), protective modes of behavior ("coping"), force of character ("coping strength"), and similar helps.[16]

As of the mid-1980s—after two decades of active social stress research—the discontents of stress scientists with their own field

---

15. Note the ironic implication that to be unstressed is to have a life without events; that is, to be dead. This theme, with its echoes of Freud, returns below.

16. Some things are hard to locate within this picture. Arthritis, for example, is both a chronic and, in its flare-ups, an acute stressor. At the same time, it produces immediate distress under both guises, and may also reduce time spent with friends (because certain activities are difficult) as well as prevent certain modes of coping. It is thus at once a chronic and an acute stressor, an unmediated source of distress, and

comprised three types of problems: with definitions, with measures, and with theories. Many of these problems had been recognized from the earliest days of the research. The very endurance of these central problems is a first hint that they arose not from soluble scientific difficulties, but from the syncretic character of the general culture's concept of stress. If the problems had been resolvable without dismantling the central concept of investigation, they would long before have been solved. Stress was simply indigestible.

Discontent with definitions began with the term "stress" itself. Some complained that it was ill defined, while others appreciated the freedom provided by precisely that vagueness, and still others bemoaned the mixture of approaches to definition. Many noted that all life is in some sense stressful and others similarly wondered why there was no concept of success in "coping" with stress. These issues—the universality of stress and the absence of a concept of

---

a determinant of both social support and coping behavior. As we shall see, the literature is by no means unaware of such complexities.

There is, to my knowledge, no scholarly history of the field of stress research. Mason (1975) offers a few tantalizing hints, while Selye (1976, pt. 1) gives a rather ego-centered account. Dohrenwend and Dohrenwend (1974:1–7) give a brief introduction to the stressful life events literature, the most active stress subfield in recent decades. One must rely, generally, on review articles from various periods, for example Cooper and Marshall 1976 on occupational stress; Jenkins 1971 on stress and cardiovascular disorder; Lazarus, Deese, and Osler 1952 on stress and performance; Vine 1981 on stress and crowding; and Kessler, Price, and Wortman 1985 on social stress systems generally. The modern stress literature descends from several tributaries. Walter Cannon founded positivistic studies of stress with his physiological work on emotions, focusing particularly on the adrenal medulla (see, e.g., Cannon 1929). From 1936 Hans Selye created and developed the model of the General Adaptational Syndrome (see, e.g., Selye 1946), a stress-interaction-response system mediated by the pituitary and the adrenal cortex that received considerable media exposure when generalized from animals to humans. A somewhat related literature on stress and performance expanded rapidly after World War II, pursued particularly within the Air Force (see Lazarus, Deese, and Osler 1952). Another source was the literature on psychosomatic medicine, which began in the 1930s as a response to the sharp separation of psychic and organic realms that had emerged with Freudian psychiatry in the 1920s. By 1950, early leaders like Franz Alexander and Flanders Dunbar had built a clinical literature on psychosocial factors in a number of diseases. Finally, the literature tracing disease to particular life experiences has its roots in the "life chart" technique of Adolf Meyer, one of the leading psychiatrists of mental hygiene and adjustment (Meyer 1948). The first life events scales appeared in the late 1950s (Hawkins, Davies, and Holmes 1957), and the now-standard Social Readjustment Rating Scale appeared in 1967 (Holmes and Rahe 1967). By the 1980s, life events research had become nearly a separate subfield of stress research (see, e.g., Holmes and David 1984:xiii–xviii).

I should note that I am not a stress specialist, and that while my selection of sources is not arbitrary, it undoubtedly seems incomplete to specialists. It will also seem dated. My review of the stress literature was done in 1987; I have not updated it because my argument is historical. If I show the stress literature to have been a fractal lineage at one point in time, that creates at least a reasonable presumption that it still is such.

positive outcome—clearly betrayed the influence of the historical stress concept. The notion that modern life is inherently stressful came directly from the mental hygiene and performance literatures, while the fruitless search for successful outcome echoed the mental hygiene literature's long-standing and nebulous definition of social adjustment as "positive mental health."[17]

Although definitional issues bothered stress researchers, most problems arose within the much more controversial area of measurement. Many worried about the mixture of self-report, performance, psychophysiological, and biochemical measures, particularly because of their diverse temporal relation to the "stress process." An immense variety of measures were used for distress, and there was little clarity about how they were to be related to each other or to the phenomenon itself.[18]

Other critics focused on the assumption that the phenomena measured were linear and unidimensional. These criticisms had begun early, as a reaction to the unexciting correlation between stress and physical or psychological morbidity, a correlation that typically accounted for 5 to 10 percent of the total variance in morbidity. Typically, the low correlation was attributed to measurement that was insufficiently specific. Two themes pervaded these general criticisms and continued throughout the critical measurement literature: the need for a finer temporal understanding of the stress process and the need to further specify measures and variables.[19]

Within the more specific areas of stressor and distress measures, many of these same complaints were repeated. Self-reports, for example, were criticized for their reliance on retrospection about stressful events, for their aggregated weighting schemes, and for their assumptions about additivity. They were also criticized for a wide variety of temporal problems, chiefly for neglecting the effects of the recency, salience, and duration of events. Other criticisms concerned confounding and contagion. It was early noted that wide conceptions of stress viewed disease (a form of distress) as a stressor, making disease an independent as well as a dependent variable. Some writers also noted direct causal shaping of conceptually inde-

17. On definitions, see Hinkle 1975, Rabkin and Struening 1976, and Baum, Gomberg, and Singer 1982. One reason for the absence of a positive concept of mental health was the recognition (see below) that even "positive" life events were stressful and hence that the lowest stress state of being was indeed death, as Freud had argued in his discussion of the death instinct in *Beyond the Pleasure Principle*.

18. See Baum, Gomberg, and Singer 1982 for a review of measurement concerns.

19. For critiques of linearity and unidimensionality, see Aiken 1961, Dean and Lin 1977, and Lundberg 1984. For general critiques, see also Rabkin and Struening 1976 and Ross and Mirowsky 1979.

pendent stressors (e.g., work status) by conceptually dependent distress (e.g., disease; if you're sick [distress] you can't work, but then you either become unemployed [which is a stressor] or you stay home without losing your job [which removes you from social supports]). Similarly, the tangled triangle of acute stressors, chronic stressors, and distress worried many writers. Still others noted the differential impact of physical and psychological distress on stressors. In responding to this confounding issue, many treated the lack of strong correlation between stress and distress as a level-of-measurement issue, seeking measures that would address the different meanings that particular individuals assign to similar events. In an extensive summary of this line of argument, Kessler, Price, and Wortman (1985) went even further, calling for "context-specific data"—measurement appropriate to a particular individual at a particular time. (This was a move toward personal narrative, a move out of the quantitative paradigm's generally analytic stance.) Similarly, earlier critics in this area had produced an extensive literature differentiating desirability (*positive* change) from mere change (positive and negative changes taken together) as stressful properties of life events.[20]

The themes of confounding and specificity appeared yet again in the measurement literature on mediating factors like social support and coping skills. Many authors commented on the need for improved definitions and measures of social support. Some called for more differentiated measures, addressing different components and functions of social support. A variety of confounding issues were also raised: that distress may lead individuals to undervalue support, that antecedent variables (e.g., ethnicity) may determine both social

---

20. On additivity, see Ross and Mirowsky 1979 and Baum, Gomberg, and Singer 1982. On temporal issues, see Rabkin and Struening 1976 and Tennant, Langelud, and Byrne 1985. On causal interdependency see Cooper and Marshall 1976. On intermingling of acute and chronic stressors see Kessler, Price, and Wortman 1985, and on differentials of physical and psychological stress, Dean and Lin 1977. On the earlier life events literature, see, e.g., Ross and Mirowsky 1979.

Complaints about the other types of stressor and distress measures—task performance, psychophysiological, and biochemical measures—mentioned many of the same themes. With performance measures, some wondered why certain particular tasks were used, while others focused on the confounding of motivation, coping, fatigue, and concentration with stressor effects on task performance. Still others focused on the familiar problem of individual variation. With psychophysiological and biochemical measures, issues of confounding again arose; catecholamine levels, for example, are partly a function of diet, age, and activity, all of which are related to both distress and other stressors. The temporal theme reappeared as well; biological measures fluctuate considerably more rapidly than does distress and therefore cannot be unambiguously temporally related to stressed states (Baum, Gomberg, and Singer 1982).

support and perception of stressors, that social support is, at least in part, a moving average of past life events. Measures of coping brought many of the same complaints; confounding and specificity were the central issues.[21]

In summary, complaints about measures of stressors, distress, and mediating factors circled around three central issues: the awkward and ambiguous temporal relation among indicators, the general confounding of measures of each family of variables with the others, and the lack of sufficient detail. In each case, the measurement criticism was closely tied to more theoretical criticisms.

The theoretical literature on stress in fact developed largely as a response to these measurement criticisms. Thus, the "mediating factors" between stress and distress—social support, coping skills, appraisal, personality variation, stressor character—were introduced when direct stress-response models proved a failure in the 1950s and 1960s. In most cases, later complaints about these mediating factors involved *their* insufficient detail. Some called for more detailed studies of stressor magnitude, intensity, and novelty. Many others called for recognition that individuals' personalities shape the meanings of stresses they suffer and urged closer study of emotional, motivational, and cognitive factors shaping that variation. Still others called for finer understanding of social support—the specific effects of isolation, marginality, ethnicity, and the nature of support providers, types, settings, and consequences. In studies of coping too, there appeared an interest in individual differences in meaning and in the various dimensions of coping, whether through altering perceptions, problems, or emotional responses.[22]

This theoretical insistence on finer specification was accompanied by an increasing desire for effective theorizing of the temporal order of stress. Some agonized over the problem of ordering stressor and response; others noted the difficulty of ordering "insidious" dis-

---

21. On definitions of social support, see Dean and Lin 1977, Thoits 1982, and various authors in Cohen and Syme 1985. On varieties of confounding, see Rabkin and Struening 1976 and Thoits 1982. Surprisingly, direct measures of distress—psychological and biological disease—received much less criticism in this literature, although the Gurin scale, for example, was from the outset known to be correlated with demographic factors independently related both to life events and to distress (Gurin, Veroff, and Feld 1960). I thank Professor Gurin for calling this fact to my attention.

22. Recommendations for study of stressor magnitude came from Rabkin and Struening (1976). From Hinkle (1975), Dohrenwend and Dohrenwend (1974), Herd (1984), and many others came calls for study of individual variation. Pleas to study social supports came from Thoits (1982) and Kessler, Price, and Wortman (1985). Barnard (1985) recommended individual-level study of differences in interpretation in the process of coping with stress.

tress and sharply demarcated life events. Many worried about the issues of causal direction, spuriousness, and reciprocal causality as well as about their relation to temporal ordering. The recognition that social support simply records a past series of life events proved particularly unnerving to theories believing in a sharp conceptual separation of the two (if you get divorced and your parents die, you not only have two life events, you also lose long-run social support). Moreover, coping, as many realized, could simultaneously ameliorate stress and perpetuate it.[23]

The theoretical literature on stress thus repeated the criticisms of the measurement literature. The central themes were temporality, confounding, and specification.[24]

3. The Quantitative Effects of a Syncresis

These self-criticisms of the scientific stress literature are easily seen to have arisen from the working out of the multivocal, syncretic stress concept within the fractal choices that make up quantitative methods. A first set of problems arose from the quantitative methodological manifold's renunciation of narrative. Stress as conceived in the image of the stressed individual was essentially a story concept; things happened, an individual struggled with them, and as a result became stressed. But the quantitative literature had no effective tools for narrative analysis. Its methods would support only narratives of variables, in which the important intricacies of individual narratives went underground as complex interactions. This inability to develop an effective temporal model was not unique to the stress literature, of course. Temporal models for the life course, status attainment, and occupational growth were no more effective than those for stress. Quantitative methods happened to prefer formal techniques unable to handle sequence and other narrative effects. The stress scientists escaped this particular cul de sac only by complexifying the narrative structure of their models. They made the "narrative of the variables" more and more complex, if not moving

---

23. On temporal order, see Chalmers 1981 and Lazarus and Folkman 1984. On the stressor response problem, see Tennant, Langelud, and Byrne 1985 and Jenkins 1971. On insidious life events see Dohrenwend and Dohrenwend 1978. On the confounding of social support and life events, see Dean and Lin 1977 and Thoits 1982.

24. Complaints about methods per se—statistical techniques—occupied a smaller part of the critical literature on stress. Writers complained about the use of retrospective data, simple statistics, and cross-sectional designs, as well as about incautious sampling, particularly once "help seeking" became defined as a means of coping, thus confounding entry into the typical stress dataset with one of the independent variables. But methods per se did not produce major complaints.

directly to study variant stress narratives within cases. Thus there
was a beginning of "comprehending the opposite" in terms of narrative, but only a beginning.[25]

A similar issue arose from the problem that stress-related variables have different meanings in different contexts. One aspect of
the univocality assumption of the quantitative methodological manifold is that causal meaning is context free. Again, stress scientists
escaped this blind alley by allowing variables to become somewhat
context dependent.

But these are simple fractal effects. They show how the distinctions of narrative versus causalism and univocal versus multivocal
measurement present important choices even deep within what appeared to its opponents as a uniformly causalist, univocal literature.
Even though in large the stress literature was quantitative and univocal, nonetheless it divided inside over issues that recapitulated its
own differences from qualitative literatures.

More important for my argument here are the direct results of
trying to analyze an inherently multivocal concept—in this case a
syncresis—within a scientific enterprise strongly committed to
univocality. In fact, the syncresis of the stress concept itself produced both conflicts and opportunities for the quantitative literature. These arose from stress's symbolic and rhetorical structure.
The dual symbolic structure of stress produced, first of all, the great
confusion over indicators of stress and distress. The literature found
it hard to choose between psychological and somatic indicators because it had inherited the cultural concept's split over mind and
body. It could not choose between performance and debility indicators because it inherited the stress concept's split between performance and anxiety. Indicators of all these kinds seemed important
to stress scientists precisely because all had been part of the cultural
concept of stress with which they began. We cannot escape these
indicators or even separate them without undermining that concept altogether. That we do not—that quantitative researchers on
stress didn't take performance and debility completely apart, for
example—tells us something about the original stress concept's cultural importance, not only for the public thinking about modernity,
but also, as the record seems to show, for stress scientists.

As its second direct effect, the syncresis of stress produced the
confounding of which the literature complains so much. Our ambivalence about whether mental defenses (e.g., ignoring cancer symptoms, for example) are coping strategies (proindividual—why notice

---

25. On narrative, see Abbott 1983, 1992b, and Abell 1987.

something that may be irremediably wrong?) or maladjustments (antisociety—why don't people catch it early when it is cheap to treat?) reflects ambivalences enshrined in the cultural stress concept since the mind cure and mental hygiene movements. For us, the stressed individual is both damaged *and* maladjusted. Better measurement is not going to change that. Similarly, the question of whether social support is true comfort (supporting the individual) or carrion comfort (concealing society's attacks on the individual) derives directly from the cultural concept's deeply ambivalent attitude about society's effect on the individual. The scientifically deadly interpenetration of stressor, distress, support, and coping came ultimately from the merging of three problematic antitheses in the stress concept: mind and body, society and individual, adjustment and anxiety. Thus, central complaints of the stress literature arose from its attempt to comprehend a concept whose absolute multivocality was deeply alien to that literature's general methodological stance.

Like most powerful concepts, stress has not only a symbolic structure (syncresis); it also has a rhetorical one. This structure too produced conflicts and difficulties within the quantitative science of stress.[26]

To begin with, to speak of stress is to assert, rhetorically, that stress exists, that there is such a thing. And for a scientist, to assert that stress exists is further to assert that it must be different from other social phenomena; there must be things that are not part of stress. (Otherwise we have a concept that is meaningless because absolutely universal.) Yet the boundary between stress and normalcy bewildered the scientific stress literature, which steadily became less and less clear about what sorts of experience are not stressful. This happened precisely because in using the stress concept, the *public* ignored that boundary altogether. For it, the nonstressful was simply the nonmodern; the ambiguities of stress pervade modern life. This belief in the universality of stress, taken over by the scientists, led them far afield indeed. Accepting the culture's term meant accepting its unscientific rhetoric of existence.

But a term's rhetorical structure extends beyond the assertion of existence. Terms like "stress" persuade by means that are implicit in how they delimit their objects. The term "profession," for example, uses the rhetorical figure of metonymy. The general culture, like most social scientists, calls occupations "professions" if they

---

26. The classic source on the social character of rhetorical figures, or tropes, is Vico [1744] 1961:87 ff.; a modern version is Burke 1969:503–17. For particular definitions, I am following Hayden White 1973:34.

resemble law and medicine. Law and medicine represent the professions just as sail represents ship or crown represents monarchy. With "stress," however, the rhetorical figure involved is synecdoche, another figure that takes the part for the whole, but not via resemblance, as does metonymy. Rather, the synecdochal term embodies the character of the whole, as in "he is all heart." In terms of my earlier analysis, we take the image of the stressed individual to epitomize the *whole* of the modern individual-society relation as conceived by the Romantic and post-Romantic account. Our other concerns about that relation are hidden, although they of course exist. We simply talk about them by talking about stress.

Like the assertion of existence, this rhetorical strategy of the cultural concept of stress had obvious implications for the quantitative stress literature. For the literature treated this symbol, which pointed to a larger whole, as if it *were* that larger whole. It therefore ignored things that might be important aspects of the "stress" phenomenon but that were not part of the image of the stressed individual. The most important of these invisible things were the social structures that generate and articulate stress (e.g., bureaucracy, mobility, competition), social structures once seen as contingent but now accepted as objectively given. In the quantitative literature, these social structures were the subjects of brief platitudes and recommendations that we "find ways to stimulate individuals to take care of their own [!] problems."[27] In short, as serious topics, social structures disappeared. Here, then, the rhetorical structure of the stress concept produced not conflict but simple avoidance.

4. The Fractal Fecundity of Stress

The syncresis that underlies our stress concept has thus had decisive effects on the quantitative stress literature. Ingested into that literature as a part of a "social scientization" of modern life, it has fueled confusion over indicators and guaranteed a fractal confounding of the various aspects of the stress process. It has also blurred the distinction between stress and normalcy and hidden from scientific analysis central aspects of modern stress. To this extent, comprehending things for which one's paradigm is ill designed proves very debilitating. Why then has so problematic a concept not been rejected altogether?[28]

---

27. Elliott and Eisdorfer 1982:137.

28. There are a number of possible answers to this rhetorical question, but they would take us far afield. Perhaps using a culturally powerful term is necessary to

The answer lies implicit in the brief discussion of narrative and contextual meaning at the beginning of the last section. The stress concept remains as a scientific term because studying multivocal concepts in a univocal fashion produces not only conflicts and collisions. It also produces opportunities. Comprehending the opposite is fruitful. A stress scholar in a blind scientific alley can always opt for the "other side" of the stress concept, using its multivocality to escape a dead end. One studies stress as "damage" until one gets into trouble; then stress as "maladjustment" permits escape. Indeed, the chicken-and-egg relation of damage and maladjustment permits escape through yet another of the fractal distinctions affiliated into the quantitative manifold, that of narrative versus causality. The conceptual move from damage to maladjustment conceptions can easily be emplotted (and indeed concealed) as a simple move within a narrative of stress.

This utility of syncresis is easily traced through the literature. The quantitative literature's response to many of its difficulties was to introduce finer and finer characterizations of variables and higher- and higher-order interaction effects. On a first reading, these strategies seemed to break the general, cultural concept of stress into smaller and smaller parts, presumably to be reassembled later. If one reads, for example, the 1985 review article by Kessler, Price, and Wortman on social factors in psychopathology, one reads dozens of statements like the following:

> At what point does heavy drinking change from a coping strategy into a symptom?

> For example, a woman with breast cancer may minimize her distress by denying initial symptoms, thus delaying treatment and reducing her chances for a favorable outcome.

---

maintain funding for the researchers involved. Perhaps those researchers simply have not got a good enough replacement yet, and when they do, "stress" will disappear. Counterexamples to this second argument, however, are easily found. In the early 1970s many cases of manic depression were found to respond to lithium treatment. The disease was essentially reconceptualized as lithium insufficiency and cases that did not respond were seen as misdiagnosed. But today, we read again of mood swings and bipolar illness; the old concept is back with new (and sometimes old) names. (This example comes from personal experience—five years' service [1973–78] as a psychologist in the Manteno [Illinois] State Hospital, a large facility for the acute and chronically mentally ill, during the period of lithium's introduction.) Syphilis provides another example; its nineteenth-century cultural image as a quasi stress disease influenced medical practice long after Noguchi and Moore had demonstrated its bacterial mechanism (Abbott 1982:363). It is probable that culturally important terms always survive scientific "reductions." When the literature "solves" it, stress will not disappear but will simply resurface in a new guise.

> By enjoining a crisis victim to look on the bright side, for example, the supporter may lead the victim to feel that his feelings and behaviors are inappropriate.[29]

At first, the authors seem to assume that these "bits" of the stress picture can be well defined out of context: that with proper conceptualization they will work in equations as independent variables. Thus, the first quote implies a three-valued variable—nondrinking, drinking as coping, drinking as symptom. But the authors' insistence on complexity shows that they do not really believe in treating such variables as main effects, but rather in particular stressed lives as experiences to be understood. They speak first as causalists who think that abstractions like "social support" actually cause things, but then reject those abstractions because they lack sufficient narrative complexity.

At a deeper level they are clearly worried that drinking may be symptom and strategy *at once*, just as the cancer symptoms could be false positives, and the cheerful supporter is damned if she does, damned if she doesn't. Their own grounding in the cultural concept of stress tells them that such multivocality calls for interpretations. This is the result of syncresis.

And the cultural concept provides such researchers, through its complex byways and ambiguities, with a hundred ways to conduct those interpretations, to complexify the simple notions with which they begin. Thus:

> We need to learn more about what is actually done when people attempt to provide support and how these actions are perceived by the recipient.

> [Examining how people cope with different problems] may clarify whether coping with one problem imparts insights or skills that can be useful in dealing with other problems.

> If the effects of life events are modified by chronic stresses in these ways, . . . explicit consideration of chronic stresses is necessary.[30]

These interpretive questions about simple situations come directly from the cultural model as internalized by quantitative students of stress. It is the source for their hypotheses, their way out of traps. Moreover, it is the cultural concept of stress that provides them with the little "plausibility stories" with which they introduce new hypotheses. For example:

---

29. Kessler, Price, and Wortman 1985:552, 552, 548.
30. Kessler, Price, and Wortman 1985:550, 558, 540.

[Brown and Harris] argue that continuing stresses can exacerbate the effects of life events. This can occur by creating stress overload, as when a person whose current life circumstances are straining his or her coping capacities is confronted with an additional difficulty created by an unanticipated life event . . . Events of this sort can be trivial in and of themselves, but they take a new meaning in the context of chronic difficulties. For example, one woman in the Brown and Harris study became severely depressed shortly after her daughter went on vacation. In her words, the daughter's temporary absence led her to "realize then for the first time that one of these days I would lose both of the children. It made me realize just how lonely I was and how I depended on their ways."[31]

These authors justify their theory on the basis of a particular story, and they clearly understand that theory within the general culture's stress concept as earlier discussed. The old and ambivalent framework of performance, fatigue, and anxiety is very present.

From the usual quantitative perspective, of course, what I am here calling "opportunities induced by the syncretic stress concept" are interpreted as "routine efforts to elaborate and test theoretical constructs." (The quote is from an anonymous referee of an earlier version of this chapter.) That is not at issue. The question is rather where the ideas for those efforts originate. The cultural concept's relation to the quantitative literature is rather like that of the three-dimensional sphere to Edwin Abbott's two-dimensional Flatland.[32] Trying to "see" the sphere, the two-dimensional mathematician sees only a circle getting steadily larger and then smaller and finally disappearing—the changing two-dimensional section of the sphere as it moves in a direction (up) that does not exist in Flatland. What syncresis allows is movement, with that sphere, into a whole new dimension, as if one of my tourists of the last chapter found a whole new area of the city.

In short, the syncretic concept of stress informs and fertilizes the quantitative literature just as it does the popular mind. Its very complexity gives it power in both arenas. The reason the cultural stress concept persists, despite the obvious disabilities it imposes on the quantitative literature, is that its fertility is far greater than those debilities. Stated in terms of chapter 1, those who would deny the multivocality of social phenomena are doomed to rediscover it and relieved when they do.

---

31. Kessler, Price, and Wortman 1985:539–40, quoting from Brown and Harris 1978:145.

32. Abbott 1956. Edwin Abbott and I are not related, to my knowledge.

5. Conclusion

In concluding, I wish to emphasize this positive quality, inverting the common position that the multivocal character of symbols like stress somehow forbids quantitative research about the phenomena they designate. On the argument of the preceding chapter, one can imagine some new turns that could be taken in this particular city of knowledge, further reversals of choices in the quantitative manifold that might lead scientific students of stress to other areas of inquiry. In the earlier version of this essay, published in 1990, I specifically recommended three main turns: choosing narrative rather than causal methods, using the syncresis of stress at a much more general level, and trying the more interpretive side of positivist methods themselves. It is useful to look at those recommendations and see whether the stress literature actually took the directions suggested. (I should be clear at the outset that, as should be no surprise, the stress literature paid no attention to this article directly. But the new directions might well have arisen from the literature itself.) I rely, in this judgment, on the magisterial review of the stress literature published by Peggy Thoits in 1995.

First, I recommended a turn to narrative. This was, in itself, nothing particularly revolutionary. After all, the idea of coping had arisen out of an essentially narrativistic attempt to make sense of weak results: what kinds of stories, analysts asked, could produce such weak correlations and yet sustain our basic idea of stress? The answer lay in granting back to the stressed individual some degree of control, some potentiality for action. Coping reemphasized an aspect of stress with direct roots in the mind cure literature of the turn of the century: the individual's power to act against stressors and distress. Formalized into variables, this new emphasis on an old theme became the basis for a renewed and improved positivistic analysis.

But I had in mind a more methodological turn. The literature's problems with measuring and analyzing the order of stress, distress, and other aspects of the stress process obviously reflected reliance on methods that were clumsy with ordered data. A movement toward more complex stochastic models and toward ideal-type models for stress narratives would help solve the ordering problem and partially avoid the specificity-interaction problem.[33] In the sequel, however, the literature made relatively few moves in this direction. In

---

33. More complex stochastic models were tried by, for example, Smith 1985. On ideal typical sequence models, see the various sources listed in Abbott 1995a.

her review Thoits still recommended the same thing as I had and for the same reasons. It had become clear to the literature itself that a move to methodological narrativism—a move to the opposite pole of a fractal distinction—would help it develop further. But few had made that move yet.

Second, I recommended using the syncresis of stress "at a broader level." By this I meant becoming self-conscious about the impact of the symbolic and rhetorical structure of the stress concept on the positivistic literature, particularly in obscuring certain central topics of analysis. In this regard, I argued first that we should study why the particular rhetorical figure of the stressed individual became culturally dominant, why we think about modernity using that image. That would be a program for the critical social and cultural history of stress. But I also suggested that we could study positivistically the phenomena that the rhetorical figure of the stressed individual obscures, developments like the coming of secularization, the problem of meaninglessness, the social structuring and social generation of stress, and, of course, our ambivalence about modern life itself. There were radical, feminist, and historical writers addressing these subjects. But the questions they considered were excluded from positivistic inquiry by the synecdochal figure of the stressed individual, which was taken as the only legitimate target of inquiry. The larger questions either disappeared from the literature or were derided as utopian.[34] Yet a positivistic literature on them— on the decline of alternative cultural representations for problems with living, for example—would have opened a whole new range of alternatives to current theories of why people react to stress as they do. Such subjects need not be the sole province of interpretive scholars, I argued. They had become so because of elective affinities among fractal distinctions.

This too became one of the Thoits's recommendations (1995:56), a fact that once again indicates both the utility of the fractal distinctions model—it predicted where the literature would see new opportunities—and the difficulty of seizing those opportunities. Seeing stress as a group rather than an individual phenomenon was extremely difficult.

My third recommendation was to try more interpretive methods within the general armamentarium of positivistic methods. After all, the importing of "interpretive" approaches was nothing new to

---

34. The "utopian" remark is in Elliott and Eisdorfer 1982:140. Some radical writers touching these subjects are Marcuse (1964), Comfort (1970), and Ehrenreich (1983).

the stress literature; it was in fact positivism's long-established strategy for freeing itself from self-imposed limits. Indeed, all the various
self-criticisms raised above are merely finer and finer specifications
of interpretive ideas within a positivistically formalized tradition—
the recognition of types of coping, of complex interactions between
stress and coping, of the backfiring of social support through
misunderstanding.[35]

Again I had in mind a "positivistic interpretivism," to coin an
oxymoron, in particular methods that formally addressed the problem of multivocality, like factor analysis and multidimensional scaling. There were few moves in this direction. But while these methods had made relatively little headway in the literature, the general
problem of meaning—the multivocal and situational character of
stressors—had clearly become an even stronger focus for the literature by the time of Thoits's review than it had been a decade before.
The problem was clearer than ever.

Thus all three of my recommendations had by 1995 emerged in
the literature—under their own steam, of course, not because of any
influence of mine. I made these recommendations not as a stress
specialist—I knew the concept's early history as a specialist, but
nothing else—but rather as an outsider reading a literature and calling on it to reverse some of the simpler fractal affinities that tended
to restrict it. The fact that these emerged as part of the literature's
own program seems confirmation, again, of the fractal model of development within literatures, both as a reality and as a normative
methodological commitment.

I have had several purposes in this chapter. My most general aim
was to support the fractal conception of knowledge by showing not
just that the customary sharp distinction between quantitative and
qualitative analysis is foolish, but exactly how and why it is foolish.
Many current writers, particularly leading theorists, seem to urge
the virtual abandonment of quantification on the grounds of its
willful ignorance of interpretation, interaction, and multivocality. It
is surprisingly common to argue that "positivism is dead" or that
we are "living in a postpositivist age." (This is positivism in the
broad sense; I myself have been using the term "positivism" in a
narrow rigorous sense and using "quantitative methodological manifold" as the more general term.) Such a position assumes a once-
and-for-all antithesis that the history of stress and stress research
belies. In fact, qualitative concerns continually operate within quantitative work to produce new lines of research. I suggested three

---

35. For further examples, see Lazarus and Folkman 1984.

ways in which that process might be furthered in the future, and strikingly all have emerged as themes in the literature.[36]

Beyond this general aim of demonstrating the utility of the fractal model, I have had three more specific aims. Empirically, I wanted to show why the quantitative stress literature—one of the most important single literatures of sociological empiricism—developed the way that it did. It is curious that in the years since I first conducted this research (1987) that literature seems to have lost at least some of its amazing impetus; although still strong, it no longer dominates the *Journal of Health and Social Behavior* like a colossus. In this sense, stress research may in the sequel turn out to be yet another of the generational paradigms discussed in the preceding chapter.

Conceptually, my aim here was to show how the process of "comprehending the opposite" unfolded. I argued in the first chapter that victorious paradigms are forced to take up the conceptual and empirical problems of work they displace. In this chapter, I have shown exactly how and why that process works. The stress literature could no more forget the agenda of problems set by the public's and the psychologists' qualitative stress concept than it could forget its own methodologies.

Practically, my aim was to begin to establish how productive is the "reversal of fractal choices." I wanted to show how even minor recrudescences of multivocality within univocal systems give rise to exciting new research. As I argued in closing the last chapter and as its own logic implies, the fractal model is at once a model for the way things *do* occur and a recipe for making real change happen. It is a model for method.

---

36. The fate of this chapter's journal version well illustrates the fractal character of the discipline. Of the early referees, one wrote from a philosophy/sociology of science position, and, although interested by the paper, couldn't recommend republishing a point so familiar (the influence of culture on science) without greater theoretical elaboration. The other, presumably a stress positivist, urged a much shorter paper with more current references and less jargon (e.g., terms like "rhetoric" and "metaphor"). A second-generation referee also argued from this point of view, calling much of the paper "overdrawn" yet at the same time "hardly new." Thus, from the perspective of the sociology of science, the paper was too weak and atheoretical an assertion of one familiar point (that cultural concepts influence scientific concepts). And from the perspective of stress positivism it was too extreme and theoretical a statement of quite another familiar point (that researchers ought to be careful with their terms). Had the paper been either more extreme or more guarded, it would have had an easier time, because it would have been clearly located in a particular subdiscipline with a particular conventional wisdom. Note that within their subfields these may very well have been a data-oriented sociologist of science and relatively reflective stress positivists; given the repetition of the larger distinction within each subfield, these would be the "proper" choices for referees.

3

The Fraction of
Construction

THE LAST chapter focused on the fractal opposition of quantitative and qualitative and examined fractal divisions largely within what is usually defined as a quantitative community. It focused on one of the several distinctions that usually separates quantitative and qualitative: positivism versus interpretation. In the present chapter, I wish to focus on a different distinction within the general opposition of quantitative and qualitative—the opposition of realism and constructionism. And I shall examine it largely within constructionist communities, which usually fall on the qualitative side of the larger opposition. So we have a different part of the same whole, and we view it, as it were, "from the other side."

As in the last chapter, I have several aims. My empirical aim is to trace the history of two constructionist moves in sociology. Conceptually, I wish to analyze in detail the fractionation process that I noted in chapter 1, at the same time fleshing out, through further examples, earlier concepts like generational paradigms and fractal cycles. (As it turns out, the fractionation process makes a historical link between the two constructionist moves here discussed, one of which arose as an extremal position against the other.) Finally, my substantive aim is to show how it has happened that although constructionism in one form or another has been a dominant theoretical stream in sociology from the 1920s to the present, much or most

I would like to acknowledge the help of Howie Becker, Rob Sampson, Jim Lynch, Pieter Slump, and Tracie Thomas on various parts of this project. I dedicate the chapter to Carolyn Williams, Associate Professor of English at Rutgers University.

of our empirical work seems to ignore it entirely, taking social reality as utterly given.

I first define the major constructionist positions and sketch their intellectual lineages. I also consider the relation of constructionist and anticonstructionist arguments. In the second section are two extended analyses of the evolution of particular constructionist positions—first within the deviance literature and second within the sociology of science. The chapter closes with a theoretical discussion.

1. Definitions and Historical Origins

As with stress, it is useful to begin by defining basic terms, in this case the social constructionist argument. That argument's first element is a commitment to idealism or mentalism. Reality (in particular social reality) is not simply there, but must at the very least be interpreted and known before one can react to it. (Most constructionisms take the stronger position that interaction is not a matter of knowing reality, but one of creating and reshaping it as one goes along.) Second, constructionism is nearly always diachronic. Construction is a process, a building up or a tearing down, a shaping or a changing. Third, this process takes place through social interaction. Construction occurs in and through the practical efforts of everyday life, principally through the negotiation or development of shared or antagonistic meanings.[1]

Historically, there have been two general versions of the constructionist argument in sociology and a third that arose outside. The two internal versions divide over another familiar distinction, that between consensus and conflict.

The consensus version of constructionism views microsocial reality as evanescent and precarious. It is therefore astounded that people manage to construct a social world in which they have substantial commonalities. Since it takes meaning as quintessentially precarious, this is normally the more radical form of constructionism. Its philosophical roots lie in existentialism, phenomenology, and pragmatism. Because of these roots, it approaches the problem of consensus through contractarianism rather than through the social domination theory characteristic of Hobbes and Durkheim. I

---

1. My use of the word "interpretation" here does not indicate a logical conflation of the realist/constructionist distinction with the positivist/interpretivist one, a problem that is discussed below. However, in practice, the constructionist position virtually always assumes the multivocality of social symbols and entities. The chapter appendix contains a history of the phrase "social construction" up to about 1990.

shall call this constructionist tradition the "constitutive" version of constructionism in what follows.

The history of the constitutive constructionism tradition in modern sociology can be quickly summarized. Chicago school writers from W. I. Thomas and Robert Park onward argued for the social foundations of knowledge and identity, partly on their own and partly under the stimulus of their pragmatist colleagues George Herbert Mead and John Dewey. Thomas's theoretical linking of social experience, individual attitudes, and community beliefs in *The Polish Peasant* and other writings was repeated in most later monographs of the Chicago tradition—in the writings of Park, Johnson, and Frazier on race, in the work of Burgess and his students on communities and families, and in the somewhat later work of Hughes and his students on occupations. At the same time, Mead's virtuosic demonstration of mind, self, and society as aspects of a single process served as the foundation for Blumer's symbolic interactionism, a rendition of constitutive constructionism that was to dominate microsociology after the Second World War.[2]

European influence on this American tradition was late but important. The German idealist tradition had addressed the issue of "socially constituted reality" for a century, Kant and Hegel providing arguments that would later be called precursors of social constructionism. Max Scheler reassembled many of these arguments in the 1920s. But the central writer for sociology was Alfred Schutz, who attempted to merge Husserlian phenomenology and Weberian sociology in the 1930s. By the time Schutz's work was translated in 1967, his students Berger and Luckmann had published their brilliant combination of Schutz with Mead, Marx, Mannheim, and Freud, a combination that introduced the phrase "social construction" to the American reader. Other students of Schutz carried his dicta directly into research practice—notably Harold Garfinkel, whose "ethnomethodology" examined in micro detail the understandings actors constructed in interpersonal interaction. More recently, Bourdieu's work often follows this tradition.

The second line of constructionist argument in sociology began from a different premise, rooted in the traditional concerns of conflict theory: not the question of how it is that people ever agree about things that seem so different, but rather the question of how it is that they disagree so much about things that appear to be common realities. This problem led to investigations of how social loca-

---

2. Thomas and Znaniecki 1918–20. On the Chicago school more broadly, see the sources listed in Abbott 1999a, chap. 1.

tions shape individuals' perceptions of the social world. Ultimately traceable to the Marxist theory of ideology, this second view includes writers in that tradition like Mannheim, Goldmann, and Hauser. In the sequel I shall refer to this view as ideological constructionism.[3]

Ideological constructionism has historically been stronger in European social thought than has constitutive constructionism. Indeed, it took its first name—"the sociology of knowledge"—from Europe. The central text was Mannheim's *Ideology and Utopia* (1936), a reaction to Scheler's exposition of constitutive constructionism. There were also more overtly Marxist studies of situationally shaped forms of knowledge: literature (György Lukács, Lucien Goldmann), art (Arnold Hauser), and science (J. D. Bernal). These studies were usually Marxist, although, conversely, Marxist work on knowledge was not necessarily constructionist.[4] Despite this Marxist heritage—which in the current configuration of sociology would lead us to expect a populist, antielite emphasis—the sociology of knowledge came to the United States as an elite, esoteric field. While their colleague Blumer founded his version of constitutive constructionism and spread it widely from the mid-1930s, Louis Wirth and Edward Shils were translating Mannheim. But Wirth returned to his work on urbanism and Shils to his esoteric studies of intellectuals. Robert Merton, Burkart Holzner, and Werner Stark also wrote strongly theoretical work in the area. Empirical work— much or most of it Marxist—dates mostly from the 1950s (it was translated in the 1960s) and had little impact until the grudging sociological acceptance of Marxism in the 1970s.[5]

---

3. See, e.g., Marx and Engels 1970, Mannheim 1936, Goldmann 1964, and Hauser 1951.

4. Thus, while the Frankfurt school's magnificent studies grounded culture and identity in social life, Frankfurt writers discussed interaction itself very little. *The Authoritarian Personality*, for example, argued that a certain family structure, in the presence of certain kinds of social changes, produced a tendency to accept fascist demagoguery. Knowledge wasn't shaped in interaction, but was simply absorbed by a character conceived in explicitly Freudian terms. Only at the most abstract level were the ideas involved seen as interacting (i.e., with the ideologies of other classes in some theoretical space, rather than with other people in actual social interactions). Similar arguments were characteristic of Gramsci and other neo-Marxists whose work became visible in the 1970s (although in many cases written much earlier). Only Habermas, of all those writing in this tradition, moved explicitly toward an interactive conception of knowledge, and that largely under the stimulus of American sources.

5. It is noteworthy that by the time Kuklick reviewed the sociology of knowledge in 1983, there was literally nothing there to review. She had to write about authors who consider themselves sociologists of art, science, or culture to find something to fit under the rubric of sociology of knowledge. The major works of the "high" tradi-

As I shall discuss in detail below, a native version of this second line of constructionism arose through political radicalization of the symbolic interactionist tradition. Chicago students like Becker combined with students of Continental traditions like Cicourel to interpret deviance as largely in the eye of the beholder, a matter of labeling. By their implicit political radicalization in favor of the subordinate, the deviant, and the despised, these studies moved Blumerian constitutive constructionism toward a more ideologically constructionist position. However, their insistently micro character left these writers ill equipped for encounter with the societal-level Marxist tradition and, as we shall later see, Marxist writers reviled them wholeheartedly.

The two sides of constructionism in American sociology were married in Peter Berger and Thomas Luckmann's *The Social Construction of Reality*, first published in 1966. But the marriage was loveless. An introductory section ("The Foundations of Knowledge in Everyday Life") set forth the phenomenological version of constitutive constructionism. The lengthy second section ("Society as Objective Reality") set forth a complex version of ideological constructionism. The two sections were little related to one another, although each was excellent in its own right. Even the authors saw the first section as philosophical prolegomenon rather than essential sociological argument.[6]

A third general approach to construction arose outside sociology. This "structuralist" approach provides the direct link between the earlier sociological avatars of constructionism and the current vogue of poststructuralism. Saussure had argued that only in speech, and hence in interaction, did language develop. But his diachronic studies of language change were complemented by a synchronic conception of language as an ensemble establishing meaning through relationships among signs. Saussure's structuralist descendants heavily emphasized his synchronic side, usually ignoring both diachrony and social interaction. For Piaget, the "construction of the real in the infant" arose out of diachronic interaction but with physical, not social, objects. In Lévi-Strauss, structuralism moved toward purely

---

tion in this area were Mannheim 1936, Merton 1973, Holzner 1968, and Stark 1958. Empirical work included Goldmann 1964, Hauser 1951, Bernal 1953, and Lukács 1969. It is interesting that Albion Small was one of Marx's early American admirers, although his admiration was not unmixed. He did, however, remark at one point that in the future Marx would be thought to be the Galileo of the social sciences (Small 1911). In general, on the subject of Marxism in early American sociology, see Calhoun 1950. Marx was far more widely recognized than Cold War sociology was willing to admit.

6. Berger and Luckmann 1967:vi.

synchronic cultural analysis, while Barthes and other literary structuralists used it to derive meaning from interrelations among synchronic signs, ignoring interacting people altogether. By way of reaction, poststructuralism sought to reground meaning in time and social space. It thereby rediscovered the other side of Saussure, and with it some of the basic insights that were widespread in other versions of the constructionist tradition.[7]

Constructionism is conflated with or opposed to various other arguments by writers considering it. It is helpful to clarify these relations. (Put in terms of the argument of earlier chapters, I wish here to dissociate certain fractal distinctions from that between realism and constructionism.) If we take constructionism as that social theory which is idealist, diachronic, and interactional, then any position sharing one or two of those characteristics is a likely candidate for conflation. Similarly, any position reversing one or two of them seems like a possible opposite.

A first conflation is methodological. So much of America's constructionist work has been micro and observational that constructionism is often assumed to be logically tied to micro observational methods. Phenomenologists and ethnomethodologists have made this position dogma. However, as historical work on socially constructed categories indicates, there is no necessity for direct observation. There does seem, however, to be near universal reliance, in constructionist work, on interpretive methods as opposed to positivist ones. This methodological reliance is not necessary in principle. That social symbols are constructed doesn't necessarily imply that they can't be constructed with single, measurable meanings; they would have such meanings under extreme forms of consensualism, for example. However, in practice, constructionists with few exceptions assume the multivocality of social symbols and entities.

Methodological conflation leads directly to theoretical conflation. Constructionism is often equated with interpretive analysis tout court. The hermeneutic tradition, for example, makes the uncovering of multiple layers of meaning central, often working "interactively" between text, author, and receiver.[8] But constructionism,

---

7. See Lévi-Strauss 1963a, Saussure 1966, and Barthes 1967. Piaget (1963) used the same words for interaction with physical objects ("assimilation" and "accommodation") that Chicago interactionists Robert Park and Ernest Burgess had used for social interaction. The move of structuralists toward synchrony was part of their more general program, derived possibly from Durkheim's *Elementary Forms of the Religious Life*, of finding the experiential roots of Kant's categories of pure reason.

8. It is ironic, given the current lineup of affiliations among our various fractal distinctions, that hermeneutics began as a positivistic technique, in the hands of historians like Leopold von Ranke.

while accepting the importance of interpretation, makes interpretations fundamentally contingent on social (not interpretive) interaction. The insistence on diachrony—on the unfolding of meanings through a social process of interaction—gives constructionism a narrative emphasis, a sense of process, that is not always present in pure hermeneutics.

We are far less likely to conflate constructionism with diachronic interactional analysis that is not idealist in its approach—with classical small group decision theory, for example. No one misses the importance of making (rather than discovering) meaning in the constructionist tradition.

The problem of a proper opposite to constructionism is likewise a difficult one. Positivism I am here restricting to the narrow sense of an appraisal of reality as measurable and univocal. I have already argued that its opposition to constructionism is a logical conflation arising out of an empirical accident. Positivism in its broad sense— what I am here calling the quantitative methodological manifold— is not inherently materialist, synchronic, and noninteractional. That is, it does not inherently reverse all three of the defining assumptions of constructionism, although the most widespread forms of sociological positivism do in fact do just that. But some do not. Thus, for example, diachronic positivism, in the guise of time series analysis, event history analysis, and other formal temporal methods, is becoming widespread.

Materialism is another likely opposite to constructionism, but it may well be interactionist (network analysis is founded on the idea of material interactions) or diachronic (as in much of structural Marxism). Therefore, since positivism and materialism are both deeply flawed as opposites to constructionism, I use realism as an opposite to constructionism. It is not necessarily true that realism is synchronic and noninteractional, but the problems are less than with the other two words. Realism will have to do.[9]

Constructionism is thus the social theory that is idealist, diachronic, and interactional. It has generally been associated with interpretive methods, but has no logically necessary connection with them. Its opposite I shall call realism, meaning here a social theory that is not only realist in ontology, but also one that tends to be synchronic and noninteractional. (The Durkheim of *Suicide* is perhaps a good example.) As I noted, there are two principal strands of

---

9. I ignore here the "realist" social theory associated most prominently with Roy Bhaskar (see, e.g., Bhaskar 1986). Bhaskar's main interlocutors, and main audience, are philosophers, not social analysts trying to explain actual social happenings.

constructionism in sociology, one emphasizing the situational determination of knowledge, the other emphasizing the precariousness of common meaning.

In a fractal system, we expect the dichotomy of constructionism versus realism to be repeated within itself. In the first chapter, I argued that this process would lead over time to a fractal cycle. But sometimes, I argued, the fractal cycle is prolonged by rapid proliferation of distinctions within one side of the dichotomy, a process called fractionation, which can stall the reaction of one major pole against another. It is this process of fractionation that I wish to examine and illustrate using the history of constructionist arguments. Constructionist arguments have broken out in sociology and social science several times this century. But they have not had a lasting effect. I aim here to find out why that happened and to what extent it is attributable to fractionation.

2. The Rise and Fall of Labeling Theory

There are two major areas where constructionism has dominated sociology in the last four decades: the study of deviance and social problems and the study of science. As it turns out, there is a loose chain connecting the two.

The Development of Labeling Theory

In the early 1960s a group of young sociologists welded many elements of constructionism into a coherent perspective called labeling theory. For them, deviance was a process that began with certain actions, then proceeded through interactive definition of those actions to a final culmination in the assignment to individuals of labels that were stigmatized by society as denoting "deviant" people. Labeling theory was thus fully constructionist: mentalist in its focus on definitions, diachronic in its insistence on process, and interactive in its concern for both actors and definers.

As editor of *Social Problems* from 1961 to 1965, Howard Becker solicited much of this work. John Kitsuse and Aaron Cicourel (1963) and Kai Erikson (1962), wrote central position papers, while a related special issue of the journal became an influential reader, *The Other Side* (1964). Meanwhile, Becker's Chicago classmate Erving Goffman produced *Asylums* (on mental hospitals) in 1961, and Becker himself published *Outsiders* (in which he coined the phrase "moral entrepreneur") in 1963. Erikson's *Wayward Puritans* (on witchcraft) and Thomas Scheff's *Being Mentally Ill* appeared in 1966 and Cicourel's *Social Organization of Juvenile Justice* in 1968.

There is little doubt that labeling became the dominant perspective on deviance by 1970. Indeed, it could lay claim to having invented the concept of deviance by grouping such diverse phenomena as physical handicaps, mental illness, sickness, transient homosexuality, marijuana use, and white-collar crime under the same conceptual system. It also established observation as the preferred methodology for the study of deviance, a preference that grew out of labeling's own origins in departments with strong ethnographic traditions like Chicago, Berkeley, and UCLA.[10]

Labeling had some direct intellectual antecedents. Frank Tannenbaum's *Crime and Its Community* (1938) and Edwin Lemert's *Social Pathology* (1951) had both made the argument that deviance lay as much in the eye of the beholder as in the acts of the beheld. And many of the emphases of the theory—particularly the concepts of deviance as a master status and of deviant careers—came directly from Everett Hughes, who had taught Becker, Goffman, and many others in the tradition.

Politically, labeling was frankly populist. It was closely identified with the journal *Social Problems*, which was itself issued by the Society for the Study of Social Problems (SSSP), a Midwestern society founded to goad and humiliate the elitist, "scientific," and very eastern American Sociological Association (ASA).[11] The battle between SSSP and ASA ranged over many fronts. It was Chicago versus Harvard and Columbia. It was ethnography versus quantification. It was overt political argument versus Olympian detachment. It was informality versus formality. It was, in a very real sense, poverty versus wealth, for Parsons and others of the eastern establishment controlled the foundations' purse strings and through them much of sociological research. (Becker and others did, however, manage to make labeling theory pay the SSSP rent by publishing journal issues as books.)[12]

Although the political connection seems adventitious at first glance, it signifies a central fact. Constructionist arguments are often employed by those who lack certain kinds of knowledge resources: young people who lack senior positions, researchers lacking

---

10. On the general dominance of the labeling perspective, see Cole 1975.

11. Ironically, the *American Sociological Review*, the principal ASA journal, had been founded in 1936 to escape what was then perceived as the elitist, "scientific," and very Chicago-dominated *American Journal of Sociology*. See Abbott 1999a:78–79.

12. On the history of the SSSP, see Skura 1976 and Lee and Lee 1976 and other essays in the SSSP anniversary volume of that year.

money to do expensive kinds of work, outsiders attacking culturally authoritative definitions of social phenomena, amateurs who lack certain kinds of technical skills. Constructionism allows these individuals to simply ignore work they could not otherwise attack for want of skill, money, legitimacy, or position. In the first place, the constructionist argument can be applied not only to objects of study like deviants, but also to opponents' arguments. (It thus legitimates what would otherwise be considered ad hominem argument.) Second, as we shall see, the constructionist argument allows those who make it to set aside the *semantics* of their opponents' work—the terms and concepts, the interpretations of everyday events, the statistical series—on the grounds that this work takes over uncritically the language of the people studied. (Note that this is, in terms of chapter 1, a way of avoiding the difficulties of ingestion of alien material.)

Labeling theory presents many of the hallmarks of what I called in the first chapter a generational paradigm. It began in a revolt against mainstream interpretations of deviance. It arrived with a flurry of new theoretical work and exciting empirical studies. It arose at least partly from remapping of old concepts into new areas—the transformation of the Hughesian analysis of work into an analysis of deviance, for example. This remapping rejuvenated ideas that were long familiar (e.g., in the Chicago tradition) but gave them new twists and interpretations. Labeling was very clearly the work of a single generation, then approaching middle age, with the aid of a few senior scholars like Lemert. It was tied up with fairly explicit attacks on dominant elites in the discipline.

The Debate over Official Statistics and the Move to Victimization Surveys

For the labeling theorists, one immediate substantive target of intellectual attack was the standard research tradition on criminology. (Since the concept of "deviance" was itself solidified by the labeling theorists, there was no prior "deviance" tradition.) The criminological establishment was wealthy through government and private funding. It was technical through its use of statistics. It was enthroned in powerful departments and professorships. And it was researching, and taking very much for granted, such phenomena as the social correlates of juvenile arrests. Thus it was inevitable that one of labeling's many attacks on the establishment would be a disparagement of official crime statistics. The labeling theorists argued that since these statistics captured only fully labeled criminal deviance, the correlation of class with criminal activity—one of the foundational findings of the literature—was nonsense. What it meant was that lower-class people were more likely to be labeled deviant.

As it happened, however, the orthodox criminological tradition was already in crisis over official statistics, less because of such class biases than because what seemed to the orthodox to be obvious unreliability. When Chicago's new police chief professionalized police practices in 1962, the city's crime rate rose 83 percent in a single year. Even the most hardened realist knew that changes in reporting were the cause. By 1960 Sellin and Wolfgang had received funding for a massive positivist project on "measuring delinquency," a project that reassembled traditional definitions of delinquency very carefully, although without taking a labeling approach. In their published report, Sellin and Wolfgang did cite the classics of labeling theory (then just appearing), but felt such works raised only problems of measurement, not of theory.[13]

Thus, in the typical fractal pattern, not only was there a realist/constructionist dispute between the orthodox and the labelers, there was also a realist/constructionist dispute within the orthodox tradition itself. But while the labelers were attacking orthodox criminal statistics on constructionist grounds as merely part of a larger critique, the attack within orthodoxy used a constructionist argument to set aside old "real" numbers in favor of new ones. Arrest statistics were simply social products; they were not close enough to the "real thing" and hence included error.

This dual critique of official statistics resulted in the idea of victimization surveys. For the orthodox critics, such surveys were an attempt to move upstream in the process of criminality, back to the "real activity," before the censoring induced by variable police practices. Self-report surveys of criminality emerged simultaneously and for the same purpose. Yet victimization surveys did implicitly draw on the larger constructionist account provided by labeling theory. For they wished to avoid the application of labels (by police) altogether. Victimization thus served as an indexical concept, meaning one thing to one school and another to the other.[14]

---

13. See Sellin and Wolfgang 1964, particularly the discussion on Kitsuse and Cicourel.

14. There is little direct evidence that labeling concerns drove victimization surveys. Of the first three victimization surveys (which appeared as background research for the crime commission report of 1967), the NORC general survey of nationwide victimization was suggested by an agricultural economist—D. Gale Johnson, then dean of social sciences at Chicago. On hearing of Chicago's famous 83 percent crime increase, Johnson asked NORC director Peter Rossi if somehow there wasn't a way

The realist vision clearly won. In the later victimization literature (e.g., McDonald 1976), victimization became a solid, unconstructed "fact" in the same way that criminal activity (shown in arrests) had been a "fact" in earlier criminal statistics. This happened above all in the massive (and continuing) victimization survey that grew out of the work done in the 1960s—the National Crime Survey (NCS). By its first major evaluation in 1976, the NCS was conceptually interchangeable with the UCR it was designed to replace. The 1976 NAS panel review of the NCS contains no theoretical discussion of the ambiguous process of criminal labeling.[15]

Thus, while the original distinction between NCS and UCR could be read as one between viewing arrest statistics as socially constructed and viewing them as transparent social facts, by 1976 it had become clear that coming to terms with constructionism within a realist research framework eventually produced just another realist analysis. In part this regression to realism reflected the need for "a number," a "real crime rate," on which social policy and social policy posturing could be based. In part it reflected the simple weight of routine practices in quantitative research. A monthly survey of sixty thousand people looking for the relatively rare event of victimization was indeed a problem whose logistics required clear lines of control and whose potential confusion required clear criteria for coding and decision. In this sense, the lesson of constructionism was negative. Ask a constructionist question in a realist way and you get a realist answer.

Yet deep in the 1976 NAS review of the NCS we find discussions of whether a series of harassing acts constitutes a single event (to count as one in the totals) or a set of discrete events (to count as more than one). We find discussions of the dangers of suggestive questions. We find worries about the way closed-form screening questions tend to force the NCS data to look like the UCR data. These are all, essentially, questions of social construction—the con-

---

to do better by a direct survey (Ennis 1967:2). Another set of surveys was conducted by Albert Biderman (Biderman et al. 1967), a private sector survey researcher who proposed them personally out of his general interest in better social indicators (Biderman 1966). The third set of surveys came from Albert Reiss, a traditional criminologist whose distrust of official statistics had been confirmed by Sellin and Wolfgang's just-published work. Like Biderman a Chicago Ph.D., Reiss (1967) followed a loose version of ideological constructionism, emphasizing the importance of institutional structures (in this case police departments) in producing knowledge. (Everyone was well aware that rising crime rates were very helpful to police department budgets.) Reiss and Biderman both knew about Kitsuse and Cicourel's work (Biderman and Reiss 1967), but viewed it as merely echoing the standard complaints, not as calling for a radical retheorization of deviance.

15. The NAS panel review is Penick and Owens 1976.

struction of a reality by interviewer and interviewee. And they generate exciting, detailed, and profoundly reflective discussion about
how to construe society. Here in the bowels of pure realism are
richly constructionist analyses.[16]

Again this shows the fractal nature of the opposition between
constructionism and its many opposites. At the most general level,
by 1976 the NCS had become simple realism, although it asked a
constructionist-suggested question within that generally realist approach. Yet even within its realism, we find analysts *again* splitting
into those who urge a loose form to the questioning (one that will
avoid excessive preconstruction of the answers), and those who urge
a strict form in order to achieve "comparability," those who regard
the facts as simply there to be discovered. Within each pole of the
constructionism/realism dichotomy, both sides reappear.

The Death of Labeling Theory

The late 1970s saw three attacks on labeling theory, one from the
quantitative realists, one from the constructionists, and one from
the left.

The quantitative realists poured an unending stream of empirical
scorn on labeling. A host of criminologists interpreted the increasing convergence of UCR and NCS figures as rejecting the idea of a
labeling process. The labelers replied that their opponents interpreted the theory too strictly by generating simplistic empirical predictions capable of direct test. Each time a labeling hypothesis was
tested and rejected, labelers offered a plausible labeling narrative
that implied the opposite hypothesis. Sometimes labelers bearded opponents in their realist dens. (For example, Scheff discussed Gove's
misinterpretations of his own and others' data.) But in general
realism seemed triumphant. By 1982, when Harris and Hill reviewed
the area, they could conclude that, empirically speaking (that is,
within realist "tests" of labeling), labeling theory was dead.[17]

This triumph was clearest in criminology. Both in replying to labeling theory and in rejecting those who favored self-report as a
measure of crime, the traditional criminologists emphasized the
uniformity of judgments of serious crime. Studies all over the world
had replicated the Sellin-Wolfgang "seriousness" scale, they argued,
and when such "serious" crimes were considered rather than the
trivial ones that made up most self-reports, class correlations with

---

16. These discussions appear in Penick and Owens 1976.
17. See, e.g., Scheff 1974 on Gove's (1970) interpretations of his own and others'
data. See also Harris and Hill 1982.

criminality held up in both victimization and arrest data. The only effective response to these claims would have been to debunk the statistical techniques themselves, as Coxon, Burrage, and others had done in the case of Donald Treiman's "universal" scale of occupational prestige. But this defense called for technical skill that labeling lacked, and so was never made.[18]

In a move that seems characteristic of constructionism under realist threat, Becker offered a broad defense of labeling, calling it not a theory but a perspective, emphasizing its simple separation of action and definition, its role in demystification of statistics, its willingness to imply moral positions. But while this argument provided a fair response to the realists, it did little to help against nonrealist attacks. The first of these was from the left (or, as Becker put it, "from left field"). For Alvin Gouldner, labelers were zookeepers who studied the downtrodden for their entertainment value, keeping them on "Indian reservations" for the weird. This blunted the potentially radical threat posed by the dispossessed and thereby supported the status quo.[19]

Although extreme, Gouldner's claim had some foundation in the fact that the labeling literature emphasized a narrow range of social problems. The social problems literature from which labeling sprang has concentrated throughout its history on a limited set of issues, the dominant ones being race and ethnic relations, crime and delinquency, physical and mental illness, family and gender, professions and work, education, and legal problems. Distinctly absent from this list were the top social problems in the public's perception: war above all, followed closely by labor and economic problems like cost of living, unemployment, and taxes. Only on race and ethnic questions did the two lists agree.[20]

But Gouldner cared less about the lack of fit between the social problems literature and the public, which was after all far to the right of that literature, than he did about that between the social problems literature and his own version of the left. Indeed, by the mid-1970s, a "critical criminology" had grown up that carried into the deviance area the banner of the *new* young generation, now that Becker et al. were the establishment. That banner was of course

18. On the occupational prestige arguments, see the books of Coxon and Jones (e.g., 1978, 1979) and the elegant paper of Burrage and Corry (1981). For a latter-day technical defense of labeling, see Hagan and Palloni 1990.

19. Becker's defense of labeling is Becker 1974, which includes the typically wonderful quote about Gouldner's criticism "from left field." Gouldner's attack is Gouldner 1968.

20. I have done my own counts of areas. See also Henslin and Roesti 1976 and Lauer 1976.

Marxism. Labeling's constructionism failed in the eyes of the critical criminologists (and those of other Marxists interested in deviance, e.g., Scull), because it was left but not left enough. (We shall see similar fractionation with respect to degree of belief in constructionism.) But while the original theoretical statements of critical criminology had considerable intellectual force, at the empirical level the critical criminology movement approached criminality ham-fistedly, accepting crime statistics at face (realist) value and then simply interpreting them as signs of oppression. This dissociation of leftness from constructionism was to lose allies (particularly feminist allies) for critical criminology and to contribute to its early demise.[21]

Far more interesting for my purpose here is the fact that by 1978 the labelers were under attack for *being* realists. Becker had argued that the whole point of labeling was simply to cross two dichotomies; (a) the doing or nondoing of a certain action and (b) the labeling or nonlabeling of that act as deviant. For some (e.g., Pollner [1978]), it was a mistake to consider the first dichotomy at all, to act as if there "really was" any action, beyond simple constructions of action. In defending himself against realists, Becker had accepted reality in a rather commonsense fashion ("it would be foolish to suppose that stick-up men stick people up simply because someone has labeled them as stick-up men").[22] For Pollner, such talk was the smoking gun of realism.

This new constructionism of the late 1970s had two sources. One was ethnomethodology, a small sect of sociologists who followed Harold Garfinkel's redaction of Schutz. The group was small, intense, and very fractious. It is striking that Aaron Cicourel, long perceived by many outsiders as one of ethnomethodology's founders, was by the inner group "not widely regarded as conforming to the mainstream of ethnomethodology."[23]

---

21. On critical criminology, see Taylor, Walton, and Young 1973 and Quinney 1977. On feminism and criminology, see Melossi 1985 and Rafter 1990. Note that it is possible to be constructionist without being left (Michael Polanyi [1958] being an example), but difficult to be left without being constructionist. Constructionism is so enticing as a weapon of the weak that a substantial group on the left will always be holding it. But this regularity must be historically conditioned, since Marxism itself is deeply realist and has itself split into fractions over the issue of how seriously to take noneconomic material facts and, more extremely, nonmaterial facts like ideologies. In the nineteenth century, left meant a certain form of what would now be called realism.

22. Becker 1974:42.

23. Atkinson 1988:443. It is also ironic that it was arch-behaviorist Donald Black (1984:14) who recognized the direct line from labeling to a purely realist theory of what he called social control and what the ethnomethodologists considered the pure

Ethnomethodology drew more strongly on Continental philosophical constructionism than on the pragmatic traditions behind labeling theory; Schutz's roots lay in Husserl and other phenomenologists. But the other major constructionist attack on labeling came from an indigenous source, one very close to labeling itself. This other source was the "social problems" literature. Labeling theory had been built in the social problems context: supported by an editor of *Social Problems,* researched predominantly by members of the SSSP, focused on the classic issues of the literature. But even as labeling reached its apogee around 1970, the social problems field was in crisis.

The first aspect of the crisis was political. The once-populist SSSP had settled down to the drudgery of professionalism, the very thing the organization had been founded to undermine. The organization had been swept up in labeling's success at drawing students and even funding during the heyday of the Great Society. By 1970 the original SSSP leadership thought the organization was just another ASA, with no focus on policy studies, no policy positions, no interdisciplinarity. A series of bitter critiques slammed the society's journal, *Social Problems*—where labeling was built by editors like Becker and David Gold—for being simply another refereed journal of standard stuff. This line of attack went beyond Gouldner's argument; not only was social problems work not substantively radical, it was no longer even disciplinarily radical.[24]

The second, and undoubtedly correlative, crisis was intellectual. Many both inside and outside the SSSP had finally noticed the disjunction between social problems as defined by the organization (and its members) and social problems as defined by the public, a public whose images of problems were themselves reforged in the late 1960s. In the early 1970s there was a spate of articles on the definition of social problems and the true scope of the social problems literature. Out of this literature came a new focus.

The architects of that new focus were John Kitsuse, a converted labeler, and Malcolm Spector. In a brilliant 1973 article later expanded into a book, Kitsuse and Spector built on Herbert Blumer's earlier speculation about social problems as collective movements. Both the civil rights movement and the antiwar movement made it obvious that social problems could be "made" by activity. Blumer

---

labeling act. One could ignore the originating actions on either constructionist or behaviorist grounds. On ethnomethodology's early structure, see Mullins 1973, chap. 8.

24. The great debate about the SSSP arose at its twenty-fifth anniversary; see the various essays in *Social Problems,* vol. 24, no. 1.

emplotted that activity as a type of "natural history," employing the
framework traditional in Chicago sociology since Robert Park.[25]
Kitsuse and Spector simply expanded this emplotment. They sev-
ered themselves from the labelers by bracketing any concern with
whether the social problems were "really there"; like Pollner, they
looked only at constructions, not at the original "real" actions or
facts. Thus, the new "constructing-social-problems" literature came
to define the labeling generation as realists. Ironically, the natural
history vocabulary they followed so lovingly came from the same
source as had Becker's analysis of deviant careers. Moreover, Spector
and Kitsuse claimed Becker's Chicago classmate Joseph Gusfield as
an important if slightly misguided forerunner of their version of
constructionism, while Becker not surprisingly saw him as an interactionist loosely under the labeling umbrella.[26]

The whole affair seemed at times to be a battle about presupposi-
tions and labels, with little impact on research. The main research
shift was of methodology, from micro, observational studies to relatively historical, often radical ones. (This shift was, of course, widespread in other areas of sociology at the time.) The main issue was
whether the new historical research would be theorized using Becker's (1963) "moral entrepreneurship" concept or using the more general natural history concept (from which Becker's concept itself
came). In fact, Kitsuse and Spector could just as easily have cited
Becker himself as Blumer.

By 1985, the new constructionist approach to social problems was
standard in the field. But despite the new view's attack on labeling's
"narrow substantive focus," the enormous expansion of constructionist arguments about social problems in the decade 1975–85 in
fact came mainly in quite traditional substantive areas. While the
new constructionists ranged a little more broadly than had the labelers, they still did not move into issues like war and unemployment.
The literature continued to work with the downtrodden, but retun-
ing itself with the new, more positive radicalism, it now stressed the
empowered nature of the downtrodden.[27]

The history of labeling thus well illustrates the processes affecting generational paradigms. Labeling began as a remapping of the
old and familiar ideas of interactionist constructionism onto the
new turf of deviance. It opened with a blaze of theoretical and em-

---

25. Blumer 1971.
26. Kitsuse and Spector 1973. Claims about Gusfield are advanced in Spector and
Kitsuse 1987:89 ff., and Becker 1974:47.
27. For a review of this literature, see Schneider 1985. There were other approaches to social problems, mainly Marxist ones, as in the work of Scull (1988).

pirical work that caught sociologists' imagination for two decades. Although it didn't defeat its realist opponents, similar fractal divisions within them helped produce the victimization survey, which itself, however, eventually succumbed to realism. (Nevertheless, even the details of survey analysis showed a concern for constructionist issues.) Finally, the fall of labeling was a classic case. First, the labelers lacked the quantitative skills to attack the realists on their own turf of standard methodologies. Second, fractionation redefined labeling as the conservative version of radicalism, under threat from both a new radical group as well as from the conservative mainstream. Third, another dimension of fractionation redefined labeling as the realist version of constructionism, while the new generation took a more resolutely constructionist line. Pushed toward the center, but still in opposition to the mainstream, labeling lost definition and defensibility.

By 1985, however, labeling's chief opponent within constructionism—the social problems literature—was *itself* under attack for closet realism. The attack came from ethnomethodologists within the sociology of science.

3. The Constructionist Sociology of Science
The New Sociology of Science

In the 1970s, the sociology of science became the chief sociological home of ideological constructionism. Before that time, the sociology of science (then under Merton's leadership) had believed scientific knowledge to be fundamentally different from social knowledge and hence not subject to ideological analysis. (There is some disagreement about the Mertonian position; see Gieryn 1982 and related comments.) But in the mid-1970s there arose in Great Britain a group of younger sociologists committed to direct analysis of scientific knowledge as situationally determined. A 1975 York conference brought together many of the central figures: Nigel Gilbert, Stephen Woolgar, Harry Collins, Michael Mulkay, Richard Whitley, and David McKenzie. The movement had echoes in Germany, where a group inspired by Habermas (the Starnberg group of Wolf Schäfer, Gernot Böhme, Wolfgang van den Daele, Rainer Hohlfeld, and Wolfgang Krohn) pursued similar intellectual aims.[28]

Barry Barnes and David Bloor published the major manifestos.

---

28. The York conference is discussed in *Social Studies of Science*, vol. 6, nos. 3 and 4. On the Starnberg group, see Schäfer 1983.

Both rebelled against Mertonian scientific exceptionalism.[29] Barnes relied heavily on Kuhn, making at least some of science socially determined. Bloor, relying more on Wittgenstein, undertook a detailed analysis of the different meanings of mathematical statements in different social contexts. The new sociology of science thus drew heavily on that body of philosophy that dismantled the logical positivists' account of science: not only Kuhn and Wittgenstein, but also Quine, Popper, Lakatos, and Feyerabend.

Like many generational paradigms the new sociology of science defined itself by bringing these "outside" sources to bear on its home turf. The issues raised, however, were not totally new. The Mertonians had in fact worried about the constructed nature of scientific knowledge, for which their favorite citation was the brilliantly idiosyncratic *Personal Knowledge* (1958) by crystallographer Michael Polanyi. Polanyi's book anticipated most of the radical arguments of the new sociologists of science, but did not spawn an empirical research tradition. Rather, it gave the Mertonians a pied-à-terre in constructionism, holding a place there without distracting them from their real interest in institutions. (The new sociologists of science dealt with Polanyi very simply, by ignoring him. To create novelty in a system of fractal distinctions, one may have to ignore existing fractal divisions, saying they do not go far enough.)[30]

Despite the philosophical emphasis of the new sociology of science, its real strength—like that of labeling in its early years—lay in its empirical studies. These studies (there is a list of the early ones in Collins 1981) were often micro and often historical, but sometimes addressed larger institutional questions. By 1981, however, there were sharp philosophical discontinuities within the group, much like those that had appeared in the study of deviance a decade before. In particular, a group of radical constructionists confronted others whom they accused, more or less, of realism. There were in fact four somewhat distinct schools by this point.

The "interests" school was closest to the traditional sociology of knowledge, with its focus on relatively large knowledge structures and their social origins. The group was centered on the original Edinburgh "strong programme" and included Barnes, Bloor, McKenzie,

---

29. Barnes 1974; Bloor 1976. It is ironic that Marx, the founder of ideological constructionism, had specifically exempted natural science from its purview, anticipating Merton's position.

30. Polanyi 1958. Shapin (1994:25) speaks of Polanyi as "notably invisible." Lynch (1993) gives him a half-page mention to dozens of pages for Wittgenstein and Habermas. Polanyi continues to be widely cited, but outside the new sociology of science.

Steven Shapin, and Andrew Pickering. Another English group had taken relativism to its extreme and so was driven to investigate "the interpretative flexibility of experimental data . . . and . . . the mechanisms through which the potentially endless debate about interpretation is limited," insisting on this as preliminary to work like that of the Edinburgh school.[31] This, the "empirical program of relativism" (EPOR), was argued by Collins and Trevor Pinch. Still another group, the discourse analysts, led by Mulkay and Gilbert, felt that even EPOR failed to get to the real preliminaries. It was necessary to analyze (and perhaps to simulate) the exact language of scientists in order to understand how interpretation really unfolded.

Karin Knorr urged a fourth, "constructivist" program. Here the focus was on the construction of knowledge in the laboratory, as in EPOR and discourse analysis. But the mode of study was contemporary enthnography more than historical reconstruction or text analysis. Central figures were Woolgar, Knorr, Bruno Latour, John Law, Rob Williams, and Michael Lynch, each associated with a particular laboratory ethnography. The "constructivists" included a group influenced heavily by ethnomethodology, which by now had become seriously interested in science.[32]

It was from this last quarter that open attacks began on the Edinburgh school, the originators of the new sociology of science. In 1981, Woolgar attacked the strong programme for its attempt at "naturalism" and for its focus on interests. Naturalism assumed an unreflective real world to be investigated, and interests were "unreflectively" imputed on external grounds. Sociologists of science ought to "turn our attention to the management of explanatory strategies in the practice of scientific argument."[33] Barnes replied for the Edinburgh group that a focus on why (Edinburgh) was not incompatible with one on how (ethnomethodology, constructivism, etc.).[34]

This was a classic fractionation attack; the Edinburgh school was attacked for not going far enough. Moreover, as in the history of labeling, attack came also from the realist side, from the larger mainstream of sociology. But whereas the mainstream attacked labeling for extremism, it attacked the Edinburgh school for familiarity. Speaking for the earlier mainstream version of the sociology of science—Merton's "institutions" position—Gieryn claimed that the strong programme's philosophical justifications had little con-

---

31. Collins 1981:6-7. The phrase "strong programme" originates in Bloor 1976:7.
32. On constructivism, see Knorr-Cetina 1983.
33. Woolgar 1981:365.
34. Barnes 1981.

nection with its empirical work. Merton had in fact written about social and cultural roots of science, about doubts and hesitancies in scientific knowledge, and even about the existence of things like paradigms. Gieryn saw the strong programme as a retreat from central empirical questions about the differences between science and other forms of knowledge, both historical and contemporaneous.[35]

Replies to Gieryn locate precisely the successive splits of fractionation. For EPOR, Collins replied that choice of problem was a matter of taste and that EPOR had decided to view science as a prototype of knowledge, precisely because if *it* could be shown to be socially grounded, then obviously any form of knowledge was so grounded. Discourse analysts Mulkay and Gilbert hastily remarked that while everything Gieryn said was probably true about EPOR and the constructivists, it did *not* apply to discourse analysis, which concerned "how . . . scientists construct their versions of what is going on in science." For the constructivists, Knorr-Cetina replied by distinguishing between "epistemic relativism" (which assumes that interpretations of nature are grounded in historical place and time) and "judgmental relativism" (which believes that there is no reality). Constructivism doesn't even assume the former, much less the latter, for it brackets all concerns about reality altogether (that is, it talks only about constructions per se; cf. Pollner's ethnomethodological attack on labeling). As in the history of constructionist approaches to deviance, the most radical of relativisms—the one that disregards the issue of reality altogether—comes out looking not unlike pure empiricism or phenomenology. By giving up duality, extreme constructionism re-creates the monolithic quality of traditional realism.[36]

Who are the True Constructionists?

Thus, in responding to a (relative) conservative, each sociology of science went to some lengths to prove that it took less for granted than the others. The scientific constructionists, indeed, felt powerful enough by the mid-1980s to assault the social problems literature on this issue, accusing it of not really being constructionist. Apparently, the sociology of science had tired of internal fractionation and had begun to move back toward the mainstream. The first object in its path was, of course, the next most constructionist group in sociology, the social problems theorists.

---

35. Gieryn 1982. Gieryn has more recently moved in a postmodern direction.
36. Mulkay and Gilbert 1982:314; Knorr-Cetina 1982. The point about monolithic constructionism has been made explicitly by Freudenthal (1984).

It was as if two groups of tourists within my city of knowledge met in the evening and started arguing about whether they had actually made it through to the very walls. One group thought that it had seen them. The other pooh-poohed them; one can get out of a maze only by always turning as far to the left as possible as often as possible, they said, and after all the others had indeed made a few right turns.

Thus it was that in 1985, Woolgar and Pawluch accused the social problems constructionists of being realists, guilty of "ontological gerrymandering." Kitsuse, Spector, Gusfield, Schneider, and a long list of others were simply "making problematic the truth status of certain states of affairs selected for analysis and explanation, while backgrounding or minimizing the possibility that the same problems apply to the assumptions on which the analysis depends."[37] They were debunking others, but not themselves.

To readers of the old sociology of knowledge—the ideological line of constructionist theory—this was of course a familiar problem. Mannheim had raised it in *Ideology and Utopia* and answered with the concept of a "free-floating intelligentsia" able to rise above the social determination of its knowledge. Although perhaps viable and indeed necessary in the darkness of the 1930s, this concept didn't really seem to convince Mannheim himself, much less his later readers. Berger and Luckmann answered the same question with an existentialist paean to the lone individual proudly positing meaning amid the wreckage of dismantled illusions. This too failed to persuade.

The problem is in fact a general logical problem of extremal positions in fractal lineages. Although their consistency confers impregnability against their opponents, they can never stand up to themselves. For example, the free-rider problem is insoluble if we hew rigidly to rational choice assumptions; one has basically to assume a solution (for an example of this see Hechter 1987, chap. 3) Similarly, the radical argument that all knowledge must ultimately unmask itself has no conceivable answer within everyday logic. Even to discuss the truth of the argument presupposes its error, for the argument itself holds that no criterion exists to govern such a discussion. Therefore those who make the argument must always presuppose its opposite in the very act of writing. An ironic example comes from Woolgar's reply to the positivist Slezak's argument that

---

37. Woolgar and Pawluch 1985:216. The reader will recognize the quote as a virtually verbatim repetition of the one from Gouldner—in 1970—in the opening chapter, itself a rough translation of Evans-Pritchard's line from the 1930s. There is *nothing* new about this position.

science done by artificially intelligent machines might challenge
the view of interests, science, and construction that was general in
the new sociology of science. Woolgar says, "I'm as much in favour
of 'the reader writes the text' as the next person. But it is nevertheless pretty frustrating that these critics just don't seem to get the
point of what's written."[38] While the strength of extremal positions
on fractal distinctions lies in their consistency, their weakness lies
in their self-negating character.[39]

But like anticancer drugs, extremal positions are expected to kill
the bad arguments before they kill the good ones. Woolgar and Pawluch therefore forcefully extended their analysis of ontological gerrymandering by analyzing in detail a constructionist article by social
problems writer Steven Pfohl. For Woolgar and Pawluch, the labelers
(whom the social problems group had portrayed as realists) had been
more correct than the social problems constructionists because they
"showed more interest in the conceptual problems that plague their
theoretical perspective."[40] (The implication is thus that at least the
labelers knew there was a problem, while the social problems constructionists, because never criticized, never saw the problem.)

But then, unlike most proponents of radical constructionism,
Woolgar and Pawluch eventually acknowledge that the radical constructionist critique applies to their own argument, that one has
in fact to assume that something objective is given because "the
theoretical tension . . . is an expression of the continual play between objective facts and representation of those facts which char-
acterizes all explanations of this kind."[41] They then speculate that
one could treat their own analysis as (1) a manual for how to write
social problems types of explanations (i.e., how to ontologically gerry-
mander), (2) a directive to be a little more careful about ontologically
gerrymandering, or (3) a directive to think more deeply about this
inevitable problem. Having begun with savagery and sarcasm, they
close by saying—essentially—that more research is necessary.

---

38. Woolgar 1989:662.
39. Slezak 1989. A particularly good example of an extremal position made into
reality is the practice of some economics departments and business schools of allocating a certain amount of "money" to each faculty member and then putting all
common services up for bids—secretarial assistance, photocopying, etc. It might
seem that free market extremism is immune to the problem of self-criticism raised
here. But of course one can explain adoption of free market ideas on the basis of
microeconomic models, arguing that the preference of economists for mathematics
is higher than that of, say, sociologists. Or perhaps we can infer that economics professors have to be paid much more than other faculty because orthodox economic
ideas are silly and hence embarrassing to espouse in public.
40. Woolgar and Pawluch 1985:222.
41. Woolgar and Pawluch 1985:224.

In responding, Pfohl loudly denied all realism. He invoked the lineage, saying that he, too, has read (he really listed them) Marx, Durkheim, Nietzsche, Mauss, Freud, Gramsci, Althusser, Barthes, Kristeva, Derrida, Baudrillard, and Spivak. He then said:

> In constructing my sociological narrative I metaphorically condensed an analysis of social practices into a discussion of "factors" and "forces." In framing my story in this fashion, I froze an indetermined conjuncture of dynamic processes into terms that seemingly imply a constancy of "things"—barriers, impediments, obstacles to seeing and the like. Woolgar and Pawluch arrest this play of metaphoric condensation. They seize the act of freezing concepts as evidence for speculating that the (temporary) backgrounding is a constitutive feature of explanatory work in general.[42]

> [Sociology must be a] reflexive sociological analysis that understands itself as effecting a provisional knowledge, positioned by the power of its relationship to other practices.[43]

Under the verbiage lie homespun truths any thoughtful empiricist might tell her students. They are, in fact, the generic response of realism; one has to simplify in order to explain; one has to break philosophical eggs to make an explanatory omelette; all knowledge is temporary. Even out on the final fringes of constructionism, the debate of realism and constructionism takes exactly the same form it does anywhere else.[44]

4. Some Conclusions and Final Theoretical Notes on Constructionism

These histories of constructionism well illustrate the peculiar dynamics of fractionation. At some point in a fractal lineage, the theoretical stage is seized by positions both extreme and consistent. There results a sudden and rapid splitting within a small sector of the total fractal lineage. In concluding, I wish to speculate about both the sources and the consequences of this process.

As fractal distinctions unfold in social science, the process that we might call alternation seems more usual than fractionation. A research tradition works in one way until a limit is reached, then tries the other. This process was a major theme of the preceding

---

42. Pfohl 1985:230.
43. Pfohl 1985:231.
44. To be sure, Pfohl does ultimately claim true relativism. He says at one point that in his work "even the safe experiential realism of phenomenology is left aside" (1985:231). Thus did the macho constructionism of the 1980s dissipate its energies in the same fractionation that had plagued constructionist theories of deviance.

chapter.[45] Thus, one might treat the social world as real until anomalies forced one to turn to constructions. In fact, such a move helped drive victimization research. Indeed, constructionist theory itself allows for the "turn" to realism. Processes of objectification mean that at any given time, much of the social world has a nominally objective character. If actors construe a certain social action as a rational actor game, then modeling it as a rational actor game is the best way to study it in the short run. (Hence the utility of rational actor models of, e.g., international relations in the modern era.) Similarly, realists unconsciously allow for the turn to constructionism. "Finding better measures," "using context-specific indicators," and "separating attitudes and behaviors" can all cover what are essentially constructionist moves.

Under certain circumstances, however, the response to limits becomes not alternation but fractionation. The result can be imagined if we think once again about a group of travelers exploring one dimension—one principal boulevard—of a city. Where fractionation occurs, we see in one direction a large mainstream (orthodox) group and in the other an extremal one. In the mainstream, researchers follow alternating strategies and as a consequence become all mixed in among themselves. In the fractionating extremal group, one direction is always chosen, and so the group's edge on its mainstream side recedes rapidly. Between extreme and mainstream there begins to appear a zone of unexplored, empty space. As I noted in the preceding chapter, one of that chapter's original reviewers (a sociologist of science) said that it consisted of platitudes, while another (obviously a stress researcher) said it consisted of extremist nonsense. It was not extreme enough for the one, but too extreme for the other.[46]

Fractionation arises in part through important intellectual virtues. To be a constructionist among constructionists is to be rig-

---

45. Most analysts of social science focus on the question of how researchers know that those limits have been reached. I am willing to assume the Kuhnian answer that limits appear when anomalies seem to prevent advance, and to set aside the question of why some researchers see limits earlier than do others. I assume this because I am more interested in why for some people the answer to such limits is not choosing the other fork of a fractal distinction, but choosing a more extreme version of the current one, why fractionation arises rather than alternation.

46. See chapter 2, note 36. To be sure, extreme positions may be more rhetorical strategy than actual guides to research. Underneath the fractional debates of the sociology of science, for example, the subdiscipline continued to produce empirical work accessible to scholars of various theoretical persuasions. Perhaps it lacked the supreme vibrancy of the 1970s—the early days of the generational paradigm—but it was steady and solid empirical work nonetheless. I am indebted to Howie Becker for insisting on this point.

orously consistent. To be an unforgiving realist or an absolutist believer in choice is to be parsimonious, logical. This simplicity of extremal positions is not merely powerful, but also intellectually virtuous and admirable. Moreover, like any unblemished reputation, extreme consistency requires only one false step to compromise it completely. Once a scholar makes one compromise with realism, there is little point in absolute constructionism thereafter. This too will tend to create a vacant area between the extremes and the compromising, alternating strategies of the mainstream.

Another important source of fractionation lies in the tendency of extremal positions to take strong political stands. This is a recurrent pattern empirically, although the politics involved varies considerably. When the extremal position is politically nonorthodox, its politics is explicit, both to itself and to others. Thus, the phrase "political correctness" originally emerged within the intellectual left to rank order the many extremist political positions there; it was only later taken up by the mainstream. But when, as sometimes happens, the extremal position has a politics of orthodoxy, that politics is generally implicit, since orthodoxy in intellectual inquiry definitionally portrays itself as without politics. Extreme rational choice positions illustrate this latter phenomenon, for they embody American culture's strong ideology that "this is the way people really are."

Conflation with politics exacerbates fractionation because it heightens the emotions involved. For example, an exchange between two sociologists of science and the feminist Evelyn Fox Keller finds the former attacking the latter for feminist essentialism, for her belief in "feminine" scientific methods. Keller replies that her attackers have mistaken biological for culturally constructed gender, an argument that is correct, but beside the point. Yet the attacking authors, rather than pointing out that irrelevance, further it by counterclaiming that they take even less for granted, regard even more as constructed than does Keller.[47] The central but unstated issue is whether feminist constructionism or constructionism tout court is the proper tool with which to deconstruct the orthodox position on science.[48] The admixture of a substantive feminist politics simply raises the stakes.

47. Richards and Schuster 1989; Keller 1989.
48. As I noted above, the same debate arose between feminism and the new criminology over how to deconstruct orthodox views of crime. The debate is really over a substantive political issue—who is "ignoring women" or "taking hegemonic orthodoxy for granted." Within orthodoxy itself, of course, such issues can be ignored—not because orthodox scholars don't have quite diverse political commitments, but

Finally, fractionation arises in what we may call the pleasures of unconventionality. Those involved in extremal, fractionating groups view the mainstream with a distant but prideful contempt. We see this emotion in sociological theorists' talk of "postpositivism" at a time when hundreds of millions of dollars are spent by government and private industry on positivist social science annually. Defining a group around strong opposition to such a mainstream is heady stuff—solitary enlightenment against the swinish muddle of eclecticism, which is of course always painted as a hegemonic orthodoxy rather than the mainstream tangle of alternating choices that it is. These pleasures of opposition make opposition per se the dominant value of the fractionating group and awards highest in-group status to those in the strongest opposition.[49]

Fractionation is thus driven partly by intellectual virtues and partly by a kind of self-righteousness that becomes a vice. These are exacerbated by the common conflation of extremal arguments with politics.

All these forces are clear indeed in the histories of constructionism reviewed earlier. Perhaps most evident is the power of political commitment. Labeling theory secretly admired the various deviants it wrote about, as Alvin Gouldner well saw. And despite their occasional denials, the new sociologists of science clearly despise the project of objective knowledge of the world, the science that seems to them so smug, so wealthy, so arrogant. But the politics is not the only thing we see in these cases. We also see in the cases of labeling and the new sociology of science the great power of the consistency that drives fractionation, a consistency that has ended up producing much important empirical work. In these cases, we

---

because being orthodox means not having to talk about your politics. On the other hand, for extremal positions, everything orthodoxy does is political. As, in such a view, is the present inquiry. This position, like all extremal ones, falls apart over the ultimate fatuity of universal predicates. See the argument above and chapter 7 below.

49. Sometimes the heady pleasure lies in opposition to some external actor. The sociologists of science play to the hilt their valor in standing up against science, the paradigm and colossus of the modern world. Yet they often pull the punch at the last minute. Epstein's (1996) book on AIDS science is an excellent example—full of tendentious assaults on scientific reasoning, but coming down, at the end, to the position that the AIDS activists (who derailed a number of important clinical trials) can really only play an advisory, corrective role to scientists who really do have the most important things to contribute. Interestingly, the book never considers the purely scientific argument that if one embedded the "compromised" studies in a simulated annealing framework (or a sequential Bayesian system), one could perhaps reach a correct answer faster by doing many such small, "dirty" studies than by insisting on a few uncompromised clinical trials; that is, that the probability theory behind the whole model of giant, completed clinical trials may be wrong scientifically, rather than being simply ethically and politically problematic.

see too the intense pleasures of opposition and a clear status competition over who will enjoy them to the fullest.

I suggested earlier that the long-run fate of fractionation is re-
absorption. I would like to discuss this issue through a discussion
of the long-term fate of constructionism.

It is clear that there are important forces driving social scientists
toward realism. All derive from variants of Samuel Johnson's stone-
kicking refutation of Bishop Berkeley. None of us really believes that
there isn't some kind of real world; the only question is how
"sticky" or how "constructed" we think that reality really is. As social science has become a successful, even an influential, part of
modern life, we have had to recognize that the mechanics of doing
social research often favor realism. Large studies do give more general conclusions, and large studies require divisions of labor that
make consistent intellectual decisions extremely precarious. Such
a research process is more easily conducted, more easily controlled—and more easily justified—on realist terms. (This suggests
that constructionist arguments must inevitably be artisanally produced, an interesting hypothesis.) Realism also has tremendous audience appeal—particularly to the politicians and marketers who
consume most social science. It gives simple answers, with simple
meanings. It has the character—to constructionists the damnably
constructed character—of transparency. The forces favoring realism—both as research practice and as social ontology—are strong
indeed. Gusfield's (1981) magnificent analysis of drunk driving research shows them very well.

We can put this another way by saying that constructions have
audience appeal, but constructionism does not. The public is always
ready for new social constructions.[50] Comparable worth is an excellent example. The "worth of a day's work" is without doubt a socially constructed fact. And constructionist arguments about the
genderedness of earlier constructions of the worth of work were central in establishing the new construction of "comparable" worth.
Once the previous view was unseated, however, the constructionist
arguments that did the dirty work were forgotten. The new, politically desired reality they made possible was established to the satis-
faction of those who used constructionist arguments to do it and,
for them at least, it was now time to treat the *new* construction they
had made as real. This is one of the great problems of constructionism; it does not in fact have a politics. Constructionism as an

---

50. Kohn 1976 argues that we can have a great effect on these constructions, even
if not on the social problems behind them.

argument is attractive for its cleansing, destructive powers until a particular end, for a particular group of people, is established. Then constructionism becomes an intellectual embarrassment to those very people.

The comparable worth case shows the ultimate utility of constructionist arguments. They empower the powerless. Once that is done, they disappear. Constructionism empowers people by negating crucial resources of the powerful—their methods, their language, their research capital.[51] But it is very difficult to imagine constructionism as a hegemonic argument in social science. That is, one cannot imagine an entire intellectual field in which all terms continuously dissolve into each other at a fast enough rate to prevent some form of objectification. This is what postmodernists tell us is coming. But their own performance betrays more than a hint of realism. Like everyone else, they argue from authorities. More important, their participation in an apparently rule-governed social science means that they implicitly believe in such an enterprise.[52]

In social science, then, constructionism is thus doomed to a perpetual succession of flare-ups. But these flare-ups have important results. Labeling drew an exciting generation into sociology, even if much of that generation soon turned to other things, among them realist analysis. Or again, constructionism can start wonderful new empirical traditions, as it started (in part) studies of victimization and new analyses of scientific practice. We see the beginnings of an exciting new constructionist transformation today in the area of occupational analysis as Desrosières, Szreter, Anderson, and others start to deconstruct our occupational statistics. All of these works will ultimately turn back toward realist analysis. For ultimately constructionism fares best when it works in alternation, getting realism out of the holes in which it often finds itself. A fractal distinc-

---

51. Nonetheless, it helps if constructionists have a few of those resources. The fact that many of the new sociologists of science were lapsed scientists meant that they had intellectual tools that labeling lacked against the mainstream empiricist students of deviance.

52. Why constructionism could not be a hegemonic intellectual view is a very interesting question that I cannot address fully here. Purely intellectual arguments about it seem to me to come down to the "what about reality" view of Dr. Johnson. How would such an intellectual system have any "system" to it? How would it be anything other than a perpetual transition of ideas without means of comparability? To put the question in a less utopian fashion, how could a social science based on constructionism produce results warrantable in the eyes of the politicians, marketers, and public who consume social science? It is ultimately of no help to either left or right to tell the National Institute of Justice that crime is simply something we imagine.

tion accomplishes the most for us when we leave it to play on and on. Extremal positions are heady and noble, but also sterile and vain.[53]

APPENDIX
A History of "Social Construction" to 1990

The phrase "social construction" and its various relatives (socially constructing, socially constructed) seem to have begun with Berger and Luckmann's 1966 book. They provide no antecedent references for the phrase and use it as early as their first page. One can easily trace the citation history of both book and phrase (I did so by hand). The book commanded around 20 citations a year in the period 1966–70 and around 50 to 60 citations per year in the early 1970s. In 1974–75 there was a sudden jump to about 120 citations per year. Citations hit a peak in 1981 at 160, then fell slightly, averaging around 140 per year into the 1990s.

As for articles with the phrase "social construction" (hereafter "SC" in this appendix) in their titles, there were none in the late 1960s and one or two a year in the period 1970–74. There was again a sudden rise in 1974–75 to five or so articles per year, a figure that endured until the 1979–83 period, in which there were seven to nine articles per year. In 1984 there were suddenly sixteen SC articles a year, and the figure has not fallen below fourteen (1987) since. As for books, Gerald Suttles (1972) was the first to use the phrase after Berger and Luckmann, whose book he tells me he had not read. In the late 1970s the phrase was used in book titles by sociologists both of science and of social problems, later entering other areas as well.

There is no easy explanation for the sudden jump in both citations and titles in 1974–75. There was no new edition of Berger and Luckmann's book nor any major conference (to my knowledge) about the book. The 1973 Kitsuse and Spector paper that launched social problems constructionism did not cite Berger and Luckmann, although many later articles in that tradition did. In any case, as the citation history makes clear, the phrase had entered the general sociological vocabulary by 1974. For example, Lauer (1976) uses the phrase "social construction of reality" without quotes and without citation.

We can get some sense of the areas addressed by the concept by coding SC articles in terms of their subjects (table A3.1). I have grouped the data in quinquenniums to make the trend of subfields clear.

What is first striking here is the conformality of these numbers to the pattern of the old social problems literature—dominated by deviance, physical and mental illness, family, and education problems. (The unimportance of race, until the late 1980s, is the only exception to this conformality.) A

---

53. See Conk 1980, Desrosières and Thévenot 1988, Szreter 1993.

Table A3.1

	to 1975	1976–80	1981–85	1986–89
Deviance, including crime, delinquency	2	5	2	4
Medicine/illness	0	1	3	5
Psychopathology	1	0	2	4
Psychology/development/emotion	0	3	14	5
Family	1	1	3	2
Gender	0	1	3	5
Race	0	0	0	4
Education	0	3	5	1
Economy	1	1	2	6
General	3	12	16	26

second striking fact is the concentrated focus on the argument in brief periods. Psychologists talked constructionism in the early 1980s, as did students of education. By contrast, writers about psychic and physical illness, the economy, gender, and race began to use the term only in the late 1980s. Most interesting, there is no evidence at all of perhaps the strongest area of constructionism in sociology in the period: the sociology of science. The sociologists of science often insisted on their own peculiar terminologies (there are several) for the constructionist argument.

In summary, this evidence indicates that Berger and Luckmann contributed the current name for social constructionism and that citations pay them well for that contribution. But the content of their book has had little impact. It was conceived very much in the old European version of ideological constructionism, the so-called sociology of knowledge. The constitutive constructionism of the opening was merely grafted onto the book. By contrast, the dominant version of constructionism in the social problems literature is precisely the constitutive one, deriving from the same general sources as labeling theory. And even though the original sources of the new sociology of science lay in ideological constructionism, that emphasis rapidly disappeared as the field developed. Thus the Berger and Luckmann book, brilliant as it undoubtedly was, seems to have been the last, elegant statement of the old dilemma of ideologies. It was an end rather than a beginning.

4

The Unity of
History

THE ANALYSES of fractal ingestion in chapter 2 and of fractionation in chapter 3 underscore the powerful and sometimes confusing effects of the unfolding of fractal distinctions in time. In this chapter, I analyze the problem of monism. What happens when groups set out deliberately to cross the boundaries of a fractal distinction and even to synthesize one of our basic dichotomies into a single concept?

I examine this problem through a detailed investigation of yet another example. The years from 1965 to 1990 saw a complex encounter between the discipline of history on the one hand and the various social sciences on the other. In field after field—economics, political science, sociology, even anthropology—historical questions moved to center stage. I examine here one among these encounters, that between history and sociology.

We can imagine this encounter as a fractal process with two aspects. The first of these concerns the opposition of narrative and analysis, which shapes both the questions and methods of the two fields. Broadly speaking, the disciplinary distinction between history and sociology concerns how problems are posed. Historians pose their problems narratively. Why is it that slavery disappeared? How did the First World War begin? Sociologists pose their problems

No special acknowledgments here; I was my own research assistant in this chapter, counting up the names and the speakers and the Ph.D.s. This chapter first appeared as a talk at the Social Science History Association meetings in Minneapolis in 1990 at the invitation of Eric Monkkonen. After a suitable toning-down, it appeared in print in 1991. As the reader will note, I am an active participant in the debate discussed here, not the distant observer of the two preceding chapters. I dedicate the chapter to Daniel Scott Smith, Professor of History at the University of Illinois, Chicago.

more analytically. What are the causes of social mobility? What variables are related to religious fundamentalism? This narrative/analysis distinction continues into the realm of methods. Historians generally choose narrative methods, sociologists analytic ones.

At the same time, the narrative/analysis distinction can also be seen as a distinction between a temporal and a static view of the very nature of social life. In this guise it concerns not questions and techniques, but objects of inquiry. Concretely, we can see this distinction as one between taking old data seriously and ignoring it. But it is more intelligible at a more abstract level, as a distinction between on the one hand assuming that social life is continuously changing and on the other assuming that change is a mere foreground within the constancy of eternal rules of social life. As we shall see, these various assumptions about objects of inquiry can entangle with those about technique in bewildering ways.

What happened in the 1960s and 1970s was reversal within the world of technique, particularly that of method. Some historians began applying analytic methods to address narratively posed questions. Shortly after, some sociologists began asking analytic questions about singular events like the rise of capitalism, a task that required a more narrative approach to explanation. Thus came social science history on the one side and historical sociology on the other.

One might have expected that this encounter would produce either a synthesis or an explicit conflict. And within sociology, one might have expected that the encounter with history would radically transform the discipline. In fact, neither synthesis nor conflict nor transformation took place. In this chapter, I show why the fractal process that produced social science history and historical sociology failed to produce such synthetic results. I begin by tracing the various rebellions that drove some historians toward the social sciences and some sociologists toward history. I then detail the institutional structure of historical work in sociology, a structure that arose in the 1970s and 1980s in response to these earlier rebellions. In this institutional analysis, I aim to show the complexities that arise when several fractal distinctions intersect in concrete research communities; we do not observe all possible combinations of all fractal choices, but rather a very limited sample of those combinations, embodied in a few mildly successful generational paradigms.[1]

---

1. I start with an institutional analysis partly because I am an institutionalist myself and partly because no one else has, to my knowledge. Concept-based studies of historical sociology, most of them more or less prescriptive, are by contrast quite common. (Examples are Skocpol 1984b; Tilly 1981, 1984; Sztompka 1986; Hamilton and Walton 1988.) But more importantly, an institutional analysis shows why histori-

My structural analysis leads into a detailed discussion of position statements by historical sociologists. There I show exactly how it was that the historical sociologists stopped short of reconceptualizing the social process in narrative terms. As in chapter 2, I close with a retrospective discussion of the reaction to the earlier publication of this paper and the status of the current debate over history and sociology.

Like earlier chapters, this one has several aims. Empirically, the chapter discusses a particular generational paradigm in American sociology. This examination is more detailed than the analyses in preceding chapters both in its data on structures and networks and in its explicit analysis of particular texts. Also, I am myself a participant in this story. In this chapter, more than any other, the mixture of description and prescription is nearly complete.

Conceptually, this chapter underscores the extreme difficulty of actually resolving a fractal dichotomy with any monistic argument. The story of historical sociology and its cross-cousin social science history is the story of a marriage that, so far at least, has failed. The failure has resulted in an extraordinarily useful mass of empirical and theoretical writing. But that writing has not resolved or really even addressed the original problem.

1. The Rebellions in Sociology and History

The border groups between history and sociology emerged as generational paradigms attacking disciplinary orthodoxies. Like most such rebellions, they involved alliances between a small out-group in the dominant generation and a larger segment of the rising one. They also reflected their times (the 1960s) in drawing some of their force from radical politics.

In sociology, 1960s orthodoxy was Parsonian functionalism. Despite its commendable interdisciplinarity and theoretical consistency, functionalism never generated an empirical research program. Moreover, it shared with its predecessors in English social anthropology an extreme disattention to social change. Opposition to Parsonian functionalism was located mainly in the remnants and descendants of the Chicago school, who concentrated on the study of deviance and community and whose customary methodologies were field observation and case study. These topics and methodologies

---

ans and sociologists together have produced so little beyond what they produced apart. The synthetic project has not been intellectually defeated. Quite the contrary. It has never been tried.

had their own disattention to macro change, even though the Chicago progenitors originally constructed interactionism in order to study the effects of macro change.[2]

The empirical vacuum left by functionalism was, however, only partly filled by the case study and observation literature. The third and soon-to-be-dominant strand of sociology was quantitative empiricism, which gradually occupied the rest of this vacuum. Ogburn had pioneered this genre with his "social trends," simple sums of individual indicators that could hardly be considered historical. Lazarsfeld and others developed survey research methods from the 1930s onward, and these received a mathematical push when path analysis was borrowed from biology and economics in the 1960s by Duncan and Blalock. Suddenly dominant in sociology, the general linear model drove the discipline rapidly away from grand theory (some would say away from theory altogether) and established, in the Wisconsin status attainment model, a basic paradigm and method for investigating social affairs. The Wisconsin model, intensely micro in focus, was historical in only the loosest sense. Real actors were replaced by variables, narrative causality by the reified causality of variables, real time by the order of the variables.[3]

Historical sociology emerged in the 1970s to attack these orthodoxies theoretical and methodological. While its leaders included contemporaries of the Parsonians (Charles Tilly, for example), the rank and file were students from the radical years. Theoretically, historical sociology was for them a way to attack the Parsonian framework on its weakest front—its approach to social change—and a way to bring Marx into sociology. Methodologically, historical sociology damned the status attainment model for its micro focus, its antihistorical and antistructural character, its reifications, its scientism. As for the Chicago interactionists, already deep in their own critique of established society via labeling theory as we have already seen, historical sociology simply bypassed them.

Central to historical sociology was its invocation of the ponderous respectability of "History." History's unimpeachable if obscure methodology and its immense factual mastery justified rejection of the Wisconsin worldview. And while History's comprehensive scope matched that of Parsonian orthodoxy, its focus on events and macro

---

2. Schwartz (1987) sees the Chicago school as more openly antihistorical than do I, while Hamilton and Walton (1988) agree more with my judgment. For my views at greater length, see Abbott 1999a, particularly chap. 7.

3. So dominant was this view that its rhetoric pervades even those historical sociologists who most actively seek its overthrow. See Abbott 1988a, 1998, for my full analysis of this approach and Bernert 1983 for a useful history of it.

change justified rejection of Parsons. Above all, History's respectability redeemed the radical politics of the historical sociologists.
Even as an evolutionist, Marx was more historical than Parsons, and
the Marx of *The Eighteenth Brumaire* was a downright storyteller.[4]

In sum, many sociologists of the 1970s—particularly the younger
ones—turned to historical sociology because it enabled a criticism
of both the conservatism of Parsonian theory and the misplaced concreteness of the linear modelers.[5] These "historical sociologists"
constituted a clear generational paradigm of the sort seen before,
produced by the simple reversal of a fractal distinction—that of narrative versus analysis—but within a single discipline. The difference
between historical sociology and the sociological mainstream recapitulated the difference between history and sociology themselves.

But while various intellectual forces produced a group successfully claiming the label of "historical sociologists," there were—at
least in principle—several other ways of imagining or constituting
historical sociology. It could also be defined as sociological work
that involved data over time, or sociological work that theorized
about social processes, or sociological work that self-consciously examined past social groups. Each of these alternatives embodied a
somewhat different move away from the analytic, causalist approach
to understanding social life and each, like "official" historical sociology, entailed a body of work and a group of people doing it.

Work involving data over time became common in sociology as
methodological change finally slowed to the point where old data-
sets could support current techniques. But the move toward old or
panel data was not accompanied by a change in sensibility. One
could hardly consider as "historical sociology" the all-too-standard
article on "blacks in the labor force, 1972–82." Such an article

---

4. John Hall (1989) notes the somewhat different emergence of historical sociology in England. There, the preceding sociological tradition of Marshall, Lockwood,
Dore, and others never accepted Parsonian theory and never lost touch with historical
workers like E. P. Thompson and Raymond Williams. This older tradition had been
receptive to the earlier historical sociology of Americans like Bendix, Lipset, and
Moore. So the younger generation, while strongly influenced by structural Marxism,
extended rather than attacked earlier work. England moreover had a long-standing
empirical tradition in historical sociology—the Cambridge historical demography
group—whose contributions to both history and sociology were of undoubted greatness. Writing a decade before Hall, Stedman Jones (1976) saw considerably less recep-
tivity to historical ideas among English sociologists, although much borrowing of
sociological ideas by historians. Perhaps Stedman Jones described the general attitudes of the discipline while Hall described a particular line of scholarship that never
lost sight of history.

5. I am using "misplaced concreteness" in the technical sense intended by
Whitehead (1925), the sense of mistakenly perceiving one's abstractions as real things
in the world. See Abbott 1988b.

merely did cross-sectional analysis with time as an index variable. It concerned trends and counts, with little sensitivity to historical context or contingency and less to qualitative change in the social categories or attributes analyzed. However, there were scholars who became convinced that techniques designed for such analyses effectively merged history and social science.[6]

Another group of potential historical sociologists were the many sociologists who theorized about social processes. Most of these, however, thought little about "historical change." Sociologists who focused directly on contingent processes were usually microtheorists like interactionists and ethnomethodologists, whose common assumption of an unchanging "social a priori" was hardly historical in the usual sense. Nonetheless, such process theorists clearly understood history's long-standing emphasis on contingency, accident, and process, even if they ignored the limits it placed on the extent of generalization.[7]

There remained a third view, that historical sociology comprised those who self-consciously studied past social groups or cultures. Although it clearly included the historical sociologists discussed earlier, this definition covered many others as well, scattered throughout sociology. (Historical demographers were the most conspicuous example.) I shall examine these "unofficial historical sociologists" in more detail below.

Within sociology, then, there were a number of groups pushing out toward history. The most self-conscious of these was the group we usually think of as historical sociologists, the group whose emergence from a standard fractal cycle I recounted earlier. The other groups of potential historical sociologists, however, were not generated by fractal cycles, with the possible exception of the microinteractionists, who in any case were more deeply characterized by their micro and intensely phenomenological stance. Thus it makes sense that the consciously oppositional group took the lead.

Curiously, the history that these historical sociologists embraced

---

6. Chief among these are the proponents of event history analysis, an approach construing history as a matter of waiting times until given events happen. The methods are of profound utility but only within a limited range of problems. For analyses of the approach see Abbott 1990a, 1992b. A better understanding of history can be found in sociology's relatively scarce formal temporal modeling literature, a literature begun by James Coleman, Harrison White, and others, but never really strong in the discipline.
7. It is precisely this dual sense of history, I argue below, that has undone the historical sociologists. They have understood what the process theorists missed—the necessity of limiting generalization—but have ultimately missed the emphasis on contingency and process that those others understood.

was in many respects an orthodoxy that their contemporaries in history departments sought to escape. Historical orthodoxy in the 1950s and 1960s was above all an orthodoxy of genre and style. As the old "new history" of Robinson and Beard had subsided under the pressure of the war and the postwar "American High," the discipline had reoriented toward "consensus history."[8] Although aware of the contributions of the Annales school, American historians showed little desire to emulate its distinctive (and to the American taste peculiar) mixture of history and the social sciences. The political tenor of American history was even and conservative, with broad acceptance of the "liberal tradition" proposed by Louis Hartz. To the retrospective eye there were clear signs of change, but even by 1980 signs of transformation in history were muted at best.[9]

Quantitative history—a direct borrowing of social science methods—was one revolt against this orthodoxy. One strand of quantitative history studied politics. It arose at the University of Iowa in the 1950s, where William Aydelotte, Allan Bogue, and Samuel Hays developed a program for "behavioral" history and adapted Guttman scalogram analysis to carry it out methodologically. With help from others, the Iowa group founded the ICP(S)R historical archives at Michigan, whose status as a center for quantitative history was reinforced by Tilly's arrival in 1969.[10]

A second strand of quantitative history studied the economy. Originating at Purdue, this strand produced the most visible products of quantitative history: Robert Fogel's counterfactual demonstration that railroads had not been necessary for American economic growth and his and Stanley Engerman's controversial revision of the historiography of slavery. Throughout the 1960s and 1970s, debates over counterfactual analysis kept cliometrics, as it was called, in the disciplinary eye.[11]

---

8. "Consensus history" as a phrase comes from John Higham in 1959 (see Hofstadter 1968, chap. 12). The phrase "American High" is William O'Neill's (1986). My account of orthodoxies in history and sociology is echoed and reinforced by that of MacDonald (1996b).

9. Hartz 1955. On muted changes, see Kammen 1980:29.

10. The 1960s and 1970s brought a methodological swing away from scaling (regarded as purely descriptive) toward regression (perceived as "causal"; see Alter 1981). This issue of causality versus description has proved central to relations between history, sociology, and their interdisciplinary offspring. For while social science history believed in causality by conversion and historical sociology believed in it by ancestry, they meant very different things by the term. My short history of quantitative history comes from several sources. The principal ones are Bogue 1983, 1990; Kousser 1980; and various essays in Swierenga 1970. For a quantitative assessment of quantitative history, see Sprague 1978.

11. See Fogel 1964; Fogel and Engerman 1974. On counterfactuals more generally, see Gerschenkron 1967 and McClelland 1975.

The third, "social" strand of quantitative history was both later and more diffuse. Quantitative techniques had long been central in demographic history, but Stephan Thernstrom's 1964 attack on anthropologist Lloyd Warner's analysis of Newburyport, Massachusetts, was the first highly visible quantitative study in social history more generally. The effort required to generate usable data from manuscript censuses and biographical databases clearly slowed the application of quantitative techniques in this area, although the ultimate results have been considerable.[12]

Institutionally, quantitative history took on the name of "social science" history. In point of fact, the social science involved was rather restricted, based on quantitative methods in general and on standard linear models in particular. Thus much of social science was left out of social science history. The serial history characteristic of the Annales school never caught on in America. Microeconomics proper, though highly (social) scientific and in its own way highly quantitative, affected only the economic wing of social science history, and in any case that wing relied on linear models for empirical analysis like everyone else. (Rational choice theory came to history only much later.) Anthropological theory, although equally social scientific, seems to have bypassed social science history entirely in the 1980s.[13] Only the full advent of postmodernism elsewhere in the disciplinary system brought anthropological writing into the world of social science history, starting a new fractal cycle whose transformations are still working themselves out.

---

12. Warner and Lunt 1941; Thernstrom 1964.

13. Despite these appearances, one might argue that history's reaching out toward social science was less methodological than theoretical. MacDonald (1990, 1996b) has traced this borrowing not only through institutions—showing the central importance of the SSRC reports on historical and social science methodologies—but also through an elegant analysis of social scientific citations in the urban history literature of 1940–85. To some extent MacDonald's methods overstate the case; authors almost always provide citations for common theories while not doing so for common methods. But other writers have also argued for separating "theoretical" history and "quantitative" history as departures from traditional practices (Kocka 1984). In Germany, for example, the two represented quite different traditions (Kocka 1984). In England too, theoretical borrowing seems to have been more powerful than methodological borrowing, at least outside the demographic group (Stedman Jones 1976).

In the long run, some have judged social science history a success, while others have judged it a failure. Quantitative training has found its way into about half the graduate curricula in the country (Kousser 1989), but Floud (1984) argues that the decline in controversy over quantitative history reflects more a conviction that it can be safely ignored than a fear that its practitioners cannot be answered effectively.

Finally, I should note a material reason for the absence of anthropology from the universe of social science history. The meetings of the primary association of the social science historians—the SSHA—often conflict with those of the American Anthropological Association. On the Annales school, see Bourdelais 1984.

The methodological foray of the social science historians into the empty space between history and sociology was complemented by substantive incursions, embodied in the various "new histories." Some of these were substantive groups emphasizing this or that concern ignored in traditional history: psychohistory, climatic history, and other such topics. But in the 1970s more important were the radical histories. Although these too argued that certain aspects of history had been ignored, they transformed this claim into a political one; ignorance was rather deliberate than merely intellectual. There was a complex development here. Unlike the turn to history in sociology, the turn to social science in history had predated radicalism.[14] Thernstrom's book, like Fogel and Engerman's, lacks the overt advocacy that would mark much later social (and social science) history. But if the historical generation of the 1950s and early 1960s had found quantitative history an effective tool in generational overthrow, it became for many of their students a more political implement.

In the United States, Marxist (or New Left) historical scholarship began with William Appleman Williams's students, who started *Studies on the Left* in 1959 and helped set forth the "corporate liberalism" interpretation of American history since the Civil War. At a more micro level, Herbert Gutman, David Montgomery, and their students produced detailed studies of working class groups in city after city. Eugene Genovese produced a brilliant analysis of slavery whose cultural emphasis owed much to E. P. Thompson's magisterial *Making of the English Working Class*, itself the most visible single work of what became an extensive Marxist historical movement in England, centered on the History Workshop of Ruskin College.[15]

The left historical community was divided by a number of issues, most of which were also central to debates between history and sociology more generally. Johnson, Selbourne, and others condemned the History Workshop, Thompson, and even Genovese for their emphasis on experience, for distrust of theory, for unwillingness to

14. I thus disagree with Skocpol's (1987) assertion that the two came simultaneously. Quantitative history was the first wave of the "new social history" and very clearly began without any radical emphasis. See also Skocpol 1988.

15. The stronghold of historical Marxism in England was at the History Workshop, whose origins as a seminar for the adult students at Labour's Ruskin College dictated its emphasis on personal experience and working-class history (Samuel 1980). The History Workshop drew relatively little on social science history, in fact being antiquantitative; its emphasis tended to be cultural, following Thompson, with Gramsci as its theoretical lodestar (Hall 1978; Floud 1984). Beyond the sources given in text, I have used Novick 1988, Wiener 1989, and Higham 1989 as background sources on radical history. I have also gone through the entire run of *History Workshop Journal* for relevant material.

make large interpretive statements, and indeed for romanticism about the past. Others saw the same problems in the incipient professionalism of American Marxists; as radical social historians marched with considerable success into the professoriat, some critics thought their work forsook theoretical focus for empirical microquarianism. This latter tendency was angrily protested by Judt and others who saw the study of detail as "ignoring politics." The Marxists were thus to some extent divided over empiricism versus theory, and to some extent divided over micro versus macro. Indeed the two distinctions were often run together, a conflation that recurred in historical sociology.[16]

Another new history exploring the gap between history and sociology was women's history. Women's history emerged in the early 1970s, taking organizational form in the Berkshire Conferences (from 1973). Articles on women and women's issues in leading historical journals ballooned from 1 percent of the total in the late 1960s to well over 10 percent by 1980. Like Marxist history, early women's history was closely tied to activism, and, as in Marxist history, more recent years have seen some conflict between the professionalized and activist wings. The gradual institutionalization of women's history also saw an intellectual shift from an early focus on domination, through an emphasis on a separate women's sphere in the early 1980s, to a renewed focus on conflict and differences in the late 1980s.[17]

Thus, in the 1960s and after, quantitative history, Marxist history, and women's history were the three most clearly distinguishable branches of history moving toward social science or paralleling major movements in the social sciences. All three eventually developed connections with various parts of historical sociology. But these connections reflected the diverse stories discussed above. The historians and the sociologists had turned toward each other for quite different reasons.

---

16. Johnson 1978; Selbourne 1980; Judt 1979. See more generally sources cited in Novick 1988:443. The Marxist historians pushed into many of the same areas as did the social science historians. Indeed, the two met on the turf of labor history, where some commentators (e.g., Floud [1984]) wondered why there wasn't more collaboration between the two. (Others expected none—e.g., Berkhofer [1983].) To say, however, that Marxist history resembled social science history in lying between history and sociology is to misspeak. Rather, Marxist history moved toward a radical scholarship that was as removed from standard sociology as from standard history. As we shall see, this radical pole attracted historical sociologists as well. Yet it did not strongly link the historians and the sociologists.

17. Background sources on women's history include Vogel forthcoming, Novick 1988, and Lerner 1989.

The sociologists were mainly younger people who saw history—radical or otherwise—as a way of attacking functionalism, which they disliked on both intellectual and political grounds. To them history meant comparative studies of particular great events or systems, and their heroes were less Charles Tilly with his numbers and variables than Barrington Moore and Perry Anderson with their comparative cases and congenial politics.[18] Quantification as then dominant in sociology was a nightmare from which they wished to awaken, and hence they defined historical sociology as a theoretically impregnated analysis that was qualitative but not quite fully narrative.

On the historical side, the quantitative historians were led by an earlier generation attacking an historical orthodoxy on purely intellectual grounds. They and their students had little love for functionalism—Thernstrom's *Poverty and Progress* was an attack on functionalism—but they had equally little love for grand narratives, however theoretical. Theory meant microeconomic theory for Fogel and North, as it meant behaviorism—what would today be called rational choice—for Lee Benson and others. The Marxist historians, meanwhile, had split. An older group, less active as the 1970s wore on, worked with general theoretical and explanatory schemes aimed at political and economic systems. The other, younger group, which increasingly dominated academic Marxism, focused at the micro level and tended toward culturalism and the study of lived experience. This last was the central connection for feminist history as it developed the concept of separate spheres in the late 1970s.

The stage was thus set for the tourists wandering through the city of knowledge to bypass each other completely. The social science historians had rejected history's intentional narration for social science's theoretical and analytic causality. They had also exchanged history's grand and often political stories for social science's breadth of interest in the economic and the social, the micro and the unstudied. They understood causality in social science terms but accepted history's insistence on factual mastery and on the limitation of explanation in place and time. Among Marxist historians, it was by contrast the group emphasizing large-scale studies that endorsed

18. Of course Tilly could not be ignored and was therefore one of the "masters" studied in the major stakeout of the historical sociology turf (the edited collection *Vision and Method in Historical Sociology* [Skocpol 1984a]). His institutional importance and string of important students made him inevitably central to historical sociology even if his work did not really fit the mold that came to be established for "comparative historical sociology," which was self-consciously Weberian and antiquantitative.

Table 4.1
Positions of Various Groups on Various Important Dichotomies

	Macro/ Micro	Narr/ Causal	Concept of History	Sci/ Exper. Theory	Political Economy Central	Conscious Substantive Politics	Quant or Qual
Traditional history	Macro	Narr	Master Narrs	Exper	Yes	Liberal	Qual
Sociological theorizing, 1960	Macro	Causal	None	Sci	No	Liberal	Qual
Sociological empiricism, 1970s	Micro	Causal	None	Sci	No	No	Quant
Social science history	Micro	Causal	Periods	Sci	No	No	Quant
Historical sociology 1	Macro	Causal	Master Narrs	Sci	Yes	No	Qual
Historical sociology 2	Micro	Causal	Periods	Sci	No	No	Quant
Macro Marxism	Macro	Causal	Master Narrs	Sci	Yes	Radical	Qual
Micro Marxism	Micro	Both	Periods	Both	Yes	Radical	Both
Feminism	Trans	Trans	Master Narrs	Exper	No	Radical	Qual

"Both" means both alternatives were represented.
"Trans" means group claimed to transcend the given dichotomy.

theory and causality (as well as, in some cases, transhistorical generalizations), while the radical social historians studied "the way things really were" in people's lived, micro experience and usually gave only limited interpretations. Women's historians were split in similar ways, although their common claim that feminist theory grew out of lived experience rang yet another change on these dichotomies.

For their part, the historical sociologists accepted from history the positive value of limiting generalizations and mastering details, but reinterpreted social science's belief in causality in *qualitative* terms, unlike the social science historians. Moreover, as we shall see below, they accepted, with the traditional and the large-scale Marxist historians, a belief in the centrality of politics and political economy.

Table 4.1 summarizes these positions. Generalizing and particularizing, quantitative and qualitative, radical and nonradical, political and social, macro and micro: each of the various groups in history and sociology represented some unique combination of choices among these dichotomies. These different combinations of choices tell us two very important things about the concept of fractal distinctions. First, they tell us that while the number of possible combinations of choices is huge, in fact the active research traditions in an area at any given time use only a few of those possibilities, because of the conflation of choices that often produces systematic opposition across all dichotomies, as we have seen with the general methodological manifolds of quantitative and qualitative. Even a minor deviation from those standard conflations (as is illustrated by nearly all these groups) is difficult indeed.

Second, these patterns show us that a narrative group that turns causal arrives at a very different place than a causal one that turns narrative. (Compare the rows for social science history and for historical sociology 1 in table 4.1.) The actors themselves were quite clear about the difference. If we consider the situation as of 1990, for example, the American Sociological Association teaching materials on historical sociology contained no substantive references (among twenty-six syllabuses and eleven bibliographies) to the work of Robert Fogel, William Aydelotte, or Lee Benson.[19] Such social science historians appeared only in the general bibliography on methods, and in fact none of the six syllabuses on historical sociological methods taught any of them, or any quantitative techniques to speak of. The Marxists were somewhat better represented—Thompson was one of the "great men" of the historical sociologists—but the micro work of the Gutman and History Workshop type was far less evident than one might expect. The ignorance was as great in the other direction. The Social Science History Association, for example, did not prove hospitable to the theory-laden papers characteristic of the comparative-historical sociologists and had no network bringing such papers onto the program until 1992. In their passage through the city of social knowledge, the social science historians and the historical sociologists had not arrived at the same street corner.

2. The Institutional Structure of Historical Sociology

That historical sociology and social science history came to such different places suggests that the image of a city of left and right turns is not as useful as it seemed. But we have so far largely ignored another group of sociologists who thought of themselves as historical. These were students of past social groups—families, occupations, and the like—who for various methodological or substantive reasons were not part of the "historical sociology" movement earlier outlined. These people make up a second large group of "historical sociologists" (hereafter "HS2" in this chapter) who augment the ini-

---

19. The 1987 ASA historical sociology materials were edited by Roy (1987a).

tial group discussed above ("HS1"). Unlike those others, most of these sociologists did arrive at a place fairly close to social science history.

The historical turn in sociology, that is, was itself divided into two separate groups. To some extent, this arose because of a fractal split within a group (historical sociology generally) that itself emerged from a fractal split (of sociologists interested in history from the rest of that discipline). But while the idea of a proliferating fractal division is analytically convenient, it is in this case historically questionable. The division of HS1 and HS2 dates from the very first emergence of "historical sociology" as a label. In fact, it reflects differences on other fractal distinctions than the narrative/analysis one central to the emergence of HS1. These other differences, as we shall see, forced history and sociology to link up within substantive areas. They distracted attention from the general theoretical question of radically rethinking sociology along narrative lines. To see exactly how this separation and distraction occurred, an easy procedure is to study the organizations with which the two groups of historical sociologists were most closely associated, the Social Science History Association (SSHA) for HS2 and the American Sociological Association Section on Comparative Historical Sociology (ASACHS) for HS1. Analyzing these groups will help us see how fractal structures work at the most detailed, individual level.

The SSHA was founded as part of the institutionalization of quantitative history in the 1970s. The 1960s had brought the ICPSR historical archives and, in 1967, *Historical Methods Newsletter.* In 1970, the substantive *Journal of Interdisciplinary History* commenced publication, and Allan Bogue, with Jerome Clubb, began to agitate for a quantitative history association. SSHA and its journal (*Social Science History*) began official life in 1976. The association is structured around "networks" of common interest: Methods, Family, Demography, Labor, Urban, Rural, Economic History, and so on. These networks plan future programs on a panel-by-panel basis, making SSHA largely member driven. Some SSHA networks had strong ties to sociology from the outset. For example, among the SSHA's numerous international connections was one to the English historical demographers. Since historical demography was not part of HS1 but was quite central in HS2, the SSHA's linkage to HS2 dates from its founding.[20]

The other institutional setting for historical sociology was the

---

20. SSHA history is scattered in a number of sources. Most generally, see Bogue 1983.

quite different ASA. A much larger organization than the SSHA
(and, unlike SSHA, a disciplinary association), the ASA has frag-
mented since 1970 into more than thirty sections, with varying degrees of overlapping membership. The new sections are usually
smaller, specialized groups that institutionalize political splits
(Marxist sociology) or methodological cum intellectual ones (Culture, Political Economy of the World System [PEWS]). Cappell and
Guterbock have used joint section membership data to demonstrate
that ASACHS is one of seven sections (the others were World Conflict, Collective Behavior, Theory, Marxist, PEWS, and Political Sociology) tightly bound by joint memberships and relatively isolated
from other sections. The members of this group are, in general, left,
theory oriented, and antiquantitative when compared to the rest of
the discipline.[21]

The importance of the ASA sections lies in their control of about
one-third of ASA program space. Most of the ASA program is dominated by the president, whose program committee loosely controls
the thematic and general sessions via personal networks. Since
there are no panel submissions, the only way for outsiders to present
intellectually coherent panels is through the sections, which divide
the remaining program space in proportion to their membership.
Most new sections therefore bespeak new paradigms craving legitimacy and program turf.[22] ASACHS was no exception. HS1 dominated it for nearly a decade.

For evidence, we must merely list, from ASA programs of the mid-
1980s, all people who either held office in ASACHS, or organized
the section sessions, or presented papers in section sessions. We can
also include organizers and speakers at the general (nonsection) ASA

---

21. On the section changes, see Ad Hoc Committee 1989. The scaling studies
are Cappell and Guterbock 1986 and Guterbock and Cappell 1990. They have been
replicated on later data by Daipha 1999.

22. This fact perhaps explains why there are seven closely tied ASA sections car-
rying out what is largely a common intellectual program. Different sections to some
extent "specialize" in rejecting different parts of orthodoxy. The Marxist section rejects conservative politics, the Theory Section rejects positivism, and so on. This
specialization explains why historical sociology can be clearly antiquantitative without ever having presented a deep analysis of the issues involved; the Theory Section
takes care of that subject (but see Skocpol 1984b). It also explains why there are
sections as specialized as PEWS. The reader will notice that the sections exemplify
"substantive differentiation" in the terms of chapter 1. They seem to show that differentiation can happen in the context of scarcity (of program space). But as Daipha
(1999) has shown clearly, new sections are often simply old sections duplicating
themselves to get more program space. At the same time, however, the ASA has
multiplied program space at will (over a third of the membership now appears on the
program), thereby inflating its intellectual currency endlessly in order to avoid scarcity. The actual scarcity at ASA is of audience.

sessions on historical sociology, although these are more open to the general membership. To these lists we can compare lists, taken from the programs of the SSHA from the equivalent period, of paper presenters who were identified as sociologists.[23]

The ensuing lists of "historical sociologists" are virtually disjoint. Only four people made four or more appearances at each venue in the period. By contrast, eighteen appeared four or more times at the SSHA but not four or more times in these particular sessions of the ASA. And fourteen appeared four or more times in these ASA sessions without appearing at least four times at the SSHA.

The SSHA group included Charles Tilly and his students, historical demographers, a group studying family and gender, and some diverse others. The ASA speakers included holdovers from ASACHS's early days (when it focused exclusively on Weber), macrosociological students of whole societies, and people who had written about Western European or American capitalism and their general effects. The only crossovers (on both lists) were two macrosociologists (Theda Skocpol and Ann Orloff) and two historical sociologists of gender and family (Barbara Laslett and Sonya Rose).[24]

---

23. The lists cover 1983–89 for the ASA and 1981–89 for the SSHA; the longer period reflects a need for comparable numbers. I omit the details of the names, all of which are given in the original article on which this chapter is based. In conversation, Margaret Somers has questioned my use of the 1980s to establish the personnel of HS1 and HS2, arguing that the actual formation of historical sociology came in the late 1970s, at Harvard, in events like the Conference on Methods of Historical Social Analysis (reported in Skocpol 1984a). That may well be true, although without undertaking more detailed historical work I cannot evaluate the judgment. Since my aim is rather to document the existence of the two groups, the later period suits my purposes better.

24. These figures to some extent conceal how absolute the disjunction was; most of the four-or-more-participations ASA people had appeared at SSHA only once or twice, most of the SSHA people once or never at the ASACHS section. There is good reason, then, to think that HS1 and HS2 were somewhat separate groups. Theda Skocpol was clearly the dominant figure in defining historical sociology as a subdiscipline, as much by her institution building (in the 1979 methods conference, for example) as by her brilliant work on revolutions (1979). It is for that reason, rather than out of some conspiracy theory on my part, that she figures so prominently in this essay. It is striking that Skocpol remarked in 1988 that she had ultimately been persuaded of the importance of gender as a central social variable. This persuasion might have been related to the presence of two historical sociologists of gender among those highly active in both ASACHS and SSHA as well as to the eventual arrival of gender as an ASACHS session topic. Gender has for the last twenty years been the central issue in ASA politics generally, and one of the four or five most central research topics in sociology. It is therefore not surprising that gender sociologists provide crucial links in historical sociology. Since I did this work originally, gender has become central in the SSHA as well. I should also note that the gradual increase of people doing HS1-type work at the SSHA meeting eventually took formal shape when a network

This difference continued in the actual topics considered in the two venues, topics that show rather clearly the organizations' respective histories. After the ouster of the Weberian faction in 1983, ASACHS concentrated on macropolitical sociology of the nation state. There was little representation of micro areas in historical sociology (demography, family, labor, urban, etc.) other than a few sessions on types of inequality.[25] From 1983 to 1989, the section sponsored seven general sessions (example: "The Resurgence of Historical Sociology"), six methodological sessions (example: "Concepts and Methods in Historical Sociology"), four sessions on national or international macrosociological issues (example: "State and Economy"), six sessions on various types of inequality and social problems (example: "Comparative Historical Research and Contemporary Social Issues"), and three sessions on topics related to culture (example: "Comparative Historical Studies of Cultural Change"). Methodologically, the section emphasized comparative work of a strongly theoretical and quasi-narrative bent, with little attention to quantitative work either of the traditional sort (demography) or of the newer sort (e.g., time series, event history).[26]

Much of sociology disappeared in this list of topics. Some areas were missing because they have their own associations; the historical sociologies of science, medicine, and religion have their chief venues outside the ASA. But strikingly, the major fields represented in the SSHA were missing as well. These included historical demog-

---

for such work was initiated at the request of the program chairs for the 1993 meeting, Margo Anderson and myself.

25. This concentration has also been remarked by Cornell (1987) although she sees even less work outside macropolitics than I do. See also Goldstone (1986:83). When they founded the ASACHS section, Ronald Glassman and others defined comparative historical sociology as work resembling Weber's empirical work and sponsored sessions on Weber and his theoretical peers; at a bitter business meeting in 1983, however, the Weber group was ousted and topics took the shape discussed here. Larry Griffin urged the importance of quantitative work at that meeting, but while his argument may have helped oust the Weber group, it had little effect on the future direction of the section.

26. I should be clear about my own position. The SSHA, not the ASA, has been my venue for historical sociology (on the lists above I appeared seven times at SSHA and never at ASA). Since my substantive work involved professions—a micro topic in ASACHS terms—it was of no interest to that section. It was of equally little interest to the labor historians of the SSHA, whose strong Marxism judged that professionals "aren't really workers." But my quantitative work on narrative was eagerly received by the SSHA, although perhaps less interesting to ASACHS because it was quantitative rather than qualitative and narrative rather than causal. Nonetheless—and this underlines my later judgment that HS1 and HS2 are not totally distinct—my first paper in that area (Abbott 1983) appears in several of the bibliographies and syllabuses in Roy 1987a.

raphy and studies of the family and migration; labor, urban, and rural history; and even the historical sociologies of education, criminality, and deviance.[27]

The SSHA history was just as clearly inscribed in the sociological work dominant there. Until 1992, there was no macrohistorical or macropolitical network, and therefore relatively little of that kind of work was presented. ("Political analysis" at the SSHA in the 1980s meant voting studies.) The work appearing at SSHA was relatively quantitative and considerably more tied to primary data than was that presented at the ASACHS sessions.[28]

Not only individuals and topics differed between HS1 and HS2, but also origins. If one considers the lists compiled above in terms of date and location of Ph.D., one finds that among SSHA-active sociologists, the dominant universities were Chicago and Michigan, then UNC and Harvard. West-coast universities were conspicuously absent, a factor reflecting SSHA's distinctly regional character.

The ASA listing tells quite a different story. Here, Harvard and Chicago were overwhelmingly, obviously dominant, in both cases reflecting the presence of Theda Skocpol. The major west-coast departments had representation better according with their general status in the discipline. And virtually absent were the quantitative powerhouses—Wisconsin, Indiana, and so on. Thus, except for the common prominence of Chicago (and Laslett was the only Chicago Ph.D. prominent in both organizations), the two groups had little in common either in pattern or in detail.[29]

One common pattern did emerge between HS1 and HS2: the explosion of historical sociology Ph.D.s around 1975. Only eight of the SSHA group preceded this date, while 1976 produced four by

---

27. It is striking that in studies of science, the interdisciplinary group shows far greater ability to merge perspectives from philosophy, sociology, history, and science than has occurred in historical sociology.

28. Two of the long-standing SSHA networks—Demography-Family and Women's History—supplied most of the sociologists presenting at SSHA. The SSHA-Tilly connection reflected Tilly's (and other Michigan faculty's) role in starting and maintaining the organization. The situation with respect to macropolitics changed considerably in the 1990s; see note 24 above.

29. Further final corroborating evidence comes from the ASA Teaching Resources Center collection of teaching materials for historical sociology, mentioned earlier. Of twenty-six syllabuses contained in that document, half covered general topics: three covered historical sociology generally, four covered "masters" of historical sociology (e.g., Weber), and six covered "historical comparative methods." (I have noted above how antiquantitative the methods syllabuses were.) Of the thirteen specialized syllabuses, seven concerned class, capitalism, development, and related historical aspects of political sociology. Ideas, demography-family, urban, and even gender rated only one apiece. The emphasis, once again, was clearly on the macrosociology and politics of capitalism.

itself. Among the ASA group, only seven Ph.D.s predated 1974, while 1975 and 1976 produced five apiece. Historical sociology thus was clearly a generational affair.

We can summarize this evidence fairly simply. Historical sociology had its major expansion in the mid-1970s, about a decade after the major expansion of both quantitative history and Marxist history, and roughly contemporaneous with women's history. It was strongly colored by its generational and political origins. Work appearing under the auspices of ASACHS in the 1980s came largely from a well-defined group, HS1. It emphasized comparative macrosociology, usually of nations and usually focused on political systems, and dealt with the quantitative orthodoxy of sociology by ignoring it. In a broader sense, however, much or most "historical sociology" then appearing at the ASA appeared outside of ASACHS and the explicitly "historical sociology" sessions, usually at the sessions of other sections: Population, Gender, Criminology, and so on. These were the ASA venues of HS2.

The institutional structures embodying HS1 and HS2 clearly had roots before the 1970s, however. It is thus merely an analytic ordering to make the fractal argument that sociologists first divided into those who take history seriously and those who do not and that the former then divided into those who follow the theoretical mainstream and those who follow the methodological one. The narrative order of fractal division was more likely the reverse; attention to history arose independently within the dominantly theoretical and dominantly empiricist communities, producing HS1 in the former case and HS2 in the latter.

But these patterns of slowly proliferating, crossed dichotomies ended up creating bridges between the two disciplines (the disciplines themselves being themselves enormous, structured labor markets) in ways shaped by arbitrary conjuncture. These links seem to follow a fairly simple rule. They joined the two disciplines (sociology and history) whenever the proliferating dichotomies produced subgroups within each that were reasonably close to one another in the "dichotomy space" that is spanned by the columns of table 4.1.

As a result, it was HS2 that provided the main link in sociology to the social science historians and, to a considerable extent, to history more generally. The HS2-social science history link arose for reasons obvious in table 4.1; the two are isomorphic on all dichotomies.[30] In many cases, the only differences were arbitrary differences

30. These people also provided the principal link between historical sociology proper and the quantitative communities in both sociology and history. It appears that Chirot was quite correct in his 1976 prediction that "the conflict [over the utility

in department of Ph.D.; Charles Tilly, for example, trained Michigan Ph.D.s in history as well as in sociology. Thus, it was the substantively diverse HS2 group that provided the major links between sociology and substantive areas in history other than macrosociology of modern states—in studies of occupations, gender, organization, population, family, and so on. Such links tended to be segmental. Many sociologists working on contemporary crime knew of the work of Roger Lane and Eric Monkkonen, but few other sociologists did.

This substantive foundation for interdisciplinary links is also evident in the increasing importance of gender studies in tying history and sociology. Gender studies have historically had their own independent institutional channels, journals like *Signs* that publish both historical and social scientific work, interdisciplinary conferences, and the like. But as the ebbing of cliometrics left the SSHA less committed to causal analysis, scientific theories, and quantitative methods, gender studies moved toward center stage within the SSHA. Again the conjuncture of positions shapes the actual alliances among research groups.[31]

The links between Marxist history and sociology, like those in gender studies, lay partly within and partly without historical sociology per se. As with feminism, there were interdisciplinary Marxist scholars' conferences, as well as Marxist journals. But there were also many direct ties within substantive areas. For example, there were historical sociologists of work who related directly to the new labor history, both within HS1 and HS2. Yet even so, there were

---

of quantitative approaches to historical sociology] is so fundamental that it is unlikely to be resolved" (1976:235).

31. Indeed, the 1990 panel on the current state of social science history (and some other unobtrusive indicators, like the size of network meetings) seemed to indicate that the quantitative emphasis of SSHA was weakening and that the organization was headed for new interdisciplinary waters in which women's studies, with its diverse but seldom quantitative methods and approaches, would play an even more important part.

Surprisingly, however, the net effect of history on sociology in the gender area seems slight. In the first three years of sociology's new (1987) gender journal, *Gender and Society*, only about 20 percent (10 of 51) of the articles had any temporal component at all. Of these, several were standard quantitative "trends and counts" articles covering recent periods, a familiar form of sociological article owing nothing to history in general or to women's history in particular. The real level of "historical" articles was probably closer to 10 percent, about the level of historical material in sociological journals generally (MacDonald 1990a). Gender may, then, not have been as strong an avenue for historical influence in sociology as one might have expected, especially given the appearance of two gender sociologists on the list joining HS1 and HS2 and the strong representation of gender scholars in HS2 generally.

complaints that Marxist historians and sociologists of labor had not transformed each other's practice.[32]

Thus, links between history and sociology tended to travel along particular substantive lines rather than along general theoretical ones. This tendency may well have been the central difficulty with historicizing sociology as a whole; the relations between the two disciplines have been shaped on a subject-by-subject (or method-by-method) basis. Links are largely ad hoc, as steady processes of fractal division within disciplines toss up groups that are near enough to each other (in their "dichotomy profiles") to make a direct link.

So far it seems that subdivisions within the two disciplines create roughly equivalent communities that then ally across disciplinary boundaries. (It should again be understood that this is an analytic, not necessarily a temporal, sequence; the disciplinary differences take priority because dominant social structures like academic labor markets follow disciplinary lines, not because those differences necessarily come first historically.) But on this model, it becomes important to understand the historical counterparts of HS1. HS2 linked up (by substantive area) with the social science historians, Marxist and feminist sociologists linked up with Marxist and feminist historians. Whom then did HS1 link up with?

To a certain extent, the answer is no one at all. When Terrence MacDonald did a citation analysis of forty-eight selected position papers in historical sociology (broadly defined) since 1957, he found that the twenty-five most-cited authors included only four historians (Stedman Jones, Bloch, Thompson, and Carr). The top figures were themselves historical (or sometimes theoretical) sociologists: Tilly, Skocpol, Giddens, Stinchcombe, Collins, and Smelser.[33]

One possible reason for this isolation was the lack of likely candidates on the historical side—a lack made evident in table 4.1. The obvious candidates were ruled out by crucial differences. The social science historians were too quantitative and often too micro. The dominant strands of Marxism—the new labor history and the History Workshop school—were emphatically micro in their approaches and fell on the experiential and factual side of the theory/facts dispute.[34] Like the social science historians, too, the new Marxists were less tied to global political analysis than HS1 has

32. Kimeldorf 1991.
33. MacDonald 1996b.
34. It is revealing that Samuel (1980) recalls Goffmanian interactionism as a decisive influence on the History Workshop; as we shall see below, HS1 saw Goffman as explicitly ahistorical.

generally been. The older, large-scale Marxist historians of the Weinstein, Kolko, or even Montgomery type were perhaps a more likely match, but they were fewer in number and less dominant among the new generation of Marxist historians. HS1's institutional heritage of Weberianism may also have hindered connection between the two sides.

The chief institutional affiliations of HS1 seem to have been less to history than to other history-minded and more or less left scholars in sociology and related social sciences. Within sociology, this meant the seven sections that made up the Young (now late-middle-aged) Turk group of the ASA. Beyond sociology, HS1 linked up with like-minded members of other social science disciplines, particularly political science. Another close group were their English counterparts, a diverse group extending across several disciplines and, now, countries: Perry Anderson, Derek Sayer, Michael Mann, and others. Surprisingly, however, links between all these communities and history proper were weak.[35]

As of 1990 then, it seemed that most of the links between history and sociology came within limited areas—either within particular analytic approaches like Marxism and feminism or within particular substantive areas like demography, studies of the family, labor history, criminology, and so on. As for the visibly defined "historical sociology" of HS1, although it had clear admiration for certain great historians, it lacked a direct connection to any particular group within history.

3. The Missing Synthesis

This discussion leaves us with a much more realistic picture of the evolution of a system of fractal distinctions than emerged from the

---

35. One could see this institutional structure by scanning the editorial boards of the major journals representing these communities, *Theory and Society* and *Politics and Society.* HS1 was strongly represented on the editorial staff of *Theory and Society.* The ASA-active group from my earlier list included nine people who had been editors or corresponding editors of *Theory and Society* since 1980, while the SSHA group included only three, all of whom were also on the ASA list. Although in its early years quite interdisciplinary, *Theory and Society* steadily moved toward sociological dominance on its editorial boards, which included many sociologists not in HS1 but active in the theory/history/politics area. *Politics and Society* was by contrast more interdisciplinary, but as with *Theory and Society,* there was minimal representation of historians on the editorial board, although nearly every article is thoroughly informed by a sense of history.

Editorial boards provide a clearer indication of linkages than do lists of authors. There have been journals in which HS1 and HS2 have been published side by side, *Comparative Studies in Society and History* and the *Journal of Interdisciplinary His-*

earlier chapters. It is true that this system is dominated by a single fractal distinction, that between analytic and temporal approaches to social reality. And this distinction is powerful indeed.

But the development of a set of communities dividing and subdividing along the lines of the analytic/temporal distinction is also shaped by other, simultaneous processes. Important among these are, first, institutional and material structures. For example, ASA organizational structure (the section system) provided strong incentives to develop generational paradigms and fractionating subgroups. Or again, the existence of an SSHA that was predefined in the somewhat quantitative mold of HS2 lessened the probability of a link between HS1 and history via the SSHA. The importance of such institutional structures suggests that we might consider whether those structures do not themselves have a fractal character, a subject to which I turn in the next chapter.

A second environment of importance is not institutional structures, but other fractal distinctions. This history shows clearly that linkups between groups in different disciplines happen when those groups' profiles—across a whole set of fractal distinctions—come close to congruence. Gender became a central link between history and sociology not because there is anything intrinsically revolutionary about studying gender (at least vis-à-vis these dichotomies), but because gender research communities in the two disciplines lined up in congruent ways on the distinctions of table 4.1. A similar lineup—not in details but in degree of closeness—had made demography an important link twenty years before. One can see a similar phenomenon elsewhere in the social sciences, for example in the emergence of the extraordinarily strong and extraordinarily interdisciplinary community studying the sociology, philosophy, and history of science.

We can also learn from this case the extraordinary power of even a slight reversing of the usual affinities between the various fractal distinctions. In the first instance, the application of basic quantitative methods to historical data produced an extraordinary flowering of work in field after field. So also did the historical turn of HS1, which in other ways remained very close to traditional sociology.

But at the same time, this example also shows nicely the extraordinary durability of the principal fractal distinction involved. For all the talk, there has never really been a direct theoretical attempt to

---

tory being the principal examples. In both cases, however, the coming together of the two schools was mediated by an active editor outside either group, Raymond Grew in one case and Theodore Rabb in the other. I thank Charles Tilly for bringing this point to my attention.

resolve the contrast between narrative and analytic stances toward the social process. That the links between sociology and history have generally been within particular areas has meant that the central issue of whether history and sociology were themselves really about the same thing or about something different has never seen sustained theoretical investigation.[36] The group with the best chance to conduct this investigation was clearly HS1. They had the name, the incentive, and the energy to theorize the links between the fields, and indeed, their progenitor Weber ably bestrode the two himself. Yet they failed to theorize the history-sociology linkage because, in fractal manner, they re-created within themselves the same history/sociology dichotomy that created the disciplinary division in the first place. The contrast of the two original disciplines proves to be fractal in a very profound way. We can see this easily by watching how the words "history" and "sociology" were used to divide intellectual turf by the spokesmen of HS1.[37]

In reflecting on the relation of historical sociology and social (science) history in 1987, William Roy saw "history" as meaning that generalizations had to be time and place specific. In her remarks at the same symposium, Skocpol took much the same position. The social historians had to learn theory (and a willingness to see "the big picture") from the historical sociologists; they had to become more "causal," less "descriptive."[38] For their part, Skocpol argued, the historical sociologists had to make theory more time and place specific, to eschew reification, to become less Western-centric. Thus, history limited generalization by emphasizing changing causal universes, while sociology provided the portable causal arguments.[39]

------

36. Of course there are lots of papers saying that it *ought* to be a subject of investigation, usually providing a few examples illustrating that necessity. Everyone in the area writes such a paper at least once in his or her career. Some people make a habit of it. (Giddens, in particular, spends a lot of time telling us how important things are and very little actually showing us how to do them.). My own version of this paper is Abbott 1983, but the reader is welcome to read Giddens 1979, or Abrams 1982, or Aminzade 1992, or Sewell 1992, or Griffin 1993, or Somers 1996.

37. MacDonald's excellent paper (1990) discusses the prehistory of this issue at length. The notion that history provides facts and sociology theory is a very old notion, perhaps because it is not without a grain of truth to its mountain of falsehood.

38. Roy 1987b; Skocpol 1987. It is worth recalling that Skocpol's argument was used by early social science historians to justify their turn from scaling to regression, *both* of which are of course anathema to HS1. That indicates the extent of misunderstanding between the two on what "causality" means; they understand the concept at different fractal levels.

39. See Knapp 1983 for a "metatheoretical" version of this argument. From the point of view of standard sociology, this is essentially an argument that "taking time

A subsequent analysis by Gary Hamilton and John Walton made this division of the turf yet more clear.

> First, historical sociology includes a variety of analytical styles that, when taken together, do not exhaust all forms of valid or useful sociological inquiry. Sociology is not "intrinsically" historical in any concise sense. Second, by implication there are legitimate forms of ahistorical sociology. These forms, such as the situational analysis developed by Goffman, are not necessarily incompatible with historical work, simply distinct.[40]

Not only did this take it for granted that historical sociology is simply the same old sociology but about past times and data. The authors also explicitly rejected the argument of Giddens, Abrams, and others that all sociology (more broadly, all social science) is inherently historical, although providing little justification for this judgment other than differences in disciplinary practices.[41]

There is a central difficulty here. Goffman's work is about the "histories" of interactions. Why did this fact escape Hamilton and Walton's attention? It did so because without noticing it they used the history/sociology distinction in a completely fractal manner. They assumed that one could move the distinction to whatever level and unit of analysis one wished and then use "sociology" to denote the causal study of phenomena that change in some systematic fashion *within* that level and unit, and "history" to denote the larger parameters whose constancy *defined* that level and unit. Since their own main concerns were with macrosociology, and since Goffman studied interaction in a much shorter time framework, Hamilton and Walton saw him as legitimately ahistorical.

But if we zoom down the fractal, we can see that Goffman's work is deeply "historical" in one of the senses mentioned earlier; it concerns process. It regards all identity as negotiated over time. It sees nothing as fully fixed. Moreover, one can narrow one's temporal focus to such a point that every Goffmanian interaction has *within it* its fixed structures, its changing conjunctures, and its trivial events; one can see all three of Braudel's temporalities within this little epoch. And what seem in such a narrow temporal focus to be the fixed structures of interaction rituals themselves change in conjunctural

---

seriously" means "controlling for time and place"—in its simplest version a matter of control variables. By contrast I shall argue below that taking time seriously means focusing on process rather than causality.

40. Hamilton and Walton 1988:189.
41. Giddens 1979; Abrams 1982.

or even "evenemential" ways if we again lengthen our epoch of interest, as did Norbert Elias in considering the history of such rituals. The notion, then, that social history should be setting limits within which historical sociology can write causal explanations simply replicates at some new level the same old history/sociology dichotomy. And it breaks down because its argument applies to itself. Each "time- and space-specific" generalization is shown to generalize ahistorically when we move to a shorter time scale.

Of course, one cannot rule out sociological analyses that define zones of temporal constancy and do "pure sociology" within them; that is what the Braudel's distinction of structure, conjuncture, and event is about. But as a general strategy, such procedures are inappropriate. An example may show why. Suppose we want to know why 95 percent of American psychiatrists worked for mental hospitals in 1880 but less than 50 percent did so in 1930. We can analyze year-to-year mobility conditions—salaries, vacancies, markets—and see the proximate forces impelling doctors to move. We can also analyze the growth, over periods of five to fifteen years, of powerful local communities of psychiatrists in major cities, local communities whose structures and enticements drove the individual mobility and yet were simultaneously created by that mobility. And we can analyze the shift of psychiatric knowledge from an organic to a Freudian paradigm, a development also conditioning and conditioned by these micro and meso changes, but one taking place over an even longer time frame. And we can analyze the change in the social control functions of psychiatry—a change that may have taken even more time than that in knowledge—a change driven in part by psychiatrists seeking jobs, but also by large changes in the society. The move toward outpatient psychiatric practice, in short, arose in a process whose several layers moved at different speeds but nonetheless conditioned each other.[42]

An analytic strategy that isolates epochal periods within which "sociological" causal judgments hold true cannot analyze such a system. Yet in fact, most processes studied by historians and sociol-

---

42. There is a standard empiricist answer to this problem, which is to break up the general phenomena or "large events" into sums of little ones. The change in knowledge becomes "now 20 percent of the people believe in Freudianism, now 30 percent, now 50 percent," etc. Few serious historians think the problem can be conjured away by such means, and in any case, the empiricist solution has its own problems. See Abbott 1990a:144. The empirical problem discussed here is from my dissertation (Abbott 1982)—which was never published because I have never figured out how to deal with this problem. My current thinking on it is in Abbott 1999b. A rare example of a quantitative study facing the multiple-levels question squarely is Padgett 1981.

ogists have precisely this shape. A central intellectual challenge in the sociology/history relation is the problem of dealing with this fact that the social process moves on many levels at once. The simplest strategy available to theorize the multilevel social process is familiar to every historian—thinking narratively. For Hempel's insistence on covering-law arguments in history called forth a long and distinguished literature defending "narrative knowledge."

In fact, theorizing the social process via narrative is a deep tradition in both history and sociology. If there is any one idea central to historical ways of thinking, it is that the order of things makes a difference, that reality occurs not as time-bounded snapshots within which "causes" affect one another (snapshots therefore subject to "sociology" in the fractal sense used above) but as stories, cascades of events. And events in this sense are not single properties, or simple things, but complex conjunctures in which complex actors encounter complex structures.

At the heart of much classical sociological theory lie exactly these same insights. The Chicago school focused on social change in the city and organized their textbook around social processes. Their students the symbolic interactionists fought the rising empiricists precisely over the meaninglessness of the idea of a variable. And Weber himself insisted that the foundations of sociology lay in social action, in the interplay of agents within structures and urged a methodology focused on ideal type narratives, not on reified "causal analysis."[43]

Yet the historical sociologists rejected the narrative tradition and with it any concept of narrative generalization. In the opening pages of *States and Social Revolutions* Skocpol explicitly separated her "comparative-historical" project from that of the "natural historians" best exemplified by Lyford Edwards (a Chicago sociology Ph.D. and student of Chicago's Robert Park). Comparative-historical sociology, she argued, was about causes, while natural history was about sequences of stages. Although the natural historians had talked about causes, "little attempt was made to use comparisons of historical cases to validate them." Her aim is to "identify and validate causes, rather than descriptions, of revolutions." Skocpol argued that "analytically similar sets of causes can be operative across cases even if the nature and timing of conflicts during the revolutions are different and even if, for example, one case culminates in a conservative reaction whereas another does not (at all or in the same way)." Skocpol's focus was therefore quite traditional in empir-

---

43. Blumer 1931, 1956.

icist sociological terms; the flow of events was not her central concern, any more than narratives of suicide were for Durkheim. Thus, the historical sociologists of HS1 did not really address the question of resolving the narrative/analysis dichotomy. The marriage of history and sociology remained unconsummated. Put another way, the fractal relation of narrative and analysis was too useful, and too taken-for-granted, to resolve.[44]

The original 1992 article on which this chapter is based closed with some predictions, mainly that the drift toward a history that emphasized "culture" in the broad sense would grow stronger. I predicted a stronger constructionism and the emergence of a rich historical sociology of culture. This prediction was so obvious, and has so obviously been borne out, that there is little point discussing it.

But an important by-product of this development, which I also saw at the time, was the conflation, even the identification of "history" with "culture." That is, the "historical turn," as so many people call it, is perceived as inevitably emphasizing social constructions, ideologies, symbols, mentalities, and other cultural apparatus. Indeed, the strongest response to the earlier version of this essay—Michael Hanagan and Louise Tilly's portrayal of my work as tiptoeing down the primrose path to positivism—identified as the crucial bridge between history and sociology new work that dis-

---

44. Skocpol 1979:38. Tilly too sometimes shows a disappointing contempt for the natural historians' attempts at "narrative generalization," even though the comparisons from which he expects so much are essentially comparisons of narratives. See Tilly 1984. At the same time, one should recall that Tilly opposed the creation of a specific "historical sociology" from the start, remarking (1981:100), "I would be happier if the phrase had never been invented." Tilly has often argued that all sociology should be historical in the sense of attending to social processes. And it is important to recall that as many people (e.g., Burawoy 1989) have noted, Skocpol's actual practice in *States and Social Revolutions* was in fact far more "narrative" and complex than her methodological prolegomenon promised. But certainly, the usual judgment on Mill's methods of agreement and disagreement (adopted by Skocpol) is that they simply don't work. See, for example, Ragin 1987 or Burawoy 1989. The historical sociologists expended most of their methodological ammunition on comparison, not narrative (e.g., Bonnell 1980, Tilly 1984, Lloyd 1986, Ragin 1987, McMichael 1990). This comparative emphasis reflects the historical sociologists' desire for higher-level generalizations (Bonnell 1980), despite the tendency some see in historical sociology toward a (quite traditional) methodology focused on particular historical problems (Goldstone 1986).

Citation provides a useful indicator of historical sociologists' disattention to the problem of narrative. The 1960s and 1970s produced a half dozen classic analyses of narrative by literary theorists: Roland Barthes's *S/Z* (1974), Seymour Chatman's *Story and Discourse* (1978), Gerard Genette's monumental *Narrative Discourse* (1980), Vladimir Propp's *Morphology of the Folktale* (1975), Robert Scholes and Robert Kellogg's *Nature of Narrative* (1966), and Tzvetan Todorov's *Grammaire du Décameron* (1969) and *Poetics of Prose* (1977). The 1980s brought Paul Ricoeur's three-volume *Time and Narrative*. If we search the social science citation indices for 1987–89, we will not find any historical sociologists citing these works.

cussed the narrative construction of identities. This relatively strong alignment of historical investigation with culturalist assumptions has provided a new defense against any attempt to directly rethink the relation of narrative and analysis or to create a synthetic, monistic theoretical framework obliterating the distinction.[45]

To be sure, the time has come for the inevitable "rediscovery," by the culturalists, of material social reality. We can soon expect our students to tell us that we have foolishly forgotten about social structure and material determination, perhaps even that we have ignored systematic causal structures. All this will need to be "brought back in." But the synthesis of history and sociology seems as far away as ever.[46]

In the present chapter, I have studied yet another set of fractal cycles and generational paradigms. But where the preceding chapter looked at fractionation, this one has focused on the workings of a system in which several different fractal distinctions play off against one another. In particular, I have tried to show the ways analysts in my "fractal city" move through its many dimensions and the conditions under which they manage to hook up with one another. As we have seen, these connections are driven to some extent by substance, but more by relatively accidental developments that bring different groups of investigators, via different trajectories vis-à-vis their own fields, into a common fractal location, a particular set of stands on the various relevant fractal distinctions. That they come to these common positions by different pathways—by different histories of disagreement with yet other analysts—means, as we have seen, that finding themselves together does not necessarily result in common understanding. Looking at a single case in detail begins to show us the complexity of the conditions behind new scholarly understandings.

But the chapter has also a substantive conclusion. Its overall lesson is that making a separation between taking time and place seriously on the one hand and ignoring them on the other is a very useful organizing practice in academic life. Historians' very labor market is organized around times and places, while sociologists' labor market is organized around paradigms, methods, and "stable" arenas of social life. It testifies to the status of "history" in sociology

---

45. Hanagan and Tilly 1996, Abbott 1996.

46. The reader will not have missed the polemical edge of this section. I should be frank in admitting that my own project continues to be "to outline an approach to generalizing about the social process that is based not on a hypothesized continuity of attributes, but rather on a visible continuity of central or causally important events" (Abbott 1983:141).

(a status as merely a method, not a universal commitment) that even while historical sociology wanes as a hiring area, rational choice—the most ahistorical paradigm possible in sociology—is slowly expanding. (In good fractal fashion, rational choice scholars dislike my work for being precisely what Hanagan and Tilly say it isn't.) Material structure itself has pulled strongly against the reconstruction of history and sociology.

With this recognition the importance of labor markets, I come again to the possibility of fractal social structures. Perhaps not only cultural systems are structured in a fractal manner, but also social ones. As a means of approaching that subject, I shall discuss in the next chapter the social structure of academic disciplines—a transition topic to the more general question of self-similar social structures, to which I turn in the subsequent chapter. Chapter 5 thus provides the substantive conclusion to this first section of the book. As it happens, the most important academic social structures are not self-similar, or rather, their self-similarity is not their most important characteristic. But it is necessary to complete the substantive analysis of academic social science with a social structural discussion before pushing ahead, in chapters 6 and 7, to generalizations of the self-similarity argument.

5

The Context of
Disciplines

THERE ARE many who believe that the intellectual world is today in a *special* ferment, one unknown in decades, one that reaches across disciplines in ways hitherto unimagined. English professors are doing anthropology and calling it cultural studies. Economists are doing sociology and calling it family economics.

The sociologist who would deny this apocalyptic vision must offer some replacement. The fractal distinctions model presented so far contains part of such a replacement, showing that the ferment is old and, in its own way, quite regular. But the fractal distinctions model is only a partial one. First, I have talked only about cultural structure. I argued in the opening chapter that intellectual life in the social sciences is organized around perennial debates that produce proliferating lineages with the peculiar properties of self-similarity, self-replication, and rootlessness. I have described in subsequent chapters the processes of drift and rediscovery that the unfolding of such perennial debates produces. But none of this has touched disciplinary *social* structures. Second, I have not discussed the larger context in which those fractal debates take place. I have, it is true, on occasion suggested that external contexts of fractal comparison can have important consequences for internal development within a sublineage. But there has been no general discussion.

In this chapter I shall consider both context and social structure in a more systematic fashion. I connect my theory of the cultural

This chapter has had several incarnations, but its first full version was delivered to the Interdisciplinary Consortium for Organization Studies (ICOR) at the University of Michigan on 9 January 1998. I dedicate the chapter to the memory of Morris Janowitz, late Lawrence A. Kimpton Distinguished Service Professor of Sociology at the University of Chicago.

structure of our intellectual life to a social structural model of disciplines and in particular a model of disciplinary contexts. I shall consider the various disciplines as what I have elsewhere called an interactional field. Given the substantive theme of chapter 4, it is ironic
that one's first inclination is to ask what this interactional field
looks like and then to ask whence it came. But the literature on
disciplines is at present largely ahistorical. We had best begin with
history, the history of disciplines. We have spent four chapters
studying the flux of disciplines. Now we must contemplate the extraordinary stasis of disciplinary social structure.[1]

1. The Disciplinary System

In the United States, for the last century, the map of disciplinary
social structures has been remarkably constant, even while the
equivalent map of cultural structures—the pattern of knowledge
itself—has greatly shifted. The departmental structure of the American university has remained largely unchanged since its creation
between 1890 and 1910. Biology, it is true, has fractured in most
universities into a number of departments. But this differentiation
reflects the immense resources flowing into biological research

---

1. I first used the term "interactional field" in my 1992 Sorokin lecture, first
published in 1997, and reprinted, with revisions, as chapter 7 of Abbott 1999a. This
is the proper place to list a few papers on disciplines. In general such papers focus on
what they see as (1) the blurring or the disappearance of intellectual boundaries between disciplines, (2) the narrowness of purely disciplinary knowledge, and/or (3) the
intensive specialization thought to be transforming academia. Geertz (1980) gave a
famous version of the blurred boundaries argument; his emphasis on the renewed
focus on texts and symbols sounds one-sided to those of us who have been enduring
the onslaughts of game theory. Writing on the social sciences, Dogan and Pahre (1989)
emphasized specialization within disciplines and hybridization (across disciplinary
lines) between subdisciplines; they see important phenomena, but lack theory for
them. Becher (1987) writes more broadly and emphasizes what he sees as determining
(and enduring) properties of a wide variety of fields, pure and applied, "hard" and
"soft." For a comparative perspective on the emergence of social science discipline
structures in Europe, see Wagner and Wittrock 1990. There is also an extensive literature on citation between disciplines.

In general, I feel that the disciplines literature misses the basic facts about American academia that seem most important. The first of these is the coupling in America
of an extraordinarily stable disciplinary social organization with an extraordinarily
fluid disciplinary cultural system. Second is the nearly constant content of the "disciplines" literature, which has been decrying narrow disciplines, urging interdisciplinarity, and foreseeing blurring of genres since the 1920s at least. The descrying and
decrying of specialization within disciplines has also been an enduring activity, often
ignoring material forces (like the explosion of the academic system after the war) that
inevitably produce differentiation. (This long-enduring constancy of the disciplines
literature is one reason for not citing it extensively; it's another fractal literature.) The
real challenge is to develop a theory of disciplines that explains these basic social
structural and cultural facts.

more than it does internal change (cf. chapter 1). In the humanities and social sciences, the departmental map has shown only marginal change in the last sixty to eighty years. Linguistics, comparative literature, and a few other small fields are the only and occasional newcomers.[2]

The basic map of disciplines is therefore very familiar. Among the humanities we find English, various other language specialties (Romance languages and literatures, Germanic languages and literatures, Slavic languages and literatures, etc.), the arts (musicology and art history and the performance and studio work to go along with them), philosophy, and classics. About the only major changes are the astonishingly slow withering of classics and the intermittent appearance of linguistics and comparative literature. Among the social sciences, we find economics, political science, sociology, anthropology, history (often listed among the humanities), and psychology (usually lumped in the social sciences despite its individual level of analysis). There, too, is little change: merger or separation of sociology and anthropology at some places and times, the occasional appearance of statistics and linguistics among the social sciences, but little else. Moreover, the relative proportions of university faculties in these departments are surprisingly constant, although the steady increase of applied or semiapplied fields—education, communication, business, accounting, engineering, and so on—has made the traditional liberal arts and sciences faculty a smaller proportion of the whole.[3]

This enduring social structure of academic labor is all the more surprising for its international uniqueness. The departmental structure appeared only in American universities, although since midcentury it has gradually spread to Europe and elsewhere. Indeed, academic disciplines in the American sense—groups of professors with exchangeable credentials collected in strong associations—did not really appear outside the United States until well into the postwar period.

A glance at other systems can help explain why the American system has its peculiar power. In its heyday, German higher education aimed at personal cultivation (*Bildung*) through intense scholarship, subordinating all to the research enterprise. The universities

2. The definitive history of the emergence of modern universities in America remains Veysey 1965. I am also relying throughout this section on sources cited in Ellingson 1995.

3. I am relying for figures on a database developed by Ronald Durnford, former associate dean of the University of Chicago Division of Social Sciences, and kindly provided by him.

were divided into faculties, each with a number of individual chairs. Most teaching faculty—"extraordinary" professors and *Privatdozenten*—fell under the official control of the chaired professors (*Ordinarien*). Chairs also organized and controlled the research institutes, which covered not the broad areas of American disciplines, but areas of particular interest to the chair involved. Germany had many universities, each relatively small and each independent of others. Expansion was slow. Taken together, these ecological and structural facts meant that academic careers advanced through the patronage of chairs, via continuous interuniversity moves seeking higher rank. Rising academics took doctorates in generic fields—doctorates of philosophy or arts rather than of English or economics, because these allowed broader ranges of opportunity for employment. When moving, professors often changed fields (e.g., from professor of physiology to professor of philosophy)[4] even though their research interests might change little or not at all. As a result the German system produced intense research dedication, but nothing resembling the American disciplinary division of turf. Within universities, the local division of academic labor reflected relatively arbitrary differences among the interests of the *Ordinarien*. There was intense cultivation of small areas, which were then surrounded by large tracts of empty intellectual space. Moreover, there was no national comparability; political economy might mean quite different things at different universities.[5]

In France, university education in the late nineteenth century was often vocational, general culture having been guaranteed by the lycée. As in Germany, chairs tended to have enormous power and impact. But France lacked the research institute structure. Academic careers proceeded by moves around the provinces aiming at ultimate return to Paris. Such careers might traverse universities, lycées, and even other areas in the civil service. In addition, the system of *grandes écoles*—parallel to and more prestigious than the universities—meant that many arrived in academic careers without ever having been university undergraduates. Central to career advance were patronage groups or clusters, which like careers tended to cross several organizations. Durkheim's group is an excellent example. In France too there was little foundation for disciplines.[6]

In England, the great universities were in the nineteenth and early

4. See Ben-David and Collins 1966.
5. Basic sources on the German university system are McClelland 1980 and Jarausch 1982. Jarausch 1983 has essays on universities in various countries.
6. On the French university system in the late nineteenth century, see Weisz 1983. On elite education specifically see Suleiman 1978. See also Clark 1973.

twentieth centuries strongly antiprofessional and, more often than not, antiresearch. Universities as corporate bodies were nearly powerless, being dominated by the smaller colleges within them. Like research institutes in Germany and patronage clusters in France, the colleges of Oxford and Cambridge were intermediate institutions organizing individuals within—and also beyond—the university. Academic careers generally unfolded within the patronage structure of a particular college, a structure reaching into secondary schools, the clinics and offices of the various professions, the civil service, the church, and the other colleges of the universities themselves. Such careers involved no formal credentialing until quite recently. The division of labor with respect to knowledge was dictated less by a structure of disciplines than by the content of the examinations that crowned the undergraduate career: the honors schools at Oxford and triposes at Cambridge. These were an unlikely foundation for disciplinary specialization, for most of them were pedagogical unities unconnected with a specific research community (e.g., Philosophy, Politics, and Economics or Modern Greats at Oxford).[7]

In the United States, however, a peculiar conjuncture fostered the growth of academic disciplines as social structures. First, as in Germany the universities were numerous and decentralized. Second, throughout the period in which the modern disciplines were formed, faculty employment was expanding at rates never thereafter achieved until the 1960s. Third, as part of their own mobility projects, aspiring professions began to view arts and sciences degrees as prerequisites of professional schooling. All these forces together meant that American universities had schools of arts and sciences that were rapidly expanding but that lacked any real internal structure. These were expected to be undergraduate educational institutions on the British model (but on a much larger scale) at the same time as they were graduate research institutions on the German model. The dual functions and rapid growth made some sort of internal organization necessary. The absolute hierarchy of the German universities, even the limited hierarchy of France, was unacceptable to democratic America. American universities compromised by creating departments of equals. The Ph.D. degree, borrowed from Germany, became specialized into a Ph.D. "in something." This specific disciplinary degree provided a medium of exchange between particular subunits of different universities. There was thus completed a subsystem of structures and exchanges organizing universities internally while providing for extensive but structured career mobility

---

7. The English university system is discussed by Rothblatt 1968 and Green 1974.

externally, between institutions. Exactly coincident with this departmentalization of the university was the formation of the national disciplinary societies, from which academics gradually excluded the amateurs of knowledge, even though the latter were often prominent among those societies' founders.[8]

The extraordinary resilience of the American system of academic disciplines lies in this dual institutionalization. On the one hand, the disciplines constitute the macrostructure of the labor market for faculty. It is at national disciplinary meetings that jobs are exchanged and it is disciplinary networks that supply the candidates. Careers remain within discipline much more than within university. On the other hand, the system constitutes the microstructure of each individual university. All arts and sciences faculties contain more or less the same list of departments. This duality means that no university can challenge the disciplinary system as a whole without depriving its Ph.D. graduates of their academic future. Carnegie-Mellon is perhaps the only major university in the United States organized in nontraditional departments. It is successful but unique. Even single departments that cross boundaries—like Chicago's Committee on Social Thought—create enormous employment problems for their graduates by denying them a specific disciplinary market. Universities can perhaps cancel a department here and there or perhaps merge two departments (like sociology and anthropology). But even these minor gestures reflect fluctuations in resources more than willingness to challenge fundamental employment structures. The most celebrated recent merger of the social sciences—Harvard's Department of Social Relations (merging social anthropology, social psychology, and sociology)—broke up as soon as its founder, Talcott Parsons, retired.

Moreover, the dual structure of disciplines also implies that even were all universities to agree to abolish one or another particular discipline, the other disciplines would just fill in the intellectual (and curricular) space that it used to occupy. The system of disciplines, that is, could easily survive the destruction of one or even several of its elements. We may call this a division of labor via "bubbling," in which disciplines like drops of oil scatter more or less uniformly over a surface and expand toward each other.

In short, as long as disciplinary academics act as the primary hiring agents for universities, they perpetuate the disciplinary system by seeking faculty *for* their own departments only *from* within their

---

8. In addition to sources noted earlier, see also Ross 1991 and Oleson and Voss 1979.

own disciplines. Occasionally, differentiation occurs within existing departments because of immense inflows of money. Or an applied field soaks up disciplinary territory, although this seems more likely in the public universities than in the privates (criminal justice and communications have taken areas of sociology, for example). But absent any radical change in the process of academic hiring, the current social structure of disciplines will endlessly re-create itself.

Even more crucial to this immobility is the role of disciplines in American undergraduate education. The most consequential single disciplinary structure—in terms of extent and impact—is not the professional association but the college major. All but a handful of American colleges and universities have majors and in all but a handful of those that do, disciplinary majors house a large share of undergraduates. The more prestigious the university, the greater this share. And among most students, the arts and science majors remain the most prestigious if not necessarily the most popular.

The system of undergraduate majors spread very quickly at the turn of this century, at exactly the same time as the departmental system. In pedagogical terms, majors were thought to be a cure for the perceived excesses of the elective system, which dominated the undergraduate curriculum in the late nineteenth century. Once institutionalized, the major system has never been questioned. Indeed, it has never really been the subject of a serious pedagogical debate, since allocating the undergraduate curriculum on some basis other than majors raises unthinkable questions about faculty governance and administration. Many universities use student numbers in majors and in departmentally taught "service courses" to allocate the most crucial resource of all—faculty positions. Only one prominent university (Chicago under Hutchins) has tried to abolish majors, and that experiment, however intellectually and symbolically important, proved a practical and financial failure. Brown's revolutionary 1969 curriculum abolished everything *but* majors, and the personally constructed majors that Brown's planners hoped would transform the system have declined over time. Even Brown's interdisciplinary majors have routinized, becoming like their disciplinary counterparts.[9]

In short, Americans seem unable to conceive of an undergraduate curriculum without majors. And of course there are no majors without disciplines. Departments can be combined, but even combined

---

9. The discussion of the history of majors rests on the work done by Steven Ellingson (1995) as part of a larger study I am conducting on college majors. On the Chicago abolition, see McNeill 1991 and the essays in MacAloon 1992, pt. 1. On Brown, see Blumstein 1990.

departments often offer separate majors, retaining the disciplinary structure. It is particularly striking that at Oxford and Cambridge, where many undergraduate programs are *not* disciplinary, interdisciplinarity is much more pervasive than in the United States. Indeed, Oxford by contrast has had difficulty in coordinating its *disciplinary* graduate programs, particularly in the social sciences, because the structure of undergraduate instruction usually does not reinforce disciplinary lines.[10]

The American system of disciplines thus seems uniquely powerful and powerfully unique. There are alternatives: the personalism of nineteenth-century Germany, the French research cluster, the ancient British system with its emphasis on small communities of common culture. But because of their extraordinary ability to organize individual careers, faculty hiring, and undergraduate education, disciplinary departments are the essential and irreplaceable building blocks of American universities.

There is an important general lesson here, one with cautionary implications for interdisciplinarity, a topic to which I turn shortly. In each of the countries earlier discussed there emerged intermediate institutions to structure the larger interactional field of the university (and beyond it the university system) into a number of lesser units. The empirical fact is that most complex interactional fields tend to break up into clusters of entities that develop internal identities. Contrary to the assumption implicit in postmodern social theory, interactional fields do not typically remain masses of flux, whether they be fields of applied knowledge (whose entities emerge as professions), of residence (as neighborhoods), of identity (as ethnicities), or of work (as occupations). To be sure, there is more flux in interactional fields than we often think, and certainly more than a language of reified social descriptors implies. But the processes of bubbling by which loosely stable groups emerge in such fields are in fact quite general. The only peculiar characteristic of American academia as an interactional field is that in academia the bubbles are held rigidly in place by dual institutionalization: on the one hand in an interuniversity labor market annually transacting tens of thousands of faculty and on the other in an intrauniversity curriculum annually "disciplining" millions of students.

Academia is not the sole location of this kind of dual institutionalization, but simply the clearest example. It is worth digressing for

---

10. I rely here on personal communications from Oxford faculty, particular from fellows of Nuffield College, who kindly welcomed me as Norman Chester Fellow in Hilary and Trinity terms of 1997.

a moment to say some more general things about dual institutionalization. This phenomenon can be observed in the relation of skilled trade unions to their employers, the relation of leading opera singers to opera companies, of physicians to hospitals, and so on. We can think of these dually institutionalized structures as "basket" structures, in honor of the simple basket-weave pattern they make.

One obvious source for basket structures is the institutional cloning by which many social systems develop new units. Where large units are repeated again and again, individuals and subunits can easily be exchanged between isomorphic positions of the larger units, creating low-level systems of exchange whose solidarity can overwhelm hierarchical solidarity within the larger cloned units. Hierarchical structures often impose internal rules to prevent precisely such systems of exchange. For example, one purpose of the imposition of strong state civil service rules in the late nineteenth century was the prevention of interstate exchange at the functional department level. The sharp separation of state mental hospital systems from each other, for example, meant that the national profession of psychiatry could not emerge within the state mental hospitals, but only in the outpatient setting. Similar forces kept railroad employees in house, preventing truly effective trans-firm occupational association. Today, such systems are evident in the nondisclosure agreements forced on their employees by high-tech firms which fear loss of proprietary knowledge through interfirm mobility.[11]

In other settings, there are different forces preventing the emergence of basket structures. In the skilled trades, for example, such structures were disassociated both by rapid technical change in manufacturing (which changed skilled workers' specialties under them) and by the increasing prevalence of unskilled labor within Fordist production (which gave them less of the division of labor to control). The basis of specialization was changing at the same time as the extent of specialized work in the labor force. It seems clear from the historical record that basket structures are usually feared by those who command cloned hierarchies, perhaps because basket structures can be particularly enduring once they are firmly in place. Certainly that has been the case in American academia, which is characterized both by enduring structures and fractious faculty.

To return to the main argument, we have seen that historicist forces—forces whose fulfillment creates conditions that in turn re-

---

11. For the psychiatric hospital example, see the detailed analysis in Abbott 1990c. On the railroads, see Licht 1983.

produce them—undergird the flexible constancy of American disciplines with their basket structure. These forces are complemented
by some shorter-lived but equally strong functional forces. Disciplines do things for academics beyond organizing their labor markets and their university social structures.[12]

The first of these functions, implied by the historicist structure
just described, is that of reproduction. Nondisciplinary intellectuals
have difficulty reproducing themselves because the American open
market for public intellectuals is incapable of supporting more than
a tiny handful of nonacademic writers and has no organized means
of reproduction and exchange beyond some tenuous referral networks. Academia is, to all intents and purposes, the only practical
recourse for American intellectuals. And being an academic means,
willy-nilly, being a member of a discipline. There have indeed been
great interdisciplinary geniuses, even within academia; Gregory
Bateson is an obvious example. But they have no obvious mode of
reproduction. They simply arise, revolutionize two or three disciplines, and leave magical memories behind.

Other disciplinary functions are cultural rather than social structural. The first of these is the Geertzian function of providing academics with a general conception of intellectual existence, a conception of the proper units of knowledge. Disciplines provide
dreams and models both of reality and of learning. They give images
of coherent discourse. They create modes of knowledge that seem,
to the participants, uniquely real.[13] Every academic knows the experience of reading work from outside his or her discipline and knows
the unsettling feeling it induces. Disciplines in fact provide the core
of identity for the vast majority of intellectuals in modern America.
It is ironic that the students of identity—currently the most vociferous critics of disciplines—should fail to see in disciplines the very
processes of identity constitution they elsewhere so easily descry.
To be sure, there are other bases of intellectual identity, politics being the most obvious. But even those who are most critical of disciplines turn out to have been profoundly shaped by them.

A second cultural function of disciplines is that of preventing
knowledge from becoming too abstract or overwhelming. Disciplines legitimate our necessarily partial knowledge. They define
what it is permissible not to know and thereby limit the body of
books one must have read. They provide a specific tradition and lin-

---

12. I am employing here Art Stinchcombe's definitions of functional and historicist accounts. See Stinchcombe 1968, chap. 2.

13. I am here paraphrasing Geertz's definition of religion from the famous essay
"Religion as a Cultural System" (1973).

eage. They provide common sets of research practices that unify groups with diverse substantive interests. Often, as I have argued throughout this book, these various limits are quite arbitrary. Sociology could substitute Ihering for Weber in its canon without experiencing much intellectual change.[14] What matters is not the particular canonical writer but rather the legitimation of knowing only the one or the other.

Thus there are important cultural functions—as well as social structural ones—served by disciplines. In a way, nothing shows the power of these functions, and the power of the historicist forces that determine the way we happen to carry them out, more clearly than the historical and current experience of interdisciplinarity.

2. Interdisciplinarity

Much recent commentary decries the disciplines and their "narrow interests." The *New York Times* announced on 23 March 1994 that "academic disciplines entwine, recasting scholarship . . . combatting compartmentalization." The trend "may also transform the university, abolishing outmoded disciplines, creating new ones, and developing ways to attack problems from more than one direction."[15] Perhaps, then, the moment of fixed disciplines is over. At the least, one can argue that the old stasis is gone.

The first hint that this is not true is the disturbing fact that, like most good ideas in social science, interdisciplinarity is old news. The first entry for the word "interdisciplinarity" in the second edition of the *Oxford English Dictionary* is in 1937, in the *Journal of Educational Sociology*. But the Social Science Research Council and the Laura Spelman Rockefeller Foundation were already focused on the problem of eliminating barriers between the social sciences by the mid-1920s. Thus, in the 1934 ten-year review of the SSRC:

> The Council has felt a primary concern with the inter-discipline or interstitial project for the reason that new insights into social phenomena, new problems, new methods leading to advances in the scientific quality of social investigation, cross-fertilization of the social

14. I first read Ihering as a graduate student in the mid-1970s, as part of a reading course in jurisprudence. Nobody in sociology had heard of him then, although it seemed pretty obvious that Weber had pirated him extensively. I should not have been surprised that a book was eventually written arguing strongly for the sociological recognition of Ihering (Turner and Factor 1994). One might, with Turner and Factor, generalize this call to a call for recognition of the whole tradition of German historical jurisprudence—not just Ihering, but also Savigny, Gierke, and many others. Weber stood on the shoulders of big giants indeed.

15. Honan 1994.

disciplines, were thought more likely to emerge here than from work in the center of established fields where points of view and problems and methodology have become relatively fixed.[16]

At the time that sentence was written (a decade *after* the foundation of SSRC), the oldest specialized disciplinary associations in the social sciences—the AHA and AEA—were just two professional generations old, about fifty years. The APSA, AAA, and ASA were all only a single generation old, about thirty years. Nor were any of these, except perhaps the historians, truly stable disciplines—disciplines complete with journals, undergraduate majors, uniformly independent departments, and national disciplinary labor markets—before the First World War. (For example, sociology and economics were combined in about a quarter of the major universities in the United States as late as 1929.) Thus, the emphasis on interdisciplinarity emerged contemporaneously with, not after, the disciplines. There was no long process of ossification; the one bred the other almost immediately. Indeed, in his history of the SSRC, Donald Fisher argues that interdisciplinarity was actually part of a deliberate policy of the Rockefeller Foundation (SSRC's chief funder) to enforce the "scientization" of the social sciences, a part of discipline creation itself.[17]

As it turned out, SSRC-based interdisciplinarity was a mirage. Louis Wirth and others expressed strong hopes for it in their review of the state of the social sciences in 1940. A roundtable discussion on "one social science or many" heard only two dissenters from a chorus of praise for interdisciplinarity. But Wirth's own view, in a contemporary self-study done for SSRC, was that interdisciplinary research was a delusion. Even the positive voices at the 1940 session—Robert Lynd prominent among them—agreed that interdisciplinarity would work only if it was trained into scholars from the beginning and that, unfortunately, there was no clear model for such training. Nonetheless, interdisciplinarism got another push from the war, which mixed the various social sciences indiscriminately in the OSS and other agencies.[18]

---

16. Social Science Research Council 1934:10. On the founding of SSRC, see Fisher 1993:39, and Social Science Research Council 1934:6, 10.

17. See Fisher 1993. On the combining of departments, see the lists in the various editions of the American Council on Education's *American Colleges and Universities*. The first two of these date from the late 1920s and early 1930s.

18. For Wirth's view, see Wirth 1937:145 ff. The Roundtable on Social Sciences was part of the tenth anniversary celebrations for the Social Science Research Building at the University of Chicago (Wirth 1940). Those who find interdisciplinarity novel might be interested to know that in the early years faculty offices in the building were scattered with respect to discipline, precisely to prevent departmental con-

The 1950s seem to have been a time of retreat for interdisciplinarity. Elizabeth Bott remarked in *Family and Social Network* that:

> Ten years ago interdisciplinary research was very much in vogue. But now its value is often questioned, partly because it has proved difficult to coordinate interdisciplinary group projects, partly too because such projects have not always produced the spectacular integration of results that was expected.[19]

Speaking of her own experience, Bott went on to remark that interdisciplinary integration did not come in the overall results, but within the modification of the views of each worker. It made one see one's own discipline differently.

The 1960s by contrast proved an interdisciplinary bonanza, as the modernization paradigm swept development studies in anthropology, sociology, economics, and political science. Enormous multidisciplinary teams took on major problems, often the very questions that had driven the first wave of interdisciplinarity at SSRC in the 1920s: population, area studies, agriculture, development, and similar topics. At the same time, moreover, the first glimmerings of social science history appeared, as discussed in the last chapter. By the mid-1970s a broad and interdisciplinary "historic turn" (MacDonald 1996a) was under way throughout the social sciences.[20]

---

centrations. The move into disciplinary contiguity came gradually after the war. Also of interest is Ogburn and Goldenweiser 1927, a long compendium of articles covering every possible pairwise combination of the basic social sciences, from "Anthropology and Economics" to "Sociology and Statistics."

19. Bott 1971:36.

20. I do not know of a serious institutional history of the modernization paradigm as it flourished in the 1950s and 1960s. The paradigm and its adherents are perhaps still too popular as whipping boys to be allowed to escape into the hands of disinterested analysis. My own sense of the period was shaped overwhelmingly by four years spent as an undergraduate research assistant in the Harvard Center for Population Studies, where oceanographer Roger Revelle presided over historians, civil engineers, demographers, political scientists, and economists in a generalized assault on everything from family planning to agroclimatology (my own "specialty") to river basin management, the green revolution, and menarche research. By comparison, current interdisciplinarity seems tame in both its ambitions and breadth, although perhaps equivalent in its self-confidence. An equally full-blown, and equally fulsome, blast of interdisciplinarity was the enormous culture and personality literature of the 1930s and 1940s, centered on anthropologists like Benedict and Mead as well as psychologists and psychoanalysts like Kardiner, Horney, and Sullivan. Culture and personality studies dovetailed with the interdisciplinarism produced by the war effort, as is shown well by Benedict's ([1946] 1989) celebrated study of Japan—sponsored by the Office of War Information.

A central 1960s text discussing interdisciplinarism was Sherif and Sherif 1969, in which the reader will find the wonderful essay of Donald Campbell, "Ethnocentrism of Disciplines and the Fish-Scale Model of Omniscience" (Campbell 1969). I think Campbell's model—which recommends that disciplines ought to tile the knowledge space like fish-scales—is too static, and thus not as strong as my conception of fractal

We can find a rough measure of recent interest in interdisciplinarity by looking at the *Social Sciences Citation Index* and comparing the relative frequency of titles including the word "interdisciplinary" to those including some generic word whose stable distribution can standardize for the increasing coverage of *SSCI*. Taking "national" as that generic reference word, we find that the ratio of the number of titles including "interdisciplinary" to those including "national" was .07 in the 1966–70 *SSCI* cumulation. This ratio was 0.08 in 1981–85, .08 in 1986–90, and .08 again in 1992–96. The 1956–66 cumulation did not separate out titles with the word "national" alone, but left them in compounds like "national-account." But this cumulation still had 144 distinguishable titles including the word "interdisciplinary." In short, over the last forty years, a serious interest in interdisciplinarity appears to be an almost stable concomitant of the disciplinary system.

This strong stability makes one suspect that the waves of interest in interdisciplinarity earlier in the century were merely apparent. Indeed, the long history and stability of interdisciplinarity—unsuspected by its current publicists—raise the interesting question of why interdisciplinarity has *not* transformed the intellectual system, even though now that it has been a permanent feature of the American intellectual landscape for so long. There seem to be a number of reasons.

In the first place, interdisciplinarism has generally been problem driven, and problems, as I have argued throughout this book, have their own life cycle. There is ample evidence that problem-oriented empirical work does not create enduring, self-reproducing communities like disciplines except in areas with stable and strongly institutionalized external clienteles like criminology. Even there, the status differences seem to keep the disciplines in superior power. Criminology departments hire from sociology departments, but seldom vice versa.

Two factors combine to prevent problem-driven interdisciplinarity from changing disciplinary structure. First, there is (again) the stability of the academic labor market. It is true that if the academic labor market were completely problem driven, disciplines might fail. But undergraduate education is generally not problem driven and it—not graduate education or research—is the driving consideration in the staffing of contemporary American universities. As long

---

rules, either as an account of disciplinary history or as a set of rules for generating new knowledge. But Campbell saw the underlying difficulties very clearly and understood the strengths and weaknesses of interdisciplinarity far better than even the best writers of today. This was and is a truly brilliant paper.

as liberal education through majors remains a central goal in American undergraduate education, faculty will be hired to teach within the majors that their disciplines define.

But second, there are far more research problems than there are disciplines—so many, in fact, that a university organized around problems of investigation would be hopelessly balkanized. Furthermore, there do exist bodies of knowledge that can be used to address many different substantive problems. Such problem-portable knowledge is precisely what disciplines generate. To be sure, any particular disciplinary knowledge works better with some problems than with others: hence the practical importance of interdisciplinarity. But an academic system based merely on problems—with Ph.D.s only in fields like women's studies, poverty studies, American studies, urban studies, population studies, criminology, and Asian-American studies—would be hopelessly duplicative and would obviously require far more "interdisciplinarity" than does the current one. The reality is that problem-based knowledge is insufficiently abstract to survive in competition with problem-portable knowledge. As Lynd and others recognized long ago, interdisciplinary studies are ultimately dependent on specialized disciplines to generate new theories and methods. Interdisciplinarity presupposes disciplines.[21]

---

21. The current wave of interdisciplinarity seems to be less problem driven or even empirically grounded than most of its predecessors, except in the various areas of identity politics: women's studies, gay and lesbian studies, and the various ethnicity studies. To some extent, interdisciplinarity may be serving as one more tool with which a younger generation tries to unseat its seniors within disciplines. Recent developments in anthropology seem a good example. Although the discipline as a whole is profoundly threatened by the theft of its major concept (culture) by professors of English and other humanities fields, the younger generation of anthropologists has borrowed postmodernism from the same sources as did the English professors and used it for the usual constructionist task of negating their elders' expertise (see chapter 3). Of course, when such people find themselves in authority—a position guaranteed by the march of age—they must either change positions or deliberately subvert the discipline they control by refusing to produce "professors in anthropology." It is not difficult to guess what they will do.

Somewhat more cynically, interdisciplinarity could also be viewed as a blind for shifting the whole university structure to a "problem-centered" one. The two are associated in that the strongest proponents of interdisciplinarity today are not the conservative scientizers who urged interdisciplinarity in the early years of SSRC, but the broad hosts of the cultural left; hence the current conservative view that the desire for a problem-centered university is driven by identity politics and an intention to study oneself and one's kind. But that argument applies mainly for undergraduates and perhaps some graduate students. The faculty incentive is more meretricious. For faculty, the advantage of a problem-centered university is that by creating a wildly duplicative system it allows many people (in different problem areas) to get credit for the same "discoveries." That is, instead of Foucault's ideas being imported into five or six disciplines, they would be imported dozens of times into the dozens of ethnic

Thus, a long historical process has given rise to a more or less steady, institutionalized social structure in American academia: a structure of flexibly stable disciplines, surrounded by a perpetual hazy buzz of interdisciplinarity. This is the enduring stability of which I have spoken earlier. However, that the system of disciplines is more or less a constant at the social structural level by no means fixes the complex cultural field that the disciplines produce, the field of academic knowledge whose evolution was the subject of earlier chapters. There we have seen a world of flux. Now we must connect the two. Between the stability of academic social structure and the swirling flow of academic ideas there is a tortured relation indeed.

3. The Interactional Field of Academic Disciplines

We can think of the ensemble of these relations as a division of labor. Now to use the phrase "division of labor" is to suggest, indeed even to assume, that disciplinary knowledge comprises a set of intellectual turfs with their controlling authorities. Such a model would make the academic disciplines parallel to the practicing professions like law or medicine, with their strong and exclusive jurisdictions of work. This concept of controlled jurisdictions provides a useful starting point, but its weaknesses will ultimately require its rejection. To emphasize the differences between the academic and practical professional worlds, I shall here refer not to jurisdiction, but to settlement. My analysis begins with this concept of settlement, by which I mean the link between a discipline and what it knows. I then consider the various structural apparatuses of settlements before turning to the central issue—the dynamics produced in the system by processes of disciplinary competition on the one hand and by the steady flow of fractal cycles on the other.[22]

Settlement

Like all divisions of labor that are not specifically planned, the division of labor among academic disciplines is established by an unrelenting process of interaction between groups. Prominent in this in-

---

and identities studies areas, with somebody getting credit for every separate act of importing. A problem-structured university multiplies the possibilities for such borrowing and rediscovery, since its potential for reciprocal ignorance across fields at any given time is far larger than that of the disciplinary university. Such reciprocal ignorance would, on a deeply cynical analysis, be good news for faculty careers.

22. An ecological model for professional knowledge is set forth in Abbott 1988a. I am here using that model as a starting point, but, as I note in text, will show how the academic ecology differs in important ways from the professional one.

teraction is competition, although there are also accommodation, alliance, absorption, and all the other processes of group ecology.

The competition is a peculiar one. Knowledge experts compete with one another through redefinition of each other's work. Academics resemble the practicing professions in this regard. Thus, English professors claim from anthropologists and sociologists the interpretation of modern cultural products like advertisements on the ground that they are written as English texts and hence subject to the "master" discipline of textual interpretation—the discipline of English. More broadly, they claim control over such metaphorical "texts" as the body and the landscape. Such disputes differ profoundly from disputes in divisions of labor that are not founded on abstract knowledge, for the plasticity of abstract argument makes the competition more fierce, more multidimensional, more subtle than is the typical labor dispute on the shop floor or construction site.[23]

Academic activity can be imagined in terms of two analytically distinct fields and a tangled net of links between them. There are on the one hand bodies of potential academic work and on the other bodies of people who do that work. At any given time, there are bundles of ties between various areas of work and various bodies of workers, bundles that make up a disciplinary settlement. For each of the various groups involved these ties embody varying degrees of connection to and control over various pieces of work being done. In such an interactional field, no individual link changes without affecting the balance of links around it. No discipline gains or loses authority in an area without displacing or enticing other disciplines. However, this ecology is nowhere near as tightly bound as that of the practicing professions, with their exclusive licensing and jurisdiction.

There are of course a host of complexities to such a model. First, there are in fact no given bodies of academic work. Bodies of academic work are perpetually being redefined, reshaped, and recast by the activities of disciplines trying to take work from one another or to dominate one another. These moves—intellectual moves of interdisciplinary deconstruction and reconstruction—are the tac-

---

23. This medium of intergroup competition—abstract knowledge—is no different in academic disciplines than in law or medicine. Whether we regard professors as applied professionals with student "clients" or as nonapplied professionals whose audience is largely themselves, it remains true that competition between academic disciplines is fundamentally similar to that between law, medicine, accounting, and the rest. It is primarily a competition in knowledge. For the moment I set aside the stakes and judges of that competition, focusing on the processes of the competitive system itself.

tical engagements of interdisciplinary conflict. Indeed, new areas emerge not only through conflict, but also from the processes of fractal combination and recombination I have analyzed throughout preceding chapters, processes that are in the first instance internal to disciplines. Second, just as these processes produce perpetual haziness about boundaries and groupings of academic work to be done, so too do processes of merger, division, and migration produce haziness about the groups doing that work. It is not only unclear what academic work is but also who the workers are who could possibly be doing it.[24]

This complexity means that we must get beyond the simple metaphor of an ensemble of groups facing a turf of tasks with links running between them like so many electric wires. It is perhaps better to think of the disciplines as amoebas putting out pseudopods as they move in a multidimensional intellectual space. In older arenas these pseudopods are somewhat hemmed in by the presence of other amoebas. It is this reciprocal constraint that I denoted earlier by the phrase "bubbling division of labor." In such arenas, most academic space has been occupied by disciplines that have expanded to meet each other. Such disciplinary blobs may have mostly convex edges to keep disciplinary heartlands compact. In addition, the removal of any one blob merely leads others to gradually fill in for it, a fact that provides extraordinary durability to the system as a whole, as I have noted.

It is important to note too that the amoebas are not really solid things with continuous external membranes, but simply densities of practitioners. We see this more clearly when we think about newer arenas of intellectual competition, where the claiming groups are in such an interpenetrating flux that their disciplinary identity is not clear. There is a distinct contrast between the relatively stable arena of "studying money flows" (which is done almost exclusively by economics—a very compact amoeba indeed) and the contested one of "studying ethnicity," which is at present done in all the social sciences and several of the humanities.

This process of pseudopodic mobility takes place in a world of many dimensions, some of which embody the fractal distinctions earlier examined, others of which capture differences of substance— differences in what is studied. And different disciplines can, like

---

24. In speaking of "merger, division, and migration," I am not here contradicting the empirical argument about the stability of disciplinary social structure that I have just made. Much of this "merger, division, and migration" is at the subdisciplinary level, and, as we shall see, much of it involves the overlapping of disciplines' connections to particular bodies of academic work.

amoebas, have quite different degrees of extension in those different dimensions, leading to interdisciplinary contact and competition in odd places over odd things. Competition between disciplines often takes the form of privileging that dimension which gives an aggressive discipline its most extensive cross-section. (This is the representation, within this metaphor, of the move mentioned above; English claiming control of everything written in texts because English thinks itself the master discipline of the interpretation of texts.) For each discipline, there is some dimension of definition along which its projection is greater than that of the other disciplines. In moments of aggression, it will emphasize this dimension, although doing so may expose it to insufferable competition.

It is common for new groups to emerge at disciplinary margins, as for example did biochemistry.[25] In other cases, bordering disciplines stably coexist, physical chemistry and chemical physics being an example. Often this leads to effective merger. Also, as in the case of engineering among the applied professions, it is sometimes difficult to specify what is the proper inclusive level of "discipline"; biochemists can be seen as chemists, as biologists, or as biochemists proper.

Recalling my earlier argument about institutionalization, however, we can see that there is one central social structure signifying full disciplinarity. That is reciprocity in acceptance of Ph.D. faculty. Border fields often employ faculty of diverse disciplines. We can think of them as having become true disciplines in the social structural sense once they hire mainly Ph.D.s in their own field. Communication is an excellent example, reaching disciplinary status, in this sense, only very recently. (American studies is still trying.) This test of social structural disciplinarity is much like the intergroup fertility standard used to define biological species.

Aspects of Settlement

By settlement then I mean the ensemble of forces that define the relation of a given amoeba to the intellectual turf that it has in-

---

25. I have discussed this process in Abbott 1995b. The important fact is that like many social objects disciplines emerge through the process whereby boundaries are assembled into things. The boundaries—in this case intellectual debates, methodological differences and other marks of differing knowledge—come first. They appear as debates (fractal debates, of course) between people not yet organized into groups. At some point, actors begin to realize that by hooking several of these boundary debates together they can create an enclosed space. This is the discipline. The speed with which boundaries get rethought in the current system—a speed driven by the processes of academic careerism—means that there are few realistic chances for new discipline creation.

vented and/or invested. Settlement has both a cultural and a social structure.

The cultural structure begins with an ensemble of research practices, evidentiary conventions, rhetorical strategies, genres, canonical works, and the like. These have been exhaustively studied by several generations of sociologists of science. I do not comment on them in further detail.

An important property of disciplinary cultural structure is what we may call a discipline's axis of cohesion. Disciplines often possess strong cultural axes, which we consider to be their central principles. Political science, we say, is about power, economics about choice, anthropology about ethnography, and so on. In the natural sciences, these axes of cohesion are aligned, to some extent, in a hierarchy of "levels of analysis." Physics concerns the atomic and subatomic levels, chemistry the molecular level, biology the supermolecular level of living things. But in the social sciences and humanities, axes of cohesion are not aligned. As my examples show, anthropology is largely organized around a method, political science around a type of relationship, and economics around a theory of action. Sociology—best conceived as organized around an archipelago of particular subject matters—presents yet another axis of cohesion. These axes do not fall in any hierarchical order, a fact that has made interdisciplinarity in the social sciences much more complicated than the simpler, linear interpenetration of the natural sciences.

Finally, to the extent that a discipline has an immediate "practical clientele" of undergraduate students, disciplinary cultural structure may also involve extensive applied knowledge, with its three characteristic processes of diagnosis, inference, and prescription. In the case of English departments earlier in this century, for example, this clientele was students to be taught how to write. For such clients, the diagnostic structure concerned the several genres of writing, the inferential structure involved reflection on pedagogy, and the prescription structure comprised actual classroom practices for teaching writing.[26]

The social structure of academic settlement has, likewise, several particular aspects. The first of these I have already discussed at length: the credential system of disciplinary Ph.D.s. This credential system dictates the disciplinary labor markets. Embodying the credential system is the familiar arrangement—virtually equivalent across all disciplines—of associations, examinations, theses, jour-

---

26. My analysis of applied knowledge systems in terms of diagnosis, inference, and prescription is set forth in detail in Abbott 1988a, chap. 2.

nals, research groups, and so on that constitute the actual social practices and organizations of disciplinary life.

Facing this internal disciplinary social organization is a second crucial set of social structures affecting disciplinary life—disciplines' audiences. Audiences are central because of their control over resources, respect, and other things necessary to academic life. Like librarians and doctors, academics require for their work an immense investment of physical capital and an immense administrative structure, both of which are provided by others. Academics also have numerous clients. These providers and clients are the principal audience for disciplinary claims.

The typical academic settlement has two levels of audiences—immediate and distant. The immediate audiences are students, administrators, and other academics. Behind each of these stands a more distant audience: parents, trustees and legislators, and the general public. These groups explicitly and implicitly judge claims by disciplines to legitimate authority over subject matters, techniques, and the like. It would seem that academics take themselves to be the most important of these audiences, for they generally address their concerns about disciplines to each other. But equally important in reality are the university administrators who control the immediately crucial resources of faculty lines. Although often drawn from faculty ranks, administrators tend to collude with students in their judgments of faculty, by steering hiring toward popular subjects. But they also, particularly in elite universities, keep a weather eye on the judgments academics make of each other.

For the natural scientists and social scientists, there is also a fourth audience, a research clientele that purchases products, ideas, and advice from academics. In some disciplines, those who serve this clientele are split off in various kinds of applied subdisciplines. Indeed, in sociology the split is sometimes so deep that departments split. Harvard, for example, has an undergraduate major in social studies as well as in sociology. The first is a popular elite major embracing qualitative and theoretical work, while the second emphasizes quantitative work of the kind typically done for governments and commercial organizations. At the graduate level, however, there is only one department (sociology) in which both kinds of work are done. This peculiar situation well shows that the research clientele's needs often diverge from those of the educational clienteles. Nonetheless, the audience that academics make for each other is so central that it calls for more extensive discussion.

The typical academic settlement involves a complex structure of relations with other disciplines. Very much unlike the practicing professions, academic disciplines—and particularly the social sciences—routinely live with what seems to any outsider like extraordinary interpenetration of settlements. It is this overlap that so frustrates the lay partisans of interdisciplinarity, for it is combined with an equally extraordinary reciprocal ignorance. If we ask academics why poor people are poor or why cities grow as they do or why certain bills fail in legislatures, different disciplines will answer these questions in their own unique ways: each with certain kinds of data, certain methods, certain habits of thinking about the problem. The social sciences in particular are quite undifferentiated with respect to actual subject matters. It is what is *done* with those subject matters that varies. And although some substantive areas see considerable cross-disciplinary knowledge exchange—the human capital literature in economics and the status attainment literature in sociology provide an example—the sheer weight of knowledge means that in most substantive areas there is what to outsiders seems like an amazing lack of reciprocal knowledge. The "discovery" of the social construction of reality by humanists twenty years after it had become dogma in large sections of social science is only one of dozens of examples of this ignorance.

Often there is a somewhat arbitrary pro tem understanding as to who is the current policy adviser to various audiences—particularly the research clientele—on this or that topic. Thus sociologists advised the state on poverty in the 1960s, but economists in the 1980s. Anthropologists and psychologists advised the state on "national character" in the 1940s while political scientists dominated the same discussion with their concept of "political culture" in the 1960s. But in the academy itself there is a substantive overlap that seems quite extraordinary when we compare it to the relatively exclusive control that practicing professions enjoy over their turfs of work.

Sometimes the sharing is open and frank. This is a common situation in area studies, where the paucity of language skills fosters interdisciplinary collaboration. Or one can have differentiation of objects of analysis without differentiation of intellectual apparatus; sociology and anthropology long split discussion of general social theory, the former basing its theories on the advanced industrial societies, the latter on the so-called primitive societies. Sometimes there are dominant-subordinate relations, perhaps with a kind of bemused tolerance of a subordinate discipline. This was the case with the sociologies of art and literature for many years until in the 1980s the dominant disciplines of art history and English decided to ingest the social interpretation of their subjects, although with quite different methods and rhetorics than the relevant sociologists had formerly used.

The extraordinary overlap between academic disciplines has a number of immediate consequences. For one thing overlap means that scholars who may seem to be in the hinterlands or backwaters of their home disciplines are often cheek by jowl with the leaders of other disciplines and hence in a position to borrow from them highly developed techniques that can reroute their own mainstreams. The flood of durational methods through the quantitative social sciences and of anthropological theory and demographic methods through history followed this pattern. The pressures of careers drive this borrowing, which is sometimes successful, sometimes not. (Vacancy chains, which Harrison White borrowed from physics, never became a standard technique in sociology, for example. But network analysis, from the same source, has done well.) Disciplines thus rejuvenate each other by a system of reciprocal theft that is facilitated by disciplinary overlap.[27]

A second consequence, unnoticed by the proponents of interdisciplinarity, is that the disciplines to some extent correct each others' absurdities. Economics and sociology, for example, have a rather curious reciprocal relationship in areas where they copenetrate, as in studies of labor markets and human capital. Economists are usually clearer and more rigorous about their theories of labor market activity. Sociologists are usually more careful about data. The two criticize each other effectively. A similar reciprocal criticism has developed between anthropology and history for the last two decades.

A third consequence, unnoticed by faculty but all too plain to students, is that teachers disagree profoundly about relatively commonplace matters. Undergraduates subject to distributional requirements learn to live with flagrant differences in the scholarly interpretation of social events. Economists tell them poverty reflects incentives, anthropologists that it arises in the culture of globalization, sociologists that it shows the potency of job migration in urban settings, and so on. The very phenomenon itself appears different in the different classes. Like their elders, most undergraduates eventu-

---

27. Nancy Tuma was the lead borrower bringing durational methods from biology and industrial reliability studies to sociology. William Sewell Jr. was one of the chief importers of anthropology to history, while the much earlier Cambridge school handled the demography importing. Vacancy chains were borrowed from electron hole theory by Harrison White (1970) and network analysis via blockmodels was borrowed by the same author from the renormalization methods aimed at Ising models in physics (White, Boorman, and Breiger 1976). My own importer experience is as the importer of alignment algorithms to the social sciences from the pattern-matching literature on DNA patterns and string editing (Abbott 1986, Abbott and Hrycak 1990).

ally learn to tune out all but one version of the problem. But curiously enough they are the ones who must live with interdisciplinarity in the first instance.

4. The Dynamics of Disciplines

Academic settlements thus have a cultural structure and a social structure. These twin structures embody the claim that a discipline has over a subject matter or a body of techniques or questions. As I have noted, this claim is quite loose by comparison with the strong jurisdiction characteristic of the practical professions like law and medicine. Even this loose claim, however, is perpetually in flux.

One reason for flux is attack by other disciplines. As I noted earlier, each major academic discipline has an axis of cohesion. This axis usually generates some kind of intellectual claim over most of human knowledge. English claims everything involving texts. Political science claims everything involving power, economics everything involving choice and utility, physics everything that involves atomic particles and so on. In each case, these properties are absolutely universal, and so the settlemental claim is in some sense universal.

Such totalizing claims embody the disciplines in their expansive mode. In their practical, defensive modes, they claim much less. English departments, for example, have actually spent most of their history teaching writing and/or the classics of English literature. English's claim to be the legitimate social interpreter of, say, modern advertising, was only implicit; most early critical studies of advertising were in fact done by sociologists, anthropologists, and historians. Or physics mainly teaches about abstract congeries of particles, not about the very particular arrangements that determined why Lincoln wrote "Four score and seven years ago" instead of "eighty-seven years ago," a rhetorical flourish that has been typically the explanatory province of English and history. Disciplines, that is, have in practice had heartlands, defined in terms of levels of analysis, subject matters, and attention to detail.

Sociology provides a nice example. In its totalizing phases, it has claimed to be the absolutely general social science; we need only recall Talcott Parsons.[28] Yet sociology in practice has comprised an archipelago of empirical work stretching from the various social problems mentioned in chapter 3 toward individual mobility studies

---

28. The reader may recall that I echoed the same claims in the opening chapter, but only in a negative way. I claimed sociology was a general social science because there was no kind of work about society that could be demonstrated to be not-sociology. The Parsonian claim was much more positive.

and studies of middle-range institutions and social structures. Crime, deviance, family, work and occupations, demography, individual attainment, race and ethnicity, communities: these have been the bread and butter of sociology. The Parsonian imperium vanished as quickly as it had been proclaimed.

Totalizing claims are less a dynamic in themselves than a rhetoric for covering more local disciplinary expansion. We should therefore turn to the forces actually conducing to local expansion and contraction. The first of these is a process I have elsewhere called professional regression, a process I mentioned in chapter 1. A good example is the case mentioned above of English faculty. In the earlier part of this century, English faculty spent their time teaching students to write (e.g., Will Strunk of *Elements of Style* fame) and to read English literature. As I mentioned above, this was "applied" academic work, in the sense of work directly with clients rather than with other academics. Today, most university professors of English have as little to do with teaching writing as they can manage, such teaching having been shifted to graduate students and hirelings steadily over the passing years. The more prestigious the university, the more extensive this shift. The trend holds despite the belief—of the parents who send their children to college, of the state legislatures who most often pay the bill, and of the students themselves— that the major reason universities have English professors is to teach students to write. English is of course hardly alone. My own university has a large mathematics faculty, few indeed of whom ever teach first-year calculus or any other form of introductory mathematics.[29]

There is a systematic reason for the paradox that professors aren't doing what the public expects them to do, one that is quite consequential within the academic social structure and that is, at the same time, common to all professions, not just academic ones. Professions are organized around abstract knowledge, and, like any social structure, they tend to grant prestige to those most closely associated with their organizing principles—those who exercise the profession's knowledge in its most pure form. But as we see in practical professions, professionals who actually deal with clients must confront the multiple complexities of client life. In the process, the purity of professional knowledge is sullied. Therefore, the most prestigious professionals in the eyes of other professionals are consultants, those who deal with cases that have already been tidied

---

29. The development of English as an academic discipline can be followed in the excellent book of Graff (1987). The subject of writing instruction is conspicuous by its absence. To read Graff's account, one would imagine that writing instruction disappeared from the task world of English professors with the death of the "old college" in the nineteenth century.

up by a front-line colleague. So, among the practicing professions, neurologists and cardiologists stand above family-care physicians, since they work as consultants and hence are more purely medical. In general, professionals who are doing what the public imagines to be the most basic professional functions are of relatively low status in the eyes of professionals themselves. It is the "professionals' professionals" who are of high status.

The same process happens in academic life, perhaps so obviously that we never think to comment on it. Professors give highest prestige to people who in fact do as little teaching as possible. Such people emphasize research, a purely professional activity. To the extent that they do teach, they deal mainly with graduate students rather than undergraduates—preprofessionalized votaries rather than demanding dilettantes. Such faculty spend as much time as possible at conferences, talking to other members of their own fraternity. In short, academics like other professionals are subject to a "regression" into professional purity.

The intellectual consequences of academic regression of this kind are considerable. First, regression explains why to academics themselves the chief intellectual structures of disciplines are not applied disciplinary practices (like teaching writing), but rather the research practices and rhetorical strategies mentioned earlier. For those are the things most concerned with disciplinary knowledge proper and those are the things that confer the most prestige. Indeed, it is this focus on purely disciplinary knowledge that has so angered the proponents of interdisciplinarity from Lynd to the present. Second, regression opens a discipline's turf to invasion. As I noted several chapters ago, it was the regression of the sociologists and others into their methodologically correct analyses of data that left the task of giving general interpretations of modern American social life to professors in humanistic fields, many of whom had what seemed to the social scientists like very hazy empirical knowledge gathered from newspapers, magazines, nonfiction, and other sources of what social scientists thought were "methodologically polluted" facts. This case also provides an interesting example of the splitting of audience perceptions of academic work. Social scientists remain completely in control of policy advice to governments on matters of American social life. It is rather the general public and above all undergraduate students who now find that the social sciences give less compelling interpretations of social life than do the less technical humanists.[30]

---

30. Graff's book on academic instruction in literature describes a textbook case of such professional regression, showing the constant tendency for literary studies to vanish into various forms of self-preoccupation, as well as the various popularizing

Professional regression is one general dynamic producing shifts in settlement power. But such shifts also arise in changes in research practices, genres, and rhetorics that can create or close off openings for other disciplines. For example, disciplines can lose power because they generate an easily portable, commodified knowledge. Statistics' loss of control of its various esoterica is an obvious case in point, as is, at the other end of the scale, anthropology's loss of control of the culture concept. But disciplines can also *develop* power by creating new and centrally important types of knowledge; one thinks of Keynesian and, later, neoclassical economics: of national character studies, of the various new histories. Cultural forces are perpetually disturbing the relations between disciplines and their areas of inquiry.

The general force behind all of these changes—whether of research practices, genres, or subject areas—is in fact the fractal dynamic outlined in earlier chapters. Here we come to the linkage between the endlessly creative, endlessly proliferating lineage structure that governs the cultural life of disciplines and the relatively stable basket-woven social structure of disciplines. To understand this linkage, we must review the entire theoretical argument to this point.

I began by arguing that knowledge in social science falls into segmentary lineages. These lineages are generated by fractal distinctions, distinctions that tend to repeat within themselves, both hierarchically at a given time and in descent systems over time. Synchronically, the indexicality of these distinctions encapsulates systems of knowledge in compact form but also generates endless misunderstandings. Diachronically, such distinctions give rise to the processes of perpetual rediscovery that I have called fractal cycles.

This argument demonstrated in cultural terms how social science could pretend to perpetual progress while actually going nowhere at all, remaining safely encamped within a familiar world of fundamental concepts. Fractal distinctions produce an illusion of progress from a reality of tradition. The reader will note that I have made a similar argument about social structure, arguing that the apparent motion of interdisciplinary relations merely emphasizes and indeed supports a networked disciplinary social structure that is of extraordinary tensile strength.

The two arguments are slightly different, however. The fractal

---

movements that have fought against this tendency. The theory of professional regression is laid out in Abbott 1981.

distinctions argument was largely about cultural flux *within* given disciplines. The present chapter's argument has been about social structural stability *between* them. Yet in the main, the two arguments capture the substantive heart of the academic disciplinary system. Its stability lies mainly in its overall social structure, and in particular in the flexible, basket-weave arrangements that guarantee the disciplines as social structural contexts for each other. Its mutability lies mainly in the cultural structure within disciplines, and in particular in the restless combination and recombination of fractal dichotomies that propels disciplinary inquirers around among the possibilities of knowledge.

In summary, the heart of the disciplinary system is stable social structure between disciplines and mutable cultural structures within them. But my earlier discussion has in fact raised the other two possible types of arguments: *intra*disciplinary social structural ones and *inter*disciplinary cultural ones.

In fact, I have throughout argued for the mutability of important social structures within disciplines. The professorial life course with its ambitions and rewards has been invoked often as a driving force, and it embodies a form of change, even if that change is organized in a regular succession whereby the young build their careers on forgetting and rediscovery, while the middle-aged are doomed to see the common sense of their graduate school years refurbished and republished as brilliant new insight. More important, the generational paradigms that have figured so prominently in earlier chapters are as much social as cultural groupings, composed of network ties and patronage links that yoke conferences and departments and faculty and students. Ever changing, these groupings articulate between the march of the professional life cycle and the unfolding fractal pattern of knowledge and thereby drive the systematic pattern of forgetting and reworking studied earlier. The regular, patterned change in intradisciplinary social structure thus makes a linkage—a slip-clutch—between the basketwork stability of the interdisciplinary social structure and the perpetual flux of intradisciplinary knowledge.

A similar argument applies to interdisciplinary cultural structure, which has also been invoked throughout my argument. Interdisciplinary theft and mutual criticism both involve complex cultural relations between disciplines and both serve to stabilize the intellectual lineages within disciplines. So too does the process of contextual redefinition, whereby internally victorious lineages find themselves in unexpected fractal relations to—and competition with—other disciplines. All these forces tend to maintain the relative separation of disciplinary cultural lineages.

I noted earlier in this chapter that differences in relatively arbitrary canons play a role in this lineage maintenance as well. To be sure, lineage endurance owes much to the fact that success within discipline has a higher relative career payoff than does success in interdisciplinary settings. But despite that powerful social structural impetus to discipline maintenance, cultural forces play a role as well. Despite the extraordinary flux of fractal lineages, cultural forces do maintain certain limits on lineages, redirecting them back toward disciplinary cores. Indeed, there is a general functional mechanism at work here. A discipline that allows its fractal divisions to proceed indefinitely would eventually lose any distinction from other disciplines and be unable to defend itself before crucial audiences—it would at that point be only a social structural, not a cultural, unit.

The overall structure thus seems virtually unbreakable. A flexible but stable transdisciplinary social structure allows all sorts of intellectual latitude within disciplines, that variety being regularly produced by fractal mechanisms. Intradisciplinary social structures articulate the cultural change with structural stasis via graded career experiences and generational paradigms, while interdisciplinary cultural mechanisms restrain the baroque variety that the fractal mechanisms induce and keep disciplines at least vaguely in separable lineages. The real question is whether anything exists that could break this system up.

The first answer to this question is clear. A change in academic hiring and/or in career structures could easily transform the system.[31] The more American colleges and universities aim at voca-

---

31. There are a number of changes in academic careers that could easily turn over the current system. The most obvious, which I mention below, are changes in the reward system. In the present reward system, academics are rewarded for publication, in particular for quantity of publication. (The forces behind this are numerous, but the important ones are growing university size, decreasing administrative trust in faculty judgment with consequent trust in "objective" [sic] measures, expansion of available journal space [see Abbott 1999a, chap. 6], and deliberate credential inflation driven by competitive pressures. Any force reducing the reward for or possibility of quantity publication would slow the fractal process considerably. A number of such developments or policies are clearly possible: abolition of tenure, award of tenure for teaching alone, or consideration of only a fixed number of pages or items at tenure time. Another possibility, given the extraordinary ease of publication on the net, would be the complete ending of all constraints on quantity, so that it would become (more than it is already) obviously meaningless. Another possible, but very unlikely, transformation would come through the ending of the cultural obsession with the new, which would end the need to pretend that old ideas are new. See Rosenberg 1959.

tional education, the more the system will attenuate, as students leave the disciplinary majors crucial to the system. The more faculty rewards are tied to teaching success (rather than to research prowess), the more this system will attenuate as success no longer flows from churning theory. The reader can easily extend these arguments. The social structural foundations of the system are plain enough and any major break in them will produce a drastic effect. It should be noted, however, that these changes must come gradually and systemwide; the disciplinary system is not vulnerable to major changes by handfuls of institutions or by one or two disciplines. What must happen is a systemwide switch in the importance of audience: from one where academics control each others' rewards to one in which students, administrators, and others control them. We are seeing a drift in that direction today.

Much more interesting is the question of whether there is a *cultural* event that could blow the system up, a Copernican or Darwinian revolution that could actually recast the symbolic structure on which it rests. Some see such an event in the much-advertised "destruction of the canon." Now the destruction of the canon doesn't matter *inter*disciplinarily because, as I have noted, interdisiciplinarity is just a standing wave set up by the disciplinary system and coextensive with it. But canon destruction does matter *within* disciplines, for to the extent that disciplines fail to enact some kind of canon (by teaching graduate students a basic set of texts), those disciplines lose one of the central forces that propels fractal cycles (you can't revolt against something you don't know) and that maintains the historicist cohesion of a set of common references (you *are* what you read in graduate school, and one discipline reads different things

---

I take no stand here on the likelihood of these things happening. Tenure is clearly under siege, in the sense that over half the student-hours in higher education in the United States are now taught by non-tenure-track faculty (Steven Brint, personal communication). Moreover, an immense new wave of commodification—the hypertext net course—is sweeping into higher education to replace the last wave of commodification (managed textbooks with their associated lectures, instructors' manuals, test batteries, etc.). But the system has proved resilient before, and it could well be that the dynamics of the elite end of higher education will change little. It is clear that in the natural sciences the interpenetration of university and commercial research is right now making fundamental changes in the structure of knowledge institutions. How this will proceed in the social sciences is much less clear. I am therefore reluctant to make predictions other than the general one that fundamental changes in the career regime will lead to transformations of the disciplinary system. I have the same reluctance vis-à-vis predictions about majors. It is true that vocational majors have swept over much of higher education in the last three decades. But the trend has not gone far at the elite colleges and universities, which support a disproportionate share of advanced degree production. Here too I can only say that a massive reduction in the place of the disciplinary majors throughout the system (including its elite end) would lead to the fall of disciplines.

than another). Simply put, if disciplines don't try to reproduce themselves culturally, they will not necessarily be reproduced in spite of themselves. Even in such circumstances, however, there are large contextual pressures maintaining any one canonless discipline in its place. If no one around you vacates his place, it is hard to spread out randomly from your own.

We see all these forces in play in the current moment of the disciplines, in which two great and general paradigms seek to reduce the whole of the social sciences to a bipolar balance. On the one hand, economics has pushed its rigorous rational choice approach into substantial areas of political science, sociology, and history. In all of these disciplines, local thieves have been busy making their reputations by bringing the good news from Ghent to Aix, reselling simplified economic ideas to revolutionize their own disciplines back home. What is unusual about this is not that it is occurring; local thievery is common, as I have noted throughout. What is unusual is rather the happening of this pattern across several disciplines at once. The same is true on the other side of the social sciences, where similar thieves are peddling Foucault, Bourdieu, Sahlins, and company to sociologists, political scientists, and historians. (Oddly enough, the new goods are sometimes pretty familiar; Habermas contains a lot of recycled pragmatism, for example.) But the situation is the same; a broad expansion, across several disciplines, of the same kind in each one.

Yet in fact the magnitude of centripetal disciplinary forces remains enormous. Initial canons are still taught in most departments in most disciplines, and even while their content changes, the intersections between them, across disciplines, do not grow appreciably larger. And the borrowing thieves themselves have very little interest in disciplinary merging. Quite the contrary. Few of those who sell rational choice outside economics could make it as economists; their self-interest is very much in maintaining disciplinary lands of the blind in which they can be one-eyed men. Put another way, a social science that had only two departments would present many fewer opportunities for ambitious intellects to produce revolutions. The rewards of revivifying a third position are too great. As this argument assumes, much rests on the initial number of disciplines, determined around the turn of this century. It is very hard to change that number now that it has hardened.[32]

---

32. The present moment is an interesting one in the history of disciplines in that the turn of much foreign graduate instruction toward English has meant that more than ever before there is an international context of comparison for cultural products (publications) even while the social structural products (Ph.D.s) are staying very

We are left, then, with the question of whether there is not some great insight that could turn the symbolic system into something new. We can see that the present battle of rational choice and culture will probably amount to little long-run change. Is there something that could? If by this we are asking whether there is something that could stop fractal cycle processes, I believe the answer is no. A couple of disciplines might combine, but that would not affect the functioning of the system. Are there profoundly new dichotomies? No, I don't think so, or, to put it another way, I think the array of dichotomies that we have means that there is no major intellectual position that cannot be expressed as what mathematicians would call "a linear combination of existing positions."

But in making this argument we seem to fall back on the fixed structuralism of Lévi-Strauss. And it is clear that idea systems do have a complex history that is in some sense more than the simple play of fractal repetition, forgetting, and rediscovery. What then is the connection between the stasis, or at least potential stasis, of the deep structure, and the perpetual flux of the surface? We can take it for granted that in some deep sense, everything has already been thought. One can find in the pre-Socratics all the basic dichotomies of modern social science: change versus permanence, atomism versus continuity, and so on. But this level of stasis is uninteresting. Of interest rather are the gradual developments of applications of these ideas to the concrete task of studying societies. At this level, the last truly great change in the social scientific imagination was the extraordinary era that came to an end around the First World War. In that era Marx, Freud, Weber, Durkheim, the classical economists, and others erected a vision of the social world that has not changed, in any foundational sense, since their time. To create a fundamental change in the arrangement of disciplines, it would in my view be necessary for someone or some group to destroy some of the foundational ideas of late nineteenth-century social thought.

For example, someone might write a work of Darwinian greatness demonstrating that history really doesn't matter to the fate of the world. Such a demonstration would need to assemble all the prior evidence to that effect and at the same time to show that all the phenomena history *seems* to explain in fact have synchronic origins. Such a work would indeed revolutionize the social sciences, for no single idea is more central to our current tradition of social thought than historicism. Antihistoricism would recast the entire

---

much within country. That creates an interesting test of the argument here, since it is the social structure that provides the great stability of the system in my view.

fractal alignments of disciplines, for it would redefine at a stroke how the various combinations of fractal positions currently in existence relate to one another.

Creature of the nineteenth century that I am, I cannot conceive of such a book. But were it to exist it would transform the cultural apparatus of the current disciplines in such a way as to reorganize them entirely. For the present, the system works surprisingly well. Disciplines borrow from each other endlessly, but train scholars more or less within consistent lineages. Fractal cycles within disciplines generate a lot of random motion, with the result of much serendipitous contact between disciplines in odd places over odd things. Incentives for thievery are high; of the major sociologists of the past generation nearly all of the methodological innovators were pirates—Duncan borrowing from biology, Coleman from engineering, White from physics. But overall the system plows along, enduring major cultural fads and vagaries without much deep structural change.

As I noted in the opening chapter, however, the system definitely produces a richer and richer knowledge of our world. It "fills the space" of possible social knowledge more and more, even though it is capable of forgetting things it used to know well, even though it spends much of its time rediscovering things, even though its surface rhetoric of perpetual progress is silly at best. The fractal distinctions model is strong indeed, both as a model for understanding social scientific knowledge and as a means for producing it.

TWO ESSAYS ON SELF-SIMILARITY

6

Self-Similar Social Structures

THE FIRST five chapters of this book make a single unit arguing that the cultural life of the social sciences evolves through an unfolding series of fractal distinctions. In the course of that argument, I have broadened the concept of fractal distinctions in various ways and have explored some other byways of the theory of social and cultural structure, developing concepts of syncresis, basket structures, and various other things. In the next two chapters, I turn away from this analysis of a single substantive topic to speculate about the applicability of fractal arguments more broadly. The present chapter examines the possibility of self-similar social structures. To it I have appended a fractal analysis of rating scales such as are commonly found both in social life and in sociological data. The final chapter examines the quality of self-similarity in some moral debates in social science.

Unlike the earlier ones, these two final chapters are speculative. I take the earlier analyses to establish the utility of self-similarity as an approach to thinking about cultural and social structures. Here I wish to push into the unknown. As a result, these chapters have much less scholarly machinery and indeed are written in a different tone. They mix examples from a wide variety of venues with illustrative formal analyses and straightforward theoretical argument. They are meant to raise questions and issues rather than to provide a comprehensive account of something. At best, I hope to per-

This chapter dates in its original form from 1988; it was the first complete paper I wrote on this subject. I dedicate it to the memory of E. E. Evans-Pritchard, Professor of Social Anthropology in the University of Oxford, 1946–70. I would like to thank Raymond Fogelson for introducing me to the writings of Evans-Pritchard and the other classic anthropologists.

suade the reader that theoretical arguments based on concepts of self-similarity could help simplify important problems in social science.[1]

1. Self-Similar Social Structures and Their Properties

Recall the examples that began the book. The MCAT examinations select the upper extreme of the college population in terms of scientific abilities and attitudes, but three years later those same selected students will choose specialties ranging from psychiatry to cardiology, replicating within the compass of medicine the humanistic/rationalistic division that the MCAT implicitly defines on students generally. Or again, the caste system relegates certain groups so firmly to the bottom as to exclude them from the four varnas altogether, yet among the untouchables an internal hierarchy exactly replicates the much larger one that places them beneath caste Hindus.

To these examples we could add dozens of others in which small-scale social structure reproduces large-scale social structure. Literature on cities separated "social organization" and "social disorganization" only to find the latter category redivided by writers who saw a "social order of the slum." Studies of labor markets divide core and periphery only to find smaller cores and peripheries within each of these. Frazier's celebrated analysis of the black elite argued that the black bourgeoisie stood in much the same relation to the black mass as whites did to blacks in general.[2]

---

1. In opening this speculative section of the book I should make an aside about the universality of fractal arguments. In the many years since I first made the arguments that undergird this book, the most common single reaction to them has been to ask whether I am not essentially making the Lévi-Straussian argument that the entire world is cognized in structural dichotomies. And whether I am thereby invoking the structuralism that we are supposed to have transcended, or, worse yet, the dangerously unrelative argument that dichotomous perception is builded into the very structure of consciousness.

It was not my intention to make such a universal argument. It is true that once I started looking for fractal structure I began to see it everywhere. But for me the utility of the fractal idea was that it made sense of many things I had never figured out. Above all, as I hope to show in chapter 7, it made sense of the endless political arguments I had with people with whom I felt I had immense amounts in common. It explained how we used all the same arguments and all the same positions and assumptions and yet managed to disagree with violence and passion. But the universality of fractal arguments grew on me only slowly, and the idea that such arguments represented some kind of universal pattern came to me only when I began to realize that a case could be made for fractal structure in language itself, an argument made implicitly in Gal 1991 and more explicitly in Gal and Irvine 1995 and Irvine and Gal 2000.

2. On community disorganization, see Suttles 1968. On the black bourgeoisie, see Frazier 1965.

Perhaps the best-studied examples today involve gender divisions. In the modern period of production, men have generally been in the labor force and women to some extent out of it. But as women filtered into the labor force, they tended to be concentrated in certain occupations, often identified with "female" attributes like caring. And to the extent that they entered "male" occupations, they concentrated in certain specialties. And even to the extent that they entered elite male specialties, they tended to be relegated to less central locations. And so on. A similar analysis holds—in the other direction—for men and housework. We start again from the association of men with work and women with home. To the extent that they *do* work for the household, men tend to do outside work, work on things that relate the home to the larger world: lawns, cars, and the like. To the extent that they work physically *inside* the house, that work is either related to this "outside home work" (fixing lawn mowers) or to the physical substrate of the house (carpentry, electrical work); it is not emotion or family work. To the extent that men *do* do actual personal work for the family (e.g., cooking) it is often identifiably celebratory work like grilling meat. Not all the affirmative action in the world can undermine this fractal pattern.

These examples should persuade us of the reality of self-similar social structures. No matter the level at which we inspect them, we find the same pattern repeated. Nor are these simply linear scales seen in merely partial detail. In particular, the gender examples are very striking. There is no simple linear scale of "degree to which types of work are defined as culturally female," running from one pole to another. Such a scale would presume that grilling meat or making beds was permanently associated with a fixed particular value of "femininity." But the whole point is that it is not. We can always make either one look feminine or masculine by changing our zone of comparison. Making beds is masculine relative to comforting a crying child, in the standard understanding, but feminine relative to working on the family car. Given a particular arena or level of comparison, we always find the same kind of structural relation repeated between men and women, a kind of perpetually nested and therefore perpetually partial division of labor.

2. A Formal Example

It is useful to think about the concept of such self-similar social structures a little more formally. Let us consider the example of gender segregation in occupations and ask how it might be conceived in a fractal manner.

Consider a population of men and women aiming at a set of potential occupations. Imagine for the moment that the occupations can be arrayed in a linear scale of prestige or some other quality. And think of careers as trajectories of branch points such that at each branch point a certain fraction of the men "go up" in terms of this prestige scale and a different fraction of the women do so. We might think of one branch point as going to graduate school versus not, another as choosing to enter business versus entering the professions and still another as choosing to work as an operative rather than as a clerk.

Before we go further, let me point out some important details. First, note that branch points are nested within other branch points, because they are ordered, more or less, in time. Second, although I have given "choice" examples, it actually does not matter, for the sake of this example, whether the branches occur because of choice or constraint. All that matters is the difference of percentages. Third, for convenience, I will assume that the split fractions are complementary in the sense that they sum to one; the same proportion of men move up as of women move down. This assumption is not necessary, but makes the analysis a little easier to understand. So also does the assumption that the percentage remains the same at each branch for each group, which is obviously unrealistic in the extreme. (We do however require some form of regular behavior for this percentage as we go through branch points if we are to get fractals instead of simple random splits.)

We will think of the ultimate occupation of each individual as generated by a sequence of these branching processes. Thus, the first choice governs whether one goes to the top half of the distribution of occupations or to the bottom. Then the second choice governs whether one goes to the top quarter *given* that one has gone to the top half *or* to the third quarter *given* that one has gone to the *bottom* half. For example, suppose 60 percent of the men move up at each branch but only 40 percent of the women. If we start with 100 men and 100 women, after the first stage there are 100 people in the top half, 60 of them men, 40 of them women. There are also 100 people in the bottom half, 40 of them men, 60 of them women. The people in the top half then face the same probabilities again, which govern their assignment to either the first or second quartile. The men go up or down in the ratio 60/40, putting 0.60 times 60 or 36 in the top quartile, and 0.40 times 60 or 24 in the second quartile. Equivalent multiplications put 16 of the women in the top quartile and 24 of the women in the second quartile. This makes the proportion male

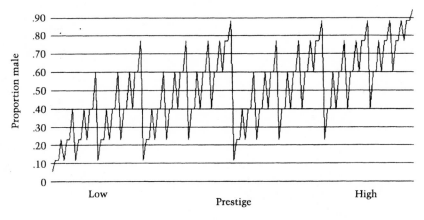

Figure 6.1

36/52 = .69 in the top quartile and 24/48 = .50 in the second. By an obvious symmetry, the third quartile percentage male is 0.50 and the fourth quartile 0.31. At the next stage, the (eight) category proportions male (from bottom to top) are .23, .40, .40, .60, .40, .60, .60, and .77. Note that the category proportions are *not* monotonically increasing. At the sixteen-category level, the proportions are .16, .31, .31, .50, .31, .50, .50, .69, .31, .50, .50, .69, .50, .69, .69, and .84. Figure 6.1 shows the result of this process after seven sets of branches. There are now 128 subgroups and the graph shows the proportion male for each of them, connecting adjacent groups so that each vertex represents a subgroup.

A number of things are quite obvious about this curve. First, it is a fractal, self-similar at intervals defined by cutting itself in half, in half again, and so on. Were we to have three percentages which we followed in the order a, b, c, a, b, c, a, b, c, we would get a more complex fractal, but there would still be strong self-similarity. This fractal character represents precisely the gender segregation discussed above. No matter at what level we consider this curve, no matter how small the section of it on which we focus, we will find the *same pattern* of gender-segregated occupations and of further gender segregation within the suboccupations. This conforms with the well-known fact that there are strongly female occupations in all ranges of occupational prestige, although fewer of them near the top than lower down. No matter what range of occupational prestige we focus on, we find wide variations in sexual composition. This continues even into the level of suboccupations. Bakers, for example,

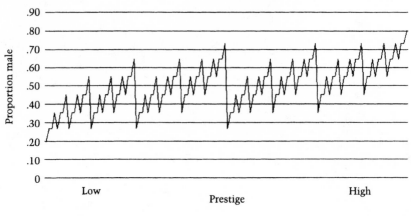

Figure 6.2

are an occupation where general parity in sex composition masks distinct internal divisions; women work in quite different settings and at different levels.[3]

Second, although there is a distinct trend toward maleness as we go to the right, the trend is quite gradual. Moreover, there is actually a quite wide dispersal of maleness. Even in the bottom quarter of the curve—the 32 low-status occupations—there are a number of occupations as much as 60 percent male. This dispersal is of course a function of my "splitting coefficient." If the splitting coefficient were .55 instead of .60, there would be only one of these, not six. But then the curve, shown in figure 6.2, would be gentler on the down side as well. Note that this general trend means that were we to undertake a regression analysis of this data, there would be a significant relation between prestige and maleness despite the quite regular pattern of departures from that relation that is evident in the curves.

Continuing in that regression vein, notice a third point; the *shorter* the range of occupations that one considers, the *steeper* appears to be the relation between status and gender segregation. That is, locally there seems a powerful relation between status and gender segregation, but globally that relation is much weaker. The fractal model produces the very odd methodological property that the narrower the range one studies, the more pronounced and distinct the

---

3. On women in the labor force see, e.g., Reskin and Roos 1990 and Honeyman and Goodman 1991. On bakers, see Reskin and Steiger 1990.

effect, precisely the reverse of the usual ecological result that throwing the net wide finds stronger relationships.

Fourth, if we raise the splitting coefficient to a very high level, in order to signify extraordinary male advantage, we will find that gender-balanced occupations will disappear. But there will continue to be some low-status occupations that are overwhelmingly male (and high-status occupations that are overwhelmingly female), a fact that is familiar from standard occupational statistics.[4]

However, these percentage figures do mask strong differences in the *numbers* of people in those occupations. The low-status occupations in which males dominate are very small occupations generally—few men, but fewer women. And similarly for female-dominated occupations at the top. When we multiply through and calculate the average status of the two genders, it turns out to be exactly in proportion to the splitting coefficient. If we assume that the scale runs from 0 to 100, and men go up or down in the proportion 60/40 (with women exactly the reverse) then the average status of men is 60 across the whole ocupational spectrum and that of women 40.

We should step back and see what this model has gotten us. As a model of the relation of occupational prestige and gender segregation, it has some strengths. Figure 6.3 shows some actual data for occupational prestige (x-axis) and percent male (y-axis), slightly attenuated vertically for ease of visualization. (Sex segregation in occupations is so strong that were this shown at the same scale as figure 6.2 the patterns would be overwhelmed by that fact.) Shown are all U.S. occupations with over two hundred thousand incumbents in 1990, located by their percentage male and their Nakano-Treas prestige score. I have connected adjacent points in order to make the similarity with the earlier figures apparent. The graph shows a number of the characteristics predicted by the fractal model. First, there is an extraordinary mixing of gender percentages across the range of prestige. Second, in the lower half of the graph, we can see several times repeated a steady rise in the low points of the curves. (There seems a very faint version of this pattern in some places at the top.) The graph also appears to have the quality that the right-hand and left-hand quarters of it seem to show a stronger slope of y on x than does the whole. With the exception of the first of these characteristics (mixing of gender profiles across the prestige

---

4. See Hauser and Warren 1997. The statistics used for figure 6.3 come from the web version of the Hauser and Warren dataset.

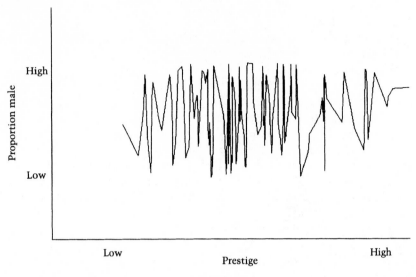

Figure 6.3

range), these are not strong findings at all. They are merely interesting appearances, suggesting that the fractal model might account for some important part of the puzzling nonrelation between gender profile and occupational prestige.

But more broadly, this model serves very well to capture the theoretical patterns that are so clear in the gender area. If we think of the scale not as occupational prestige but as measuring what we normally think of as a linear scale of the genderedness—from female to male—of certain kinds of activities, we see at once that a fractal model provides a very clear understanding of many aspects of the gender division of labor. It provides a simple account of why we see gender divisions of labor no matter what the scale at which we inspect social life or the particular area of the general division of labor chosen. It explains the intensive and systematic variance around what we try to imagine as a regular, linear scale of genderedness. It explains the paradox that our detailed studies—ethnographies, localized quantitative work—often find extreme gender differentiation even though we are all well aware that men and women act together throughout society. And, finally, it explains why the relation of gender seems, under normal methodological assumptions, to be so easy to linearize, despite its systematically messy qualities.

All this arises out of the fairly simple assumption that at any scale men and women tend to sort themselves out slightly in a division of labor. A 60/40 division is not a powerful one, yet it produces very marked fractal structures. This seems an extremely powerful account of such patterns.

3. Self-Similarity and Its Social Properties

Thus we see that there is a common form of social structure that takes a self-similar form. Its small structure recapitulates its large structure. No matter the level at which we inspect it, we find the same patterns repeated. These structures present a maddening challenge to our methods, because they contain information that cannot be captured in linear form. They also seem completely undertheorized. Let us then consider their properties.[5]

Self-similar structures are based on a unit that repeats itself. To us, the most familiar case is that of the ideal typical bureaucracy. The unit here is a simple hierarchy placing one individual in a position of authority over several, a unit we customarily illustrate as a tree with the subordinates strung out as roots and the supervisor as the stem (fig. 6.4a). If we take a group of such trees and place their supervisors in a similar relation under a further supervisor, we have created a structure similar to itself in two obvious senses (fig. 6.4b). First, the various lower trees are similar to each other. Second, the lower trees are similar to the larger upper one. I shall call these parallel similarity and nesting similarity, respectively. Note that this kind of dual similarity is characteristic not only of bureaucracy but also of its more traditional cousins vassalage and clientelism.[6]

---

5. Note that a given unit can resemble another unit of different size even when the two are not part of the same social structure. The dyadic cold war, as Simmel would have us note, is rather like some marriages: divisive but intimate and reciprocal. The implications of such resemblance are considerably weaker than those of self-similarity, however. The case of similar units on a given level loosely tied by a superordinate structure not resembling their internal ones is what Durkheim and others call "segmental social structure."

6. The question may be raised whether all hierarchical structures are self-similar. In practice, the answer is clearly no. Often, principles of hierarchy differ at different levels enough that the personal experience of supervisors and subordinates does not really resonate across levels. Or a hierarchical organization can pull together units whose internal organization is functional with units whose internal organization is not. This view assumes that the essence of self-similarity lies in its consequences for individual experience and solidarity, points I discuss extensively below.

The relations between the nested and parallel parts of self-similar structures have been the subject of some investigation in the specific area of formal organizations. Crozier (1964), for example, focused on the conditions leading to the emergence of

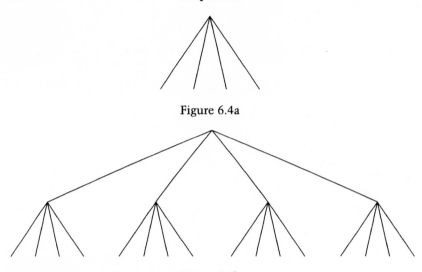

Figure 6.4a

Figure 6.4b

Parallel similarity is familiar in the anthropological literature from the concept of segmental social structure. Many social structures consist of similar organizations yoked together in some fashion. Voluntary associations often take this format, as do consortia of universities or social service agencies. In the recent past, American professions commonly existed as congeries of local professional associations tied together from place to place by state professional associations of a somewhat different form.

But segmental organizations are not necessarily self-similar. It is nesting similarity that produces the quality of self-similarity. In mathematical terms it is called contraction mapping—the producing of structures within structures by replacing the parts of a larger structure with smaller ones similar to it. Sociologists of an older generation will recognize nesting similarity immediately as the generating mechanism for Talcott Parsons's AGIL scheme. This was a theoretical model of society couched as a contraction mapping; every level of social structure had four functions, each of which was then itself broken down into four functions, and so on. In the examples given above, such contraction mapping is most evident in

---

unifed strata in organizations, attributing this in part to cultural factors. I think it preferable to theorize this in terms of self-similarity. The weaker the subordinate similarity—that is the similarity between units at different levels—the more likely the emergence of strata. I shall elaborate this point in the discussion of solidaristic implications of self-similarity below.

the gender differentiation examples. The larger gender-segregated social structures can be replaced by parts, each one of which is in turn gender structured and made up of parts that are themselves gender structured, etc.[7]

These various examples suggest an important point. The image of hierarchy limits our conception of self-similarity. There is no need for the units of a self-similar structure to take the form of domination over equals. They may, for example, be functionally differentiated systems. An industrial organization may be divided into marketing, information, operations, financial, and other divisions, all being functionally interdependent. Each one of these divisions will then have its own internal differentiation of functions, much of it replicating the larger one. An information services division has to sell its services to other divisions (marketing), to monitor its financial position in the internal accounting system (information), and so on.[8]

Units of self-similar social structures may also be exchange systems. In many ways, the economy itself can be regarded as a set of nested markets, relatively but not absolutely differentiated from one another. At each level these markets can be distinguished into high- and low-risk exchanges, fixed and probabilistic exchanges, short- and long-term exchanges, and so on. The stock and bond markets essentially embody different approaches to capital development, but each has within it submarkets that have the qualities of the other.

In our society, status systems also usually work in a self-similar fashion. College students choose occupations in part on the basis of rewards, but once in those occupations (whether these be low or high reward), they aim at specialties with the highest rewards within occupation. Once in a specialty (again whether low or high), they

---

7. For a firm mathematical introduction to the fractal literature, see Barnsley 1988. Other sources are cited in chapter 1. It is ironic that Parsons chose as a theoretical generating principle for his resolutely antiempirical social theory a social structural principle that is quite common empirically. Some readers of this manuscript have seen a close resemblance with Parsonian theory. I am at a loss to understand this. Parsons's use of self-similarity was unselfconscious, theoretical, and static, whereas mine is self-conscious, empirically grounded, and dynamic. I have also been advised that my theory ought to be related to that of Luhmann, presumably because Luhmann too spoke of systems and subsystems (see, e.g., Luhmann 1982, esp. chap. 10). On rereading Luhmann, however, I feel—as with Parsons—that he was working on a level of abstraction far above my own.

8. It is important to note that the experience of superordination does not always involve the ability to give orders to those more than one rank below. This issue was always a problem for feudalism. Organizations in which this "transitive" hierarchy does not exist are self-similar in an extraordinary way. Louis XV, king of the most centralized state of the Old Regime, is said to have once remarked, "If I were Lieutenant of Police, I would ban cabriolets" (Cobban 1957:30).

may pursue further rewards within some subspecialty (neurology, tax law, psychiatric social work). This principle holds for other values than money. Medicine has generally been considered a more altruistic profession than law, but of course within medicine some specialties (family practice) are seen as more altruistic than others (gynecology). Of course, the system is hardly perfect and determining; many people switch occupations and specialties. But the occupational reward system does have a fractal quality; although most people are worried about achievement within their sphere, they are aware only of the gross features of the status and reward systems outside their own narrow area of concern.[9]

These various examples of social "contraction mappings" suggest a set of questions about the units of self-similar social structures. What are the principles typically generating them? What is the typical degree of contraction or spread? Is that contraction uniform or are self-similar systems sometimes unbalanced?

The first of these questions is the most important. As the examples so far suggest, the most familiar self-similar generating principle we know is hierarchy. Hierarchical structures are typically produced by self-similar principles, whether they be in modern organizations, in kinship systems, in feudal land tenure, or in third-world clientelage. In all of these the principle is that certain individuals hold command or status over others, who in turn hold command or status over still others, and so on. Hierarchy is not a fixed overall structure, but rather a particular practice for expanding a social structure: expanding it by subordination of new units to the control of existing ones.

What distinguishes hierarchy from functional differentiation, as

---

9. The racial status system has this quality as well, as I mentioned earlier (Frazier 1965), although it is interesting to note that blacks originated the locution of "white trash" to denote the lower end of the upper part of the caste system (see the sources, including the journal of Fanny Kemble, listed in the *OED* supplement s.v. "white trash"). Morland (1958) discusses a southern United States example of internal differentiation in a lower-status group, reminiscent of the harijans (Moffatt 1979).

There are indeed many examples of such subdivisions, splitting "the poor" into further subgroups. The Elizabethan Poor Law (39 Elizabeth c. 3, 1597; 43 Elizabeth c. 2, 1601) insisted on the distinction of the able-bodied poor (capable of work) from the truly destitute, a distinction that exactly replicated the larger social distinction of those able to succeed in the larger economy and those unable to do so. (There is nothing new about the concept of workfare!) Indeed, within the whole not-for-profit (NFP) area in modern America, we find replicated the same complex of institutions that function for commercial organizations in the larger society. There are NFP "banks" that arrange large and complex loans from multiple public and private funding streams that enable small social service agencies to undertake large projects like housing developments for seniors. The whole NFP sector has a set of financial institutions recapitulating the commercial sector outside.

a generating principle for self-similar structures, is that in simple hierarchy the focus is on the contentless parallel fact of subordination under a head. In functional differentiation, by contrast, there is substantive content to the resemblance between levels. Each new unit replicates not merely the skeletal structure of subordination, but also a set of functional units of which the dominant unit (the unit being differentiated) itself represents only one type. There is "horizontal content" to the structure, not merely the "vertical content" of hierarchy.

Note that we need not assume an actual process of functional differentiation or construction; the functional structure could be implicit. Thus, Parsons's AGIL scheme was implicitly based on a theory about the infinite scalability of functional analysis. The multiplication of AGIL boxes within AGIL boxes reflected the Parsonian assumption that the imperative functions of adaptation, goal attainment, integration, and pattern maintenance were present no matter what the social scale analyzed. To the extent that we accept imperative functionalism as a position, such nested functions too will generate self-similar social structures. The difficulty lies in the slide from function to structure. That structures have similar functions by no means guarantees that they have similar social shape.

Nor should we assume that self-similar systems are generated only by differentiation of one sort or another. They can also be generated by true "contraction mappings," that is by the replication within a smaller unit of patterns of larger units beyond. This is common in legislatures elected under proportionate representation rules, for example, which are deliberately designed as self-similar structures. The legislators are meant to be a statistical microcosm of the polity.[10] A similar process produces self-similarity in deviance systems. We think of religious communes as setting behavioral standards far exceeding our normal ones, yet within such communes the content of "deviance" simply becomes redefined to cover behavioral differences that would be considered trivial outside.[11] (This is an example of what I will later refer to as reparameterization, although in social space, not social time. See the appendix to this chapter.) On the other end of the scale, mental health systems, loosely speaking, contain people who deviate from society, and certain hospitals within those systems contain those who can't function in the more open ones, and certain wards in the special hospitals contain patients who can't function in other special hospital wards. Each con-

---

10. It should be noted that it can take very elaborate voting systems to guarantee proportional representation. See Levin and Nalebuff 1995.
11. See Zablocki 1971.

centric system is similar to the others, yet each constitutes its own social group, with its own special repository for deviants. Again, let me note that these examples are all produced not by differentiation, but by deliberate social construction.[12]

Thus one basic question about self-similar systems is the nature of the principles generating them. The examples given so far have involved several such principles. The first is hierarchy. As I have remarked, hierarchy is so common that we often see it as the only form of self-similarity, even though it is in fact merely one form among several. The implications of this conflation in the interpretation of such phenomena as gender roles are well known. The presumption that self-similarity necessarily involves hierarchy is itself an ideological presumption, as we shall see in the next chapter.

The second generating principle I have mentioned is functional differentiation, exemplified by the Parsonian imperative function model and by practical examples of subdivisions of divisions in traditionally organized commercial firms. Functional nesting seems common, but is seldom deeply nested, at least by comparison with hierarchy, which is often so. A third generating principle is what we may call microcosm, in which structures are deliberately created as concentrically representative. Because of their importance in politics, such systems are extremely common. Often they can be strongly nested. The American system of legislative committees within legislatures within polities is an example; party representation obtains at all levels, concentrically.[13] Affirmative action is another designed microcosm system, again aiming at concentric representativeness. It is clear that representation is in part a moral structuring of self-similarity, a topic I return to in chapter 7.

Although the generating principles mentioned so far are all more or less conscious systems—systems designed into place—many, perhaps most, self-similar systems are not so designed, but rather arise naturally out of social processes. I shall turn below to the variety of historical processes that produce such systems. But here I wish to

---

12. This concentric system describes one of my field sites as a graduate student, the Jackson I ward at Illinois's Manteno State Hospital.

13. Political systems tend to be microcosmic whether designed so or not. There is little question that classical political machines took a fractal form in which internal economies of favors between "leaders" and "subleaders" (the terminology is Dahl's [1961]) exactly replicate structures of favors between subleaders and constituencies. Grimshaw (1992:10–12) notes this as well. Microcosmic systems can also be oppressive. The Pilgrims fled England to achieve religious freedom and promptly imposed on Massachusetts a religious despotism more strong than the Stuarts'. See Erikson 1966, which makes clear, as I do below, the fractal nature of religious divisions.

go on to the second basic analytic question about self-similar systems, that of the spread or contraction in a self-similar structure, familiar from the literature on hierarchies as the question of "span of control." Where the number of individuals supervised is high, we speak of a wide span of control and a flat organization; where it is low, a narrow span and a steep organization. For some self-similar systems, this terminology works; for others, it does not. In a self-similar functional system or division of labor, for example, span refers to the number of internal functional subsystems at each level (e.g., four in Parsons's AGIL scheme, many more in most divisions of labor). To a certain degree, this span can vary from level to level without the structure's losing the property of self-similarity. Clan-type lineage groups, for example, commonly produce differing numbers in different generations, yet retain the property (except in dual-descent systems) of self-similarity. As Evans-Pritchard noted, however, this self-similarity may require forgetting a good deal of the ancestral lineage.[14]

In the context of microcosm, system span refers to the fineness of the microcosm. At each move toward microcosm, definition can be lost. Indeed, it is the character of certain voting systems (the winner-take-all constituency system of the United States, for example) to shed so much information as to make the second-level institution (in that case, the legislature) only faintly a microcosm of the lower-level political structure. Affirmative action rules—and the contest to become listed as subject to them—indicate the importance of the span or detail of the process of microcosm. Only those who are defined as independent groups are retained at each microcosmic level as "required" representation.[15]

The span of the unit clearly influences a structure's character. A structure in which each unit consists of a superior and two subordinates acquires the peculiar properties Simmel saw in dyads. Sometimes there is the tendency toward opposition, what Bateson called schizmogenesis. At other times, there is a tendency to immediacy and reciprocity between subordinates. In the first case, the structure produces strong vertical bonding, for in each subordinate unit one individual will be closer to the superordinate than to the other individual. Repeated throughout the structure, this process produces vertical strings. In the second case, bonding has no such means of

---

14. Evans-Pritchard 1970, chap. 5, esp. 199–201. It is necessary to forget the past in order that the (minimal) lineage can always be about five generations deep.

15. On voting systems, see Levin and Nalebuff 1995. Affirmative action is logically equivalent to a special type of vote-counting scheme.

propagating through the structure. And with larger numbers of subordinates, these clear patterns break up into much more complex ones.[16]

Thus the relative span of the generating principle of a self-similar social structure has important implications for the structure produced. So too does its degree of "balance," my third basic analytic question about self-similar social structures. In the strict sense, any "line of descent" in a self-similar social structure should resemble any other. In some cases, however, it seems useful to loosen this requirement. According to Dumont, the classical varnas of India illustrate one possible variant. Shudras are opposed to the three upper varnas because they are not "twice-born." Within the upper three, Vaishyas are opposed to the other two because they have dominion only over animals. Of the upper two, Kshatriyas are opposed to Brahmans because the former have political dominion and the latter spiritual dominion. (Harijans are excluded from the classical varnas altogether, being opposed to all four of the classical varnas.) Here only one branch of each division in turn divides. Yet the system has distinct self-similar qualities; the phenomenon of ritual purity undergirds and sustains all of these distinctions and enables caste Hindus to negotiate the system without difficulty.[17]

The military ranks of the United States Army provide another illustration of an unbalanced self-similar structure. A first distinction opposes officers to enlisted men, the latter being further divided into NCOs and privates. NCOs are in turn divided into sergeants major and other sergeants.[18] Officers are divided first into regular commissioned officers and warrant officers; the commissioned are divided into the three groups of general, field grade, and company grade. Although this fairly complex design does produce a single hierarchy of precedence, the system is strongly self-similar. Second lieutenants, the lowest-ranking commissioned officers, have a good deal more in common, experientially, with PFCs, the lowest regular enlisted rank, than they do with general officers (the highest of the high) or sergeants major (the highest of the low). Both second lieutenants and PFCs are relatively young and new to the Army. Both tend to spend much time in settings where they are ordered to do things. More important, the system is distinctly unbalanced.

---

16. Bateson 1958:171–97.

17. Dumont 1980:67, 288.

18. The rank of corporal, lying between privates and sergeants, is rare in the modern Army. I should also note that paralleling the enlisted ranks from levels four to seven are the "specialist" grades for technical workers without command authority.

There are more systematic distinctions among officers than enlisted men. The span of the internal subclassifications varies.

The questions of content, span, and balance thus begin to tell us something about the nature of any particular self-similar social structure. More interesting, however, is the historical question of its origin.

4. Origins

One reason why the relational content of self-similar structures varies so widely is the variety of processes that produce self-similar structures. Some of these processes we have encountered earlier. Others are new acquaintances.

As we have just seen, self-similar structures can be deliberately constructed. Various political theories have endorsed self-similar structure. Parliamentary democracy, for example, rests on citizens' casting votes for representative individuals who then cast votes for leaders and policies; the legislature is felt to be similar to the polity. Indeed, classical political theory spilt much ink on this issue— Locke arguing that such representation was impossible but better than any alternative, Burke arguing that direct representation was a serious problem, Rousseau rejecting representation altogether. Such political systems need not necessarily be formally constructed. In classical China, for example, the various governmental levels from the local yamen to the whole empire were conceived as a set of concentric families, each analogous to the family itself. Managerial and other hierarchies provide extensive examples, as do ancient professions like the clergy and the military. All these examples remind us that self-similarity often coincides with hierarchies or differentiation of functions.

Self-similar structures also appear by means of fission, a common result in multiparty political systems. A political system divided into right and left often produces right and left versions of each of those and then yet further subdivision within the subdivisions. Late nineteenth-century France produces excellent examples, as do both left and right in contemporary America. Fission is also the source of the "deviance" within the religious communes noted above. Communards leave the "bad" society by choice and then find within themselves a new kind of "bad." As the examples suggest, fission ultimately divides groups into so many potentially overlapping subgroups that possibilities of recombination are endless. Nor need such "recombiners" join immediately adjacent groups. On the contrary, alliances may be sought with distant but similarly situated groups for help against near neighbors. The dizzying divisions and alliances among the parties of the French Revolution—the Jacobins, Brissotins, Girondins, Cordeliers, Feuillants, Dantonists, Hebertists, and so on—are an excellent example.[19]

Fission itself can arise from a bewildering number of social processes: division of labor (Durkheim), exacerbation of contradictions (Marx), schismogenesis (Bateson), and so on. The central empirical question concerns the conditions under which such division produces self-similarity rather than, say, mere segmentalism or completely nonparallel structures. Clearly self-similarity requires the survival of several "layers" of such divisions into a single coincident present. Mere differentiation, for example, simply leaves a finer and finer social structure. But if earlier, less finely divided structures survive into a present that also contains later division, we begin to see self-similarity.

This theme of survival leads into a second general historical process producing self-similar structures: ossification or, in the usual sociological word, institutionalization, a process well illustrated by the various councils and courts of the English kings. The Plantagenets had councils of personal advisors. Some of these, of course, had to actually run the affairs of state while the kings were fighting or enjoying themselves. By the time of the first Tudor king, the king's council had already split into a large body of senior administrators and a smaller executive committee of central advisors, including the chancellor, treasurer, and lord privy seal. The latter group formed the nucleus of the Privy Council, an advisory body within the larger council. Under Elizabeth I even the Privy Council had become large; governance moved into the hands of *its* executive committee. (The chancellor, for example, was by this time purely a legal official, having once been the king's chief administrative deputy.) Under James I, membership in the Privy Council itself had become completely honorific; numerous standing committees within it actually conducted the business of state. But since none of the earlier bodies had been abolished, there existed under the earlier Stuarts (and has later expanded) a series of concentric, self-similar advisory bodies conserving the whole history of advice to the throne.[20]

In the modern era, cost acounting provides a similar example. Cost accounting began around the turn of this century because ear-

---

19. See Cobban 1957:200–241.
20. On the earlier Tudors, see Mackie 1952:202 ff., 435 ff. On Elizabeth's council, see Black 1959:207–10. On the earlier Stuarts, see Davies 1959:30–31. The ossification of the Court of Chancery—which was first founded to provide flexible, equity-based justice—was proverbial by the time Dickens skewered it in *Bleak House.*

lier means of internal record keeping were cumbersome or routinized. For several decades cost accounting provided much more accurate and useful figures about business management. By the late twentieth century, cost accounts were themselves so ossified and rule driven that manufacturers began seeking new vehicles for realistic shop floor information. Yet the earlier systems persisted, since it is generally easier to leave them than uproot them. Note that ossification generally produces unbalanced systems.[21]

Analogous to ossification is capture. We see this in regulatory systems. Various American commissions were created to regulate certain industries in the name of the people. But they were then typically "captured" by the very industries they were to regulate, for those industries provided expertise the would-be regulators lacked. Once captured, however, these very regulatory commissions had themselves to be "regulated" by committees of Congress and offices in the executive department. A two-layer self-similar structure of regulation resulted.[22]

Another producer of unbalanced self-similar structures is fractionation, discussed in chapters 1 and 3. Fractionation is an unbalanced fission in which only one part of a self-similar structure maps itself down to the next level. In fractionation within the fractal dichotomies discussed in chapter 1, for example, only one side splits at each generation. The result is a proliferation of extremal viewpoints, more or less ordered. In the case of the French Revolution, while division continued in all parts of the political spectrum, power tended to flow toward the extreme factions, at least until the Terror.

Fractionation can be seen as ossification in reverse, ossification viewed from the strategic side rather than the ossifying one. The force driving fractionation is the need to breathe new life into a distinction that has lost it. In the various left politics examples, this force is the need to re-create a "true left," when there have become too many false or flabby ones. In the case of deviance in communes, it is to re-create the deviance necessary to a rhetoric of guilt and redemption within a community that has given up the usual forms of deviance. In credential inflation (another familiar example), it is to rebuild distinctions that have been undermined by the gaming activities of those who gave grades or wrote letters implying that all of their students were terrific. In all these cases, we see the production of unbalanced self-similar structures because earlier versions

---

21. On cost accounting early in this century see Abbott 1988a:230–33.
22. An early argument concerning regulatory capture was Bernstein 1955.

have lost their ability to accomplish social functions that had been
assigned to them.

There are a number of similar processes of seeming infinite regression that result in self-similar systems. Insurance systems are
one, with their infinite regress of guarantees. Thus, to take a homely
example, up until the early 1980s, home buyers did their own in-
spections, insofar as they were able and interested, of properties
they were about to purchase. But this proved too risky, so home inspectors emerged. (I'm not clear why this should have happened
then rather than earlier, but that's beside the point for my example.)
But of course the unscrupulous and the incompetent got into the
home inspector business, so there had to be licensing and certifica-
tion of home inspectors—that is, insurance for the insurance provided by an inspection. Undoubtedly, as with many professions, this
move toward "guaranty" was itself a business strategy, and hence
the public needed yet another level of policing to get around it. Thus
we have structure produced by a sort of infinite regress of trust-
generating mechanisms. Such regress structures are common. Sub-
contracting relationships—themselves often nested deeply in a
self-similar structure—are subject to similar sorts of policing
requirements.

Similar regress structures arise from "creaming" processes. Thus,
in areas like debt collection, the credit card companies cream the
easy credit risks and sell collection rights on the bad debt to leaner
and meaner organizations that can survive at lower collection rates.
These squeeze as hard as they can, then sell to yet another level, and
so on. Creaming processes operate in the social services sector as
well. The easier community services (the more common and easily
served ones) are provided by large scale agencies, leaving the more
specialized and difficult services to smaller, more specialized, and
more ephemeral agencies.[23]

One of the great examples of this ossification-fractionation process is of course the Christian Church. At the Church's center are
processes of drift and differentiation that built two major strands of
catholicism, but around those two stand dozens of reformist movements like the one we call Protestantism. And reforms against the
reforms: against the (reformist) Church of England, for example,
both the Oxford Movement (toward Roman Catholicism) and Meth-

---

23. I owe the debt example to my graduate school classmate William Brandt Jr.,
who currently serves, among other things, as a master in bankruptcy. The social service example comes from my own experience with United Way. Creaming is of course
related to free riding, which also can produce infinite regress. A large literature ad-
dresses the problem of policing free riders.

odism (toward evangelicalism). And indeed we also see reforms inside the catholic tradition against all these external "reforms" (the Counter-Reformation, later movements like Opus Dei) and so on and on. As a result, the words "catholic" and "protestant" are very nearly indexical expressions, despite their supposedly firm definition in American social science. As for fractionation, the various anabaptist communities provide perhaps the very best examples— the concentric varieties of Amish and Hutterites. The endless dialogue of institutionalization, reform, and fractionation has produced in Christianity a whole host of self-similar organizations, all of which see themselves as wildly different, but which are produced by a set of fairly simple self-similarity-inducing processes.[24]

We see fractionation also in simple processes like credential inflation, just mentioned. At the turn of the century, high school degrees carried significant worth. So everyone tried to get one in order to achieve comparative advantage. As a result, high school degrees lost their differentiating capacity, which passed on to college degrees. The same process is now replacing college degrees with graduate ones. Note that we still get *all* of these credentials and that the content of material taught has not expanded equivalently (nor has the material learned—students learn in college today things that were learned in high school years ago). Like the councils of the English kings our degrees embody a history of credentialing institutionalization and renewal.

There are, then, several potential mechanisms producing self-similar social structures: design, fission, fractionation, ossification. These mechanisms may involve various contents. And the repeated unit in them can take a variety of shapes. The origins of self-similarity are complex indeed.

5. Individuals in Self-Similar Social Structures

We must now consider the way the individual parts of a self-similar structure interact. For this interactional structure is in many ways what makes self-similarity so important. Self-similarity has two broad kinds of consequences for the individual; some of these concern the individual's understanding of his own experience; others concern communciation with others.

Let me begin with hierarchy, the most familiar example of a self-

24. The splitting of the various Christian churches can be followed through any standard source. Doctrinally, the best source is Pelikan 1971–89. Liturgically, the classical source on Christian divisions is Dix 1945. On the American anabaptists, see Hostetler 1993:25–49, 280–99.

similar social structure. The consequence of self-similarity for individuals in hierarchical structures is to place many of them in what we can call fractal role conflicts. For example, people who are low in highly placed units and people who are high in lowly placed units experience a particular kind of conflict. The problems of these individuals are a byword in social science. One line of argument emphasizes their tendency to pass on abuse and problems: the boss who passes on her own boss's rage to her subordinates, the activist who turns another's criticism of himself onto some one still less active. Another line of argument emphasizes the obsession of such conflicted individuals with status: medical students conflicting with senior nurses, senior professors dominating at minor universities, the black bourgeosie's tortured relations with "white trash," and so on. Such individuals are, to a certain extent, free to choose "which way to look"; whether to emphasize their highness vis-à-vis those below or their lowness vis-à-vis those above. In social scales like the stratification scale that behave in this concentric, self-similar fashion, individuals often look both ways, but with different ideologies; one attributes one's highness to one's own hard work and one's lowness to oppression from above. As this example suggests, fractal role conflict is endemic in so-called achievement societies. In societies where individual status is given by ascription, such conflict may be lessened, since individuals are absolved of responsibility for their own status. But the example of the black bourgeoisie—or that of the harijans—implies that this is by no means necessary.[25]

With respect to interaction with others, the fundamental consequence of self-similarity for individuals is that they find themselves in "similar positions" with people who are in most ways very different from them. The second lieutenant and the private both share the experience of being at the bottom of a large structure, even though they differ immensely in income, status, education, and, of course, direct power. The "deviant" of the religious commune— whose "sin" has been to ask for shampoo from the commissary in a voice deemed too demanding—shares the experience of sin with the lapsed Catholic whose misfortunes have reawakened her faith, even though the entire world of this layperson is sinful in eyes of the communard. The scientist who narrowly misses the Nobel Prize shares the experience of failure with the scientist who doesn't get

---

25. "White trash" provides an interesting example of a status fractal that has been reinterpreted. Originally the term began as an insult blacks used for low-status whites (it dates from the nineteenth century). But in the last twenty years it has been adopted as a positive cultural image. See Otter 1998.

tenure, even though the achievements of the one far outshine those of the other.

As we shall see below, there is no guarantee that these "common" experiences will be shared equally. They may become the basis of coerced communication or miscommunication. But they produce *some* sharing because of the indexicality of social structure. When the second lieutenant and the private share a moment of grumbling together about their superiors, both can agree to bracket the overall distribution of authority that makes many of the private's superiors inferior to the lieutenant.[26]

This indexicality means that interactions both numerous and substantial can take place in a self-similar structure between people whose positions are "objectively" quite different. Those interactions may require quite conscious bracketing of visible differences. Or conversely they may take place without interactants' being aware of the differences at all. What matters is that they crosscut the visible arrangements of the structure with interlevel ties, ties that bypass the normal relations that define position in the structure.

These communication possibilities of self-similarity are not by any means inherently free. An excellent example of the nexus of coerced communication, mixed communication, and indexicality in a self-similar social structure comes again from the French Revolution. Old Regime French society was a complicated system of classes and orders hierarchically nested at dozens of levels. The fundamental ideas of the revolution concerned the "rights of the people." To the aristocrats, this (indexical) phrase meant the authority of the First and Second Estates as against that of the centralizing monarchy. To the Third Estate, the same phrase meant the privileges of property and substance against a taxing monarchy and against the untaxed class of nobles and clergy. To the mass of the French, it meant affordable food irrespective of the wishes of king, nobles, clergy, or Third Estate. Each group, that is, drew two lines—one above itself, one (where possible) below. The line below distinguished "real people" or "good citizens" from "mass" or "rabble." The line above distinguished the "oppressors" from the "oppressed." In all cases these lines were drawn with the same rhetoric; but to the various concentric groups, they meant quite different things.[27]

Of course, the historical outcome reflected the actual locus of

26. And of course we don't know the meaning of weak or strong agreement or disagreement with the statement "we do have enough money for our basic needs" until we know where the respondent is located in terms of wealth.

27. See Cobban 1957.

power. The aristocrats began the revolution by undermining the royal finances and forcing the convocation of the Estates General. The Third Estate seized the revolution when the nobles and clergy refused to accept their leadership and dominance. The mass dictated much of the revolution as the chief allies of the Jacobin clubs, but ultimately failed when an internal squabble left them leaderless. This case illustrates a number of important aspects of self-similarity. Most important, it is ultimately a matter of power who defines the "appropriate" level within a long, graded set of self-similar structures. In this case, it was ultimately the middle class that defined whose rights were really meant by the indexical phrase "rights of man."

At the personal level, an interaction between fractally similar individuals begins with a phase of "parameter setting," in which it is decided at what level the indexical terms will be defined. This is most easily seen in the case of self-similar ranking scales. There the "proper parameterization" is posed by one speaker. In a political discussion, for example, an initial speaker may complete a statement like "I'm a conservative" with remarks like "I think insurance should be deregulated" or "I think we should abolish Social Security and workmen's compensation." Clearly, these two alternative completions suggest quite different levels of conservativism, and a listening conservative, having located himself relative to the speaker, may choose to contest the general parameterization by contesting the implied definition of "conservative." Or he may accept the overall implied level of conservatism and argue the details of content. Or he may "fake" acceptance and engage in the discussion as if accepting the implied level, but in fact rejecting it. In the first case, both parties are forced to recognize the indexicality of the word "conservative" and to acknowledge their own different positions. In the second, the two are similar enough to avoid worrying about indexicality. In the third, only the listener is aware of the differences. Thus, while the dominant interactant has the option of defining the level at which a fractal scale is seen to be anchored, the nondominant usually has the equally powerful option of maintaining a metastance outside the interaction altogether. There is thus a curious asymmetry in self-similar interaction, one that grants different kinds of powers to the two interactants.

Second, within a hierarchical self-similar system interaction between fractally similar individuals puts superior and subordinate in markedly different positions, irrespective of who is the dominant interactant. The superior often enjoys a pleasant feeling of condescension, sometimes even forgetting the objective state of affairs, while the inferior always remembers that state of affairs quite clearly. In the French Revolution, a number of liberal French nobles paid for this condescension with their heads. And it is against the dangers of such condescension that the military promulgates its rules against "fraternizing with the enlisted men" and separates the on-post leisure clubs of the various ranks (down to the point of having separate clubs for the three private ranks). The inferior person always remains much more aware of the bilevel character of the interaction—the mixture of a fractal similarity with "objective" inequality. This fact is of course one of the staples of the current literatures on oppression. Yet it is undercut to some extent by the fact that oppression is itself usually organized self-similarly, in many levels, rather than in the vast horizontal units theorized by Marx. Most of the oppressed find subordinates of their own to oppress.[28]

The endemic indexicality of self-similar systems gives rise to an enormous potential for miscommunication. In the French Revolution, the obvious example of this is the complete misunderstanding between the First and Second Estates and the Third on the question of whose rights were at stake. Miscommunication—often so great as to produce rage and terror—arises in several ways. It may arise, as we have seen, because individuals who differ on some self-similar scale mistake their differences because of the indexicality of their statements. Two spouses may mean utterly different things by the phrase "I would like some time to myself" yet may repeat such routine phrases to each other for years before one spouse discovers that the other has felt completely trapped by a togetherness that seems just right to the first. Miscommunication can also arise because one interactant is aware of these differences but conceals them.

The impact of self-similarity on the individual is thus complex. For many it is a source of role conflict, for they can see themselves as high, middle, or low depending on what part of the structure they attend to. It also has a profound impact on communication. On the one hand it facilitates communication between quite different levels of people. On the other it provides extensive opportunities for miscommunication, both unintentional and intentional, and for the exercise of certain kinds of interactional power.

Most of the examples I have used here concern hierarchical systems, which, as I have noted, are only one of the broad classes of self-similar social structures. An interesting nonhierarchical ex-

---

28. As many feminists argued against Marxists in the 1980s, holding that the labor movement had oppressed women in important ways (see, e.g., Gabin 1990). Similar arguments were made about the racism of unions (see, e.g., Hirsch 1990 and various papers in *New Politics* 1, no. 3 [1987]).

ample comes from sociology itself. Disciplinewide, there is a theory community specializing in a body of material called sociological theory. But within many subdisciplines are smaller groups, each of which serves as a theory community for its subdiscipline. Organization theory, for example, is part of the organizations community, not part of the theory community. Sometimes, as in the sociologies of organization or science or gender, this situation arises because the subdiscipline has strong connections outside sociology. At other times, as in the sociology of professions or the family, it follows simply because of discipline-internal self-similarity. The whole situation is a classic example of fractal social structure.

The interactional relation of the "local" theory communities to the disciplinewide one is in fact quite awkward. The disciplinewide theory community focuses on works, both classic and modern, with relatively few empirical implications and relatively little connection with data. The local theory communities by contrast grow directly out of empirical work. The citations of the former are to other general theories, those of the latter to other local theories. The classical literatures of the two are somewhat similar, since everyone looks back to the same turn-of-the-century greats. But the later major figures of the general theorists are recent general theorists like Habermas while those of the local theorists are specialized theorists like John Meyer or Eliot Freidson or Manuel Castells. There is surprisingly little exchange between the two levels, and indeed hybrids—a "structuration" theory of organizations or a "garbage can" theory of social life in general—are occasionally proposed but never go very far. (The most common examples are hybrids "down"—Giddensian organization theory, for example. Such views are usually proposed by ambitious juniors.) Nor do careers traverse the divide. Few indeed are those who have moved from local communities to the general one; the reverse move is almost inconceivable.

We find within this relation many of the same potentialities for communication and miscommunication that we saw in the hierarchical case. The word "theory," for example, means markedly different things in the two settings. So discussion between them often proceeds at complete cross-purposes. Much of this miscommunication reflects the different criteria used by the two, the general theorists looking for consilience with other general theory (or, more commonly, with particular philosophical positions), the local theorists looking for ability to comprehend large bodies of local facts. Indeed, the somewhat hopeful picture that emerged above of interaction between individuals in self-similar structures seems considerably darkened by the case of theory in sociology. In many cases, self-similarity provides possibilities for identification and sharing across widely separated units of social structure. That has not been the result with sociological theory.[29]

6. Solidarity: Social Consequences of Self-Similarity

Yet self-similarity does seem to have important solidaristic consequences. Two things, Durkheim argues, hold social groups together; resemblance and mutual dependence. This dual approach to solidarity has ancient roots. Indeed, Durkheim quoted Aristotle's dictum on the subject (*Politics* ii.1.1261a24) on the title page of *The Division of Labor*. And current theory and research often follow the Durkheimian lead as well. Studies of working-class formation, for example, emphasize both the resemblances induced by the "great transformation" and the exchange of variegated support among working-class groups. Studies of developing professions emphasize both the common careers of individual professionals and the interdependence born of specialization.

Over the years, a number of modifications in Durkheim's model have been suggested. Perhaps the most thoroughgoing is that arising among network analysts. Early forms of network analysis emphasized actual connections as the basis for social groups, an approach that falls under Durkheim's second major category, the organic solidarity of mutual dependence. Among network analysts, the interdependence has not always signified exchange of different, mutually beneficial goods, as in the division of labor. Rather, interdependence has most often meant exchange of like things: political support, money, friendship, and so on. More recently, network analysis has emphasized a different concept of connection, structural equivalence. Structural equivalence combines both of Durkheim's solidarities, resemblance and mutuality. Individuals are structurally equivalent who have *similar* patterns of *ties* to others. They resemble one another, that is, in their patterns of organic solidarity.[30]

The solidarity arising out of self-similarity is essentially a weaker and hence broader version of structural equivalence. Individuals are solidary, as we have seen above, if they have similar relational patterns to others, where "similar" means merely similar in shape, not necessarily in scale. In a bureaucracy, for example, this solidarity affects everyone who has both a superior and subordinates. Only those at the very bottom (who do not supervise at all) and those

---

29. The concept of consilience comes from William Whewell. See Whewell 1989.
30. The classic work on structural equivalence is Lorrain and White 1971.

at the very top (who have no superiors) are uninvolved. Where the repeating unit is functionally differentiated, individuals (groups) with equivalent functional positions are solidary; the people selling a firm's products to outsiders are solidary with those selling internal technical services to its line divisions and so on. Clearly this is a weaker form of solidarity than Durkheim's classical two, for it links people who often have little direct relation to one another and, among those who do, is often overwhelmed by objective differences in level.[31]

But in a larger sense, this solidarity is extremely important. It is, for example, at the heart of viewers' identifications with television characters, as it is of readers' identifications with fictional characters. Therefore it plays a fundamental role in modern societies. The viewer of a television situation comedy or soap opera enjoys the show and accepts its various ideologies because he is able to find similarities between characters' lives and his own. Often these are not similarities of content at all, but similarities of form or shape: similarities in the valence of family relations, work relations, in the balance between desires and rewards. Indeed, as the "wealth shows" illustrate, often these formal similarities serve as vehicles for wish fulfilment in terms of content. Thus, from a critical point of view, the solidary force of self-similarity can be manipulated to make people content with oppressive circumstances.

Perhaps more important, this mechanism underlies the impact of media on politics. When politics lacked mass media, several layers of self-similar communication structures intervened between national leaders and the public. Local representatives heard the many complaints and discussed, acted on, and compromised on them with other local representatives. Above them sat party leaders for whom these local representatives were in turn the equivalent of a public constituency, and above them still stood the actual leadership cadre. By the time issues reached the top they had been reshaped by several levels of compromise. At each sucessive level participants knew, from their own experience with those above and below them, that compromise and restructuring were necessary. When this system is shortcut by fireside chats and their descendants, the potentialities of politics are completely reshaped. Following the lure of self-

---

31. An interesting negative example of self-similarity is provided by the American Civil War. Several writers have noted the self-similar phenomenon that the South split from the Union over the issue of states' rights and that the Confederacy itself then fell apart, as a government, over precisely the same issue. It was hard to create an effective confederation when you were revolting against the idea of federalism. See Stokesbury 1995.

similarity and microcosm, voters are led to think that running a national economy is analogous to balancing their checkbooks.

There is thus some significant reason to think self-similar solidarity of importance. It supplements the classical Durkheimian solidarities. More important, at times when communication becomes suddenly common across varying subcultures and social structural units, such solidarity plays a crucial role. We are entering such a period at present. It should be clear why places and times of suddenly increased communication make self-similar solidarity more important. For what communication accomplishes is to bring into contact similar parts of structures that may not have been in contact before. So imperialism, for example, hinges often on aligning metropolitan elites and local elites. The strength of imperialism as a social form lies precisely in its taking advantage of concentric similar forms. The emergence of team-based organization in the advanced commercial sector is another example. Contemporary technology firms are organized in large, self-similar team structures charged with accomplishing massive projects. General project functions like process integration and project management have whole departments dedicated to them, but portions of those responsibilities are then parceled out to smaller groups and even individuals. These groups and individuals are as likely as not to be formally located outside those departments. The entire structure floats free of the official management hierarchy and requires intensive communication between similar parts of the project structure both in the nesting direction (up and down) and between parallel units.

Both of these examples illustrate the fluctuation of self-similar solidarity with communication. One of the most familiar facts of modern commnications experience is the use of personal forms of address in impersonal situations. This too is an invocation of self-similarity, a punning on social structure that brings first names and familiarity into larger and more public spaces, making the claim that they are identical with the private and small.

There is then ample reason to take self-similarity seriously not only in cultural systems, but also in social structures. Important parts of social structure are dominated by self-similarity, which brings with it forms of solidarity and interaction that have systematic consequences for social systems. Once we understand the basic properties of self-similar systems we can begin to see how and when they shape or even dominate more traditionally imagined kinds of structures. This fruitful concept also proves helpful in thinking about moral dilemmas in social science, as I argue in the next chapter.

APPENDIX
Fractal Scales

In 1996, *U.S. News and World Report* cited a survey of university professors finding that 94 percent of them thought they were better at their jobs than their average colleague. We are all above average. A similar finding is that only 10 percent of Americans think they are in the upper or lower class, the remaining 90 percent locating themselves in the working or middle class. We are all average.[32] Why are we all both average and above average?

A simple view is that desire clouds judgment. In a professional group where excellence is valued, members want to think themselves excellent. In a society obsessed with equality, members want to think themselves equal. In both cases, people perceive themselves favorably with respect to certain core values.

Such shifts are obviously consequential for social scientists because value-laden cognitive maps shape many forms of social scientific data. However, such shifts actually seem to be examples of a much broader category, one of "shifts toward familiarity." As psychologists and cognitive mappers have often argued, people's perceptions tend to emphasize the familiar over the unfamiliar. But perhaps all these examples in fact proceed from the habit of thinking with fractal patterns.[33]

Suppose we tend to judge social situations by finding a relevant fractal generator, deciding a level of application for it, and then making a judgment. When we say, then, that "nurses are not of high status," or "Hispanics are oppressed," we start with a concept of high and low status or a concept of domination and oppression, then decide a zone of relevance, and then finally apply the distinction. But our interlocutors—be they questionnaires or interviewers—do not really know what our statements mean until they know for sure what the range of comparison we chose was. One who knows the full status systems involved might guess that we are comparing nurses to doctors rather than janitors, and Spanish-speakers to whites rather than blacks. But in general, even if our interlocutors believe in such a "true" scale (as social scientists think they do), they cannot tell whether our judgment that "nurses are not of high status" conveys information about the true comparison or simply about the range of our own comparison set. It is as if we had really said "nurses are near the bottom of whatever comparison set I happen to have chosen."

In interaction, most comparative judgments are like these. They are partial judgments comparing particular pairs. As I have noted, they are always indexical judgments, because we need the comparison zone or reference

---

32. On being above average, see Whitman 1996:26. The finding about middle-classness is generally known, but see the useful discussion of the confusions of class terminology in Evans, Kelley, and Kolosi 1992.

33. The argument made here is a mainstay of literature in cognitive psychology. The effect is referred to variously, under such terms as outgroup homogeneity or availability heuristic.

categories to know what is actually being asserted. Yet it is worth asking what map of social space is implicit in such judgments. I shall therefore take up a single example for which a fractal perception model seems appropriate, and then investigate its methodological and substantive implications. Consider an example familar to most social scientists, occupational classification. Figure A6.1 contains a selected portion of the new Standard Occupational Classification system promulgated for use in government agencies in 1998. I have included four of the twenty-three general headings, and under each of them have included two randomly chosen subcategories, and under each of them two randomly chosen detailed occupations. (There is actually a fourth intervening level, but I have collapsed it here.) Again, bear in mind that this is a tiny fraction of a huge classification system.[34]

In general workers themselves know only a small portion of this system. And in fact they will tend to make many more distinctions in the part of the system close to them than further away. Actuaries know very well that they are different from statisticians, but they may be hazy indeed about the difference between accountants and budget analysts or the difference between machine tool operators and machinists. By contrast, the machinists know very well that they are not machine tool operators, but may not make any serious distinction between accountants and budget analysts, or perhaps even between the higher-level categories of business operations workers and financial specialists.

We can formalize this notion in the idea of "tree distance." Suppose that we think of the distance between two places in this classification system as the number of hierarchical steps required to go from one place to another in it. So for barbers, say, one step takes them just to the general category above them—personal appearance workers. We might think of this as meaning that at one step, barbers are aware that there are other kinds of personal appearance workers. Two steps take barbers to manicurists (up to personal appearance workers then back down to manicurists—that is, the barber now distinguishes *types* of other personal appearance workers) as well as up to the more general heading of personal care workers (two steps up—that is, by this distance the barber is aware that there are other kinds of personal care workers than personal appearance workers). Three steps take the barbers to other personal care workers (two up to personal care workers, then one back down to other personal care workers) as well as to the (implicit) general node under which the four broad classes are located.

By distance 4, the barber will be distinguishing the four general classes of occupations as well as all the particular occupations within the personal care class. By distance 5, the barber will distinguish the subcategories within the four general classes, and by distance 6, all sixteen detailed level occupations. Now suppose we ask barbers how many different kinds of occupation there are, making the assumption that reaching a general heading can be thought of as knowing that there are others under it besides those in

---

34. The argument to be made here is much like that of Evans-Pritchard 1970:200–203, for lineage distance.

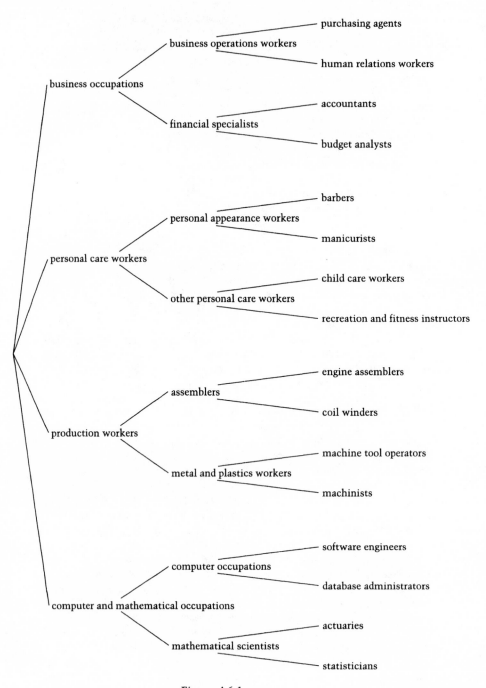

Figure A6.1

"one's own lineage." At distance 1, barbers think there are three occupations: barbers, other personal appearance workers, and others. At various distances, and omitting general categories when their subcategories are known, barbers recognize:

distance 2, four occupations: barbers, manicurists, personal care workers, others

distance 3, four occupations: barbers, manicurists, other personal care workers, others

distance 4, seven occupations: barbers, manicurists, child care workers, recreation and fitness instructors, business occupations, production workers, computer and mathematical workers

distance 5, ten occupations: barbers, manicurists, business operations workers, financial specialists, child care workers, recreation and fitness instructors, assemblers, metal and plastics workers, computer occupations, mathematical scientists

There are, of course, many other ways to assess tree distance and many other trees distinguishing occupations in other ways. But they all imply that on the assumption of limited, tree-structured knowledge, each individual will produce a vastly foreshortened view of the whole system. This will make the foreground very large, wherever it is in the system, and the background quite small. The general result will be, for each individual, a type of distortion familiar from the previously mentioned New Yorker's map of the United States with its huge Manhattan and foreshortened heartland. The same pattern—for occupations rather than cities—appears in the fractal classification system we have just seen. People make many distinctions close to themselves and few far away.

The New York map, however, has a particular dimensionality, which my example here does not. But suppose we return to the case of occupational prestige, considered earlier, and consider tree distance as a means of judging prestige. Suppose, that is, that there is an underlying prestige ordering of these occupations, but that no single individual knows it fully because no one has enough tree knowledge to get down to the details. And suppose that individuals assign prestige to occupations linearly, but only to the extent of their own knowledge. That is, they behave as if they all made New Yorkers' (or Chicagoans' or Angelenos') maps and then regarded the distances on those maps as the real ones.[35]

---

35. Of course the average worker doesn't have such a map lying around. My argument is that it is implicit in the structure of the fractal reasoning used to produce distinctions among occupations. In practice, individual judgments about occupations in natural interaction are produced as necessary by invoking the fractal system to the extent needed and employing a zone of comparison *defined by the interaction*. It is only sociologists who ask respondents to come up with systematic, structured responses. Two graduates of Ivy League universities who meet in conversation will argue about the relative merits of their alma maters. That fact that these institutions are more or less indistinguishable to 90 percent of the college-going population is irrelevant to them. By contrast, two graduates of, say, Princeton and Michigan will argue about a broader zone of the classification system. In fact, one might venture

If this position is correct, there follow distinct methodological implications. It is customary in social science to ask people ranking questions without specifying any zone of comparison. Yet to the extent that the responses are generated by the mechanism here proposed, we don't know what the respondent has actually told us until we know that context of comparison. But we never ask for this. As a result, variation in ranges of comparison contributes much variability to such rating scales. It does not bias those results, since effects are symmetrical about the midpoint (at least in this model), but it does contribute enormous and quite systematic variability. People may well agree a good deal more on rating scales than they appear to. What makes the disagreements appear large is that people do not bother to store information on an entire rating structure. Rather they store the structure in the guise of a single fractal pattern that they use to regenerate the structure as necessary. In fact, work on perception of occupational status has shown distinct effects of the kind predicted by this model.[36]

The implications of this process of fractal cognition are not simply methodological, however. They are also substantive. Consider again the system that gives rise to a New Yorker's map and what happens when New Yorkers' maps interact with Chicagoans' maps or Angelenos' maps. I again consider a one-dimensional system for simplicity's sake. Assume that there are 101 individuals uniquely located on a status scale, spread out evenly over the points from 0 to 100. (Such an underlying reality undoubtedly does not exist for any ranking, but assuming it is useful to demonstrate the consequences of fractal distinctions for interaction.) Each individual gives us *his* New Yorker's view of the ratings, expanding his foreground and squeezing his background. Rather than going through the laborious process of generating

---

the prediction that in interaction the zone of fractal comparison is often chosen strategically. To make all participants feel good, one invokes comparisons wide enough to put them all in the top categories. To be aggressive, one chooses a zone locating one's interlocutor as low as possible. What matters is by no means the absolute level—were any such thing to exist—but rather the fractal structure of the comparison.

The argument made here is somewhat like the model proposed by Evans, Kelley, and Kolosi (1992). They were more interested in beliefs about egalitarianism, arguing that respondents would envision a class system and then locate themselves in it, whereas I am more interested in the general effects of the perceptual mechanism itself and therefore do not consider beliefs about the shape of class. My central interest here is providing a motivation (via the fractal theory) for the observed fact of foreshortening.

36. Reiss 1961, chap. 8; Coxon and Jones 1978:53 ff. Even the classic Hodge, Siegel, and Rossi 1966 (see, e.g., table 2) contains some evidence of the shifts predicted here. Evans, Kelley, and Kolosi 1992:472–73 presents strong evidence for them, although, as I noted, without the same theoretical motivation. For elegant examples from an earlier tradition of class analysis, see Davis, Gardner, and Gardner 1941:65 and Dahl 1961:29. Beyond the class analysis area findings of such foreshortening are common throughout sociology, e.g., Hummon's (1990) finding that "urbanists" think towns of ten thousand are no different from rural hamlets and that rural residents think towns of ten thousand no different from major urban aggregations.

this with fractals I use a simple symmetric formula, which approximates the fractal result continuously.[37]

Figure A6.2 illustrates four such views. The positions of the four raters—at points 10, 20, 30, and 40 along the original scale—are shown by letters along the ruler at the bottom, which shows the entire scale from left to right in its original, regular spacing. In the upper array, each horizontal line represents the scale as viewed by one individual. The *order* of rated positions is exactly the same in all four rows; but each individual has spread the scale close to him and squeezed it far away. I have then rescaled the resulting modified scales so that they all take up the same space (the "whole space" of the status system). Each individual's new view of his own position is marked on the horizontal line by a circle; note that it has shifted from the position on the bottom scale. The vertical lines between adjacent scales connect similar positions; that is, they show where each of the 101 rated persons on one scale is located on the adjacent scale. (For simplicity, only the lines between adjacent individuals in the original list of four are shown.) Thus the vertical line at the left connects all the 0s and that at the right all the 100s. (These coincide tautologically; each person rates the "whole system" and one "whole" must equal another.) The slanted lines connect equivalent positions as rated by the four raters. Figure A6.3 shows individuals with slightly stronger "spreading" parameters around themselves.

A number of conclusions leap out from these diagrams. The first and most obvious is that people move themselves toward the middle of the scale. There is a simple reason. The fractal argument says that people expand the status intervals near them relative to those far away and do so in a symmetrical fashion. Because of the symmetry, we can match intervals in

---

37. There is no particular importance to the function used to do this. I have used the function:

$$N(i) \ = \ \frac{1}{\left| i - o \right|^{x}}$$

where

        o is the scale point of the individual
        i is an index running from o to the edge of the scale
        x is a parameter influencing the "degree of spread"
        $N(i)$ is a factor by which the given distance $\left| i - o \right|$ is expanded.

We create a spread scale by making the distance between the ith and $(i + 1)$th individuals equal the difference between the ith and $(i + 1)$th members of this series. (Note that we have to do this to both ends of the scale, both above and below the individual.) Since these distances *do not necessarily* sum to 100, we add them and rescale. Since the transformation given is extremely powerful, even for very small x, we allow for a constant term in the sum.

$$\text{Sum} \ = \ \sum \left[\text{dis}(i) + y \right]$$

The rescaling is then simply accomplished by multiplying each distance unit by 100/Sum. The parameters in figure A6.2 are $x = .01$ and $y = .001$. Figure A6.3 presents the same four individuals with the parameters $x = .01$ and $y = .01$.

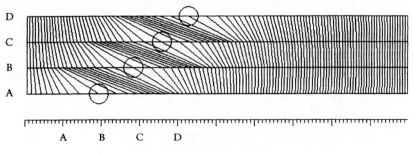

Figure A6.2

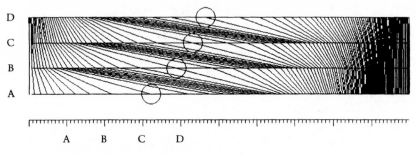

Figure A6.3

either direction as we move out from the individual toward the edges. But we reach the endpoint first on one side (call it the "short side"—this is the side to which the individual "really is closer"). But when the short side is thus exhausted, there are still many more intervals—smaller ones—to come on the "long side." Thus the *average* interval width on the long side is less, with the consequence that individuals move themselves to the middle. This simple model, then, explains the old saw that everyone in the United States thinks she is middle class. In figure A6.2, a 10th-percentile individual sees herself at the 19th percentile and a 90th-percentile person sees herself at the 81st percentile.

A corollary of this first conclusion is that the movement to the middle grows more and more pronounced as the spreading of intervals around oneself increases. The stronger the "New Yorkism," the more middle we all become. In figure A6.3, the spread factor is greater; the 10th-percentile individual moves herself to the 32nd percentile and the 90th-percentile individual moves herself to the 68th. A further corollary is that the effect is more pronounced at the edges. The middle person doesn't move herself at all, since the transformation is symmetrical. But as one looks from points of view further and further from the original center, small intervals are effectively subtracted on the short side and added on the long one, with a conse-

Table A6.1

| | | VIEWED | | | | | | |
| | | Figure A6.2 | | | | Figure A6.3 | | |
	10	20	30	40	10	20	30	40
VIEWERS								
10	19	39	49	57	32	66	74	80
20	9	28	48	57	8	39	70	79
30	8	17	36	55	5	13	43	74
40	7	15	24	43	4	9	17	47

All numbers refer to percentiles.

quently increasing disparity in average interval width on the two sides and consequently a greater shift to the middle.

Thus, we see that the idea that we store scales as fractal patterns accounts for several important facts. It accounts for the well-known shift through which everyone regards herself as middle class. It also predicts that such effects grow more and more pronounced as we move from the actual middle toward the edges. But this idea also makes some predictions about interaction. To see these, we must look at where individuals see each other. Table A6.1 shows these reciprocal views for figures A6.2 and A6.3, with viewers on the rows and the positions viewed on the columns. The main diagonals are thus self-judgments.

It is evident from the figures that the shift effects are most drastic near viewers themselves. Far-off statuses are relatively unshifted. The major disagreements between two individuals lie between them, a fact very clear in the figures. Even in figure A6.2 with its relatively mild shifts, an individual at the 20th percentile places the 30th-percentile individual at 48, while an individual at the 40th places the same person at 24. Yet they agree on the 10th-percentile individual, placing her at 7 and 9 respectively.[38]

This gives us the interesting and at least anecdotally correct prediction that individuals in interaction establish their general sense of social location by discussing distant reference points that they agree on and then settle down to disagreeing about issues in the foreground. Put another way, as-

---

38. A quote from Trollope captures this well:

The need of [a thick skin] in our national assembly is greater than elsewhere, because the differences between the men opposed to each other are smaller. When two foes meet in the same Chamber, one of whom advocates the personal government of an individual ruler, and the other that form of State, which has come to be called a red Republic, they deal, no doubt, weighty blows of oratory at one another, but blows which never hurt at the moment. They may cut each other's throats if they can find an opportunity; but they do not bite each other like dogs over a bone. But when opponents are almost in accord, as is always the case with our parliamentary gladiators, they are ever striving to give maddening little wounds through the joints of the harness. . . . It is the same in religion. The apostle of Christianity and the infidel can meet without a chance of a quarrel; but it is never safe to bring together two men who differ about a saint or a surplice. Trollope 1983, 1:296.

sessing the zone of agreement helps each individual figure out the location and "spread factor" of alter.

There are some regularities to these relative shifts. An individual tends to see himself as higher than those above him think he is and lower than those below him think he is. This too is an effect familiar to sociologists. It increases with the underlying distance between one individual and another; the higher individual B is relative to individual A, the more lower than A sees himself does B see him. Thus, in figure A6.3, the 40th-percentile person puts the 10th-percentile person at the 4th percentile, where the 20th-percentile person puts him at the 8th. The facts that we overestimate relative to those above and underestimate relative to those below are a pervasive source of miscommunications in status systems.

It is important to recall that these effects arise without any lèse-majesté or putting on of airs. I make no *differential* assumptions about individuals; they all behave in exactly the same simple and motivationally innocuous way. It is rather the structural combination of this between interactants that leads to a higher-standing person's judgment that a lower one is putting on airs and the lower one's judgment that the upper one doesn't know the extent of his good fortune.

Within triads, the principles are continuations of the foregoing. If one individual lies far away from the other two, they will agree about him but disagree about each other. Three closely grouped individuals will, in some sense, have the most to disagree about, even though their ratings of those far away will all be relatively conforming.

To return to methodological issues for a moment, we should note that the lowest Pearson correlation between the scales in figure A6.2 is 0.98; even in figure A6.3, the equivalent value is 0.93. (This is in part a function of where the individuals were to start with, but even if we located individuals at points 20 and 80 in figure A6.3, the correlation of their scale values would still be a massive 0.81.) These high correlations hide the very strong regularity of status *disagreement* in the model. It is therefore clear why scales of occupational prestige worldwide find such great agreement, even though there is immense debate about the details. Most of the correlation reflects constancy of gross order. But the high correlation masks spreading effects that are both regular and consequential. In the present scales there is much to disagree about, yet this is hidden because the exact preservation of order from scale to scale keeps the correlations high. If we were to combine fractal spreading with order perturbations, the correlation might fall considerably.

Such processes need not involve rating scales. Consider the example of tonsillectomy. A study in the *New England Journal of Medicine* in 1945 reported on a random sample of 1,000 New York City schoolchildren, of whom 61% had had tonsillectomies. The remainder ($n = 389$) were sent to a set of screening physicians, who said 174 of them (45%) needed tonsillectomies. The remaining 215 were then sent to another panel of physicians, who said 99 of them (46%) needed tonsillectomies. The remaining 116 were sent to still another panel of physicians, who recommended 51 (44%) of them for tonsillectomies. At that point, the study was ended for want of further panels of physicians. Here again we have a simple rule, applied fractally. Whatever population doctors saw, a little less than half of them seemed to need their tonsils out.[39]

The examples so far all involve deploying fractal distinctions under an assumption of "idle perception," a construing of our world when we are not particularly invested in our own location in that world. The alumni who forget about the distinctions between distant universities are only lazy, like the physicians working with a mere fractal rule of thumb. But as I have suggested, when we have a particular interest, we may choose zones of fractal comparison strategically. It is such an interest that causes 94 percent of faculty to think themselves above average. Such strategic use eventually causes shifts in the entire fractal system.

An interesting case is the move to finer and finer timing intervals in various sports. The historical rate at which records got broken had slowed considerably by 1980. The hundred-meter dash time of 9.9 stood for decades, for example. By moving the measurement to hundredths of a second, timers continued to feed the public a more steady diet of world record breaking.[40]

A simple example is grade inflation. A recent *Harvard Crimson* editorial complained that all students at Harvard *ought* to get A's for all their work[41] because, after all, they had gotten into Harvard. Here we see a deliberate argument *against* fractal comparison. On this account, the grade scale should be an absolute national one, such as the sociologists dream of for occupational prestige. The sheer plausibility of the argument—and the anguished howls of Harvard faculty—show how deeply we believe in fractal structures for our rating scales. For faculty, grades are a local differentiating structure, designed to motivate student performance, not a national comparison scale. The issue concerns the *range* of application of a fractal generator. Harvard students want a broad range, Harvard faculty a narrow one.

But when they write recommendation letters, such faculty become well aware of the broad range of fractal comparison. In their letters, all students become above average, indeed very many of them are said to be the best in several years. As a result, *readers* of recommendations themselves apply fractal *decoding* interpretations, making distinctions between layers and types of superlatives to try to retrieve the original local information hidden beneath the sales pitch. The point of credentials is to make oneself stand out, but the acquisition of credentials by everyone obviates this distinction. Hence new distinctions have to be made within a smaller space. In this case, the fractal levels are being made, then concealed, then rediscovered.

---

39. This delightful (hilarious?) paper is Bakwin 1945. I thank Bernice Pescosolido for bringing it to my attention.

40. Undoubtedly most of these records were produced, effectively, by moving of the measurement interval to within the error of instrumental measurement. Various forms of electronic timing were introduced to offset this effect. The point is that the rate of world record breaking is by no means proportionate to the increase in human running or swimming speed. Interestingly, however, the curve of world records for the mile run (across time) is indeed a straight line!

41. In practice, they all get A's and B's, according to J. B. Reiter (1993).

The overall result of this, of course, is credential inflation, because the encoders and decoders are playing a continual game to fool each other. We see such temporal transformation of meaning in many contexts. For example, the indexicality of self-similar scales can in fact be used for explicit political purposes. The ideology of contemporary feminism provides a good example. While one cannot maintain that late twentieth-century gender relations fit under the word "patriarchy" as that word would have been understood by the nineteenth century, or that modern gender relations aren't substantially more egalitarian than those of the nineteenth century, the use of the word "patriarchy" to describe the present situation, by implying that no change has taken place, can serve to mobilize discontent that otherwise would lose political force. To use the word is to reparameterize, to reset the level of a powerful comparative word while retaining its power. Or again, by no stretch of most people's imagination could the United States be considered either a fascist or a communist state. Yet there are those who have called it each, because in some ways the country might be analogized to communist countries (because it is in some respects a welfare state rather than a nineteenth-century free-trade state) and, on the other side, to fascist countries (because it has recently been willing to used armed force to disperse peaceful protest). Self-similarity can therefore serve as a powerful political tool.

This phenomenon of reparameterization is endemic in the cultural world. It might seem that it arises simply in the metaphorical nature of language. But in underlining the fractal nature of many of our conceptions, I am asserting something more than that they are metaphors or metonyms. Fractal distinctions have a number of characteristics that pure metaphors lack. The most important are their extraordinary scalability and parsimony. A fractal distinction captures an entire structural classification in a single figure.

7

The Selfishness
of Men

IN THIS final chapter I turn to moral questions. I do this partly because they pervade social science and partly out of a desire to push
the idea of self-similarity as far as I can.

Let me start with an example. Consider the statement that
"women are less selfish than men."[1] There is a sense in which this
statement is obviously true. That is, we can imagine asking male
and female survey respondents to tell us how often they do certain
behaviors and then having those behaviors rated for degree of
selfishness by independent judges. Or we can imagine field studies
getting information on the actual behaviors of men and women,
which we can then refer to an independently ranked scale of selfishness. And in both cases we can be pretty certain ahead of time that
women will come out looking less selfish than men.

Why should this be? Suppose we rule out biological accounts for
the moment, discussing the matter purely on the turf of the social
sciences. There, the quick answer involves cultural belief. On this
argument, there is a long-standing cultural ideology that women are
less selfish than men and hence the behaviors characteristic of
women have come to be labeled unselfish in the period since gender
roles diverged sharply in the mid–nineteenth century. Therefore, the
statement "women are less selfish than men" is true, but more be-

I dedicate this chapter, fumbling as it is, to the memory of Harry C. Bredemeier,
Professor of Sociology at Rutgers University, 1949–85. I wish he could read it.

1. It was Paula England who said this—without meaning much by it, I should
add—at a dinner in Washington's Adams-Morgan district after an ASA Publications
Committee Meeting in December 1994. I took issue with it and the whole committee
immediately got into an excited, friendly debate in which I was roundly worsted. I
thank my colleagues for both their fine committee work and their stimulating
conversation.

cause of an overarching cultural process of definition than because of an inherent difference.

Nonetheless, this account does accept the existence, at least in the present, of a real difference between the sexes. But do we want to accept the position that women "really are" less selfish than men? I do not. For it seems to me that selfishness is a morally defined category and I will not accept that any group or type of people has preferential access to any form of moral righteousness. Whites, blacks, Asians, men, women, gays, straights: they all have the same potential to be selfish or unselfish as far as I am concerned. It cannot be the case that women are less selfish than men. For to me that is saying "women are better than men," and I find such a statement morally reprehensible.

In this judgment, I am joined by many others. Not in the judgment that women cannot possibly be less selfish than men, but in the judgment that statements or states of affairs assigning an a priori inequality to certain categories of human beings are not morally acceptable. Many colleagues would, of course, put this presumption of equality to a different use. For them, women's selflessness is real, but is forced on them by an unequal gender role system. The locus of the "disturbing" inequality is thus the system of material rewards and social structure, not the individual actor conceived in what these colleagues would regard as an unjustifiably transcendent way. They see inequality, but judge it differently because they see it in a different place.

1. Politicians and Moralists

This difference is heightened by the usual language for denoting it, according to which my position is a "moral" one and that of my colleagues is a "political" one. (Because these words are common ones, I shall capitalize them throughout the rest of the chapter whenever I use them in my technical sense: hence, Moralists on the one hand, Politicians on the other.) In fact, both of us suffer from the same problem: an inability to keep judgments about the rightness of things separate from judgments of their actual nature. Among my colleagues the Politicians this inability appears as their quiet assumption that a particular state of affairs—substantive equality—is the natural state of human society. Often, such a belief is not perceived by its adherents as a value judgment at all, but rather exists in their minds as the simple presupposition that any deviation from equality requires explanation. (Cognitively, of course, there is no reason why this should be true.) At other times, to be sure, this Politi-

cal view is quite explicit. Historically, it derives from the Rousseau-
ian version of classical liberalism with its devout belief in an equal
state of nature.[2]

The Moral position on women's selflessness is only slightly different. It makes the same equality judgment, but seemingly a level
further down. No matter what inequalities exist in practice, it argues, no matter what the social positions in which people find themselves, they are everywhere equal in some absolute moral sense. All
have the potential for right action. This argument derives not from
classical liberalism, with its structureless state of nature, but rather
from Christianity, with its celebration of fishermen and tax collec-
tors and whores, its salvation for the downtrodden, its projection of
a world transcending inequality.[3]

In both cases, then, the question is one of mixing value judgments with scientific ones. Only the level and location of the mixing vary. We see here the first hint of a fractal structure to value
judgments. Social science is ostensibly the study of social life without value judgment; its canons of evidence and argument deny, or
at least strenuously resist, such judgments. Even the most strongly
political of my Politician colleagues follows a far more rigidly disciplined mode of inquiry than is characteristic of those outside social
science. But although career trajectories separate the value-laden
(nonacademic) from scientific (academic) study of social life, profound value commitments reappear within the supposedly value-
free world of academe.

The results of this reappearance of value judgments differ considerably in the two positions given, however. My Politician colleagues
find Moralists to be quietist or conservative, while we Moralists in
return attack the Politicians for their "politicization of the academy," even though our own position entails a clear value judgment,
albeit one at a different level.

Moreover, both versions of this argument are subject to the "remapping" discussed in chapter 1. That is, both the Politicians and
the Moralists see returning—*within* their own arguments—the positions that they vehemently deny vis-à-vis the other side; the fractal thus moves to yet another level. Among Politicians, the endless
decrying of inequality inevitably breeds a de facto belief that the

---

2. The late Bruce Mayhew made a career of attacking the baseline assumption of
equality, a fact that no doubt accounts for the minimal impact of his brilliant work.
His many papers on this topic are collected in Mayhew 1990.

3. In working out this example, I was somewhat surprised to realize that my Moralist position was in fact derived from my religious beliefs, which I had thought were,
despite outward appearances, pretty threadbare.

oppressed are indeed not full human beings. Of course Politicians
are quick to say that this stunted development is not the fault of
the oppressed. But in practice, when one invariably takes social reality to be rife with inequality, one comes to *expect* subordinate
people to always lack central personal resources like skills, efficacy,
power, and the like. From this position it is a very short step indeed
to the working presumption that subordinate people are *not* in fact
equal to others, that for "social" or "structural" reasons they are in
fact not full people, not able to "reach their full potential." This is
the direct opposite of the Moralist's position that humans are always
fully moral beings no matter what their social position.[4]

The Politician who has thus come to expect a lesser humanity
from the subordinate, "even if it is not their fault," is eventually re-
volted by his beliefs, and the inevitable result of this revulsion is the
concept of "resistance," the notion that subordinate groups are never
incapable of talking back to their oppressors. Starting from the example of overt sabotage, the concept of resistance embraces anything that can possibly be construed as foot-dragging. For example,
American blacks' retention of a dialect is defined under this argument not as a barrier to advancement or even as a mark of oppression but rather as a conscious refusal to accept subordination.

The concept of resistance is thus a remapping of the basic assumption of the Moralists (people always are free to act) into the
world of the Politicians, a return of the repressed side of the fractal.
Of course resistance must always be the subordinate argument for
Politicians. The fact of inequality (which, it should be recalled,
needs explanation because of the Politicians' hidden value presumption that social equality is the expected state of human affairs) always remains the dominant assumption in Politicians' positions.
But the idea of resistance is necessary lest the focus on inequality
degenerate into a real belief in inherent individual inequality, a degeneration many Anglo-American Marxists (often former liberals)
saw in the mainline of European structuralist Marxism.[5]

The same thing happens, perhaps in a less obvious way, on the

---

4. This entire story can be reversed in valence, so that the oppressed group par-
takes of some positive quality. Hence, one could take the position that women are
more selfless than men because they are forced to be so, but even so *really are* more
selfless. Note that Politicians would be much more likely to accept this argument
than the one proposed in text even though they are, logically, mirror images of each
other.

5. One could use my own earlier conceptual armamentarium and argue that resistance is essentially a syncresis, yoking two opposite things in a fixed, positive way.
My only argument against that is that viewing the resistance position as located in
a fractal system accounts not only for it but for the other existing positions as well.

Moralist side. Moralists stake their position on the absolute dignity and humanity of all people, social situations irrespective. This allows them to slide all too easily—by an analogous mechanism to that affecting Politicians—into complete acceptance of social inequality. Indeed, several versions of Christian social theory—certainly those of Aquinas and Luther—show this tendency quite clearly. But here too there is a return of the repressed—the very familiar phenomenon of liberal guilt. Everyone is believed equal, in some immediate, absolute sense, but existing social inequality so challenges that personal equality that it must be expunged. Like believers in resistance, however, guilty liberals put their main claim first. Equal freedom of action is, in their case, the bedrock principle; social inequality and the consequent reaction of liberal guilt are only the modifiers.

Just as the resisters oppose the structural determinists on the side of the Politicians, the liberal guilt position is opposed on the Moralist side by the classical liberalism of traditional economists, for whom unequal outcomes are simply the product of a "free market" operating on differences in taste and talent taken to be exogenous to the system. For the free-marketers, inequality exists because people choose to do other things than strive to equal their fellows. Even within the free-market position, however, there is a return of the repressed; an example is economist Robert Frank's discussion of how people choose their zones of activity so as to minimize their feelings of oppression and degradation (or to maximize their feelings of success). Thus the distinction replicates at even another level. As we have seen throughout, such replication is the mark of fractal systems.[6]

To avoid thinking fractally, we might consider attributing this pattern of positions to the crossing of three dichotomies: social and individual, equality and inequality, and is and ought. In such an array, the Politician position is that social inequality does exist but should not, to which "resisters" add the (subordinate) belief that individual equality (at the level of potentiality for action) both ought to and does exist. Conversely, the classical Moralist position is that individual equality in potentiality for action both ought to and does exist, to which guilty liberals add the subordinate belief that social inequality (which impugns that individual equality) does exist but should not.

The problem is that many of the potential combinations of belief on the three dichotomies don't exist in practice. It is more parsimo-

---

6. Frank 1985.

nious (and moreover captures the hierarchy of beliefs) to express the situation in terms of a single fractal dichotomy. The dichotomy is in fact one between social determinism and individual freedom, or, as it has become fashionable to relabel it, between structure and agency.[7] The debate between Politicians and Moralists seems then to be a standard fractal structure in which the moral concerns of social scientists divide them first into determinists (my Politicians) and freedomists (my Moralists). Then each of these divides further. The Politicians divide into determinists (e.g., Marxist structuralists) who oppose the concepts of resistance and agency, and freedomists ("resisters") who support such concepts. The Moralists divide into the guilty liberals (determinists) and the classical liberals (freedom-ists: e.g., free-marketers). Everyone in the system (except the abso-lute extremists on both sides) is working with the same distinction, but locating himself by applying it several times at different levels, and with respect to different opponents. Indeed, the whole system of distinctions flows from an *original* opposition of social scientists to others. Social scientists, broadly speaking, think of human social behavior as determined, indeed determined enough, irrespective of human volition, to be worth thinking about rigorously and compre-hensively. Hence, they are determinists by comparison with those who believe that people are completely free to act as they please and that they are therefore only loosely scientizable.

On a first pass, then, a fractal distinctions approach provides a quite parsimonious description of political conflicts in academia. The contrast of individual freedom and social determinism so famil-iar to all of us is less a single overarching linear scale than a complex cultural tool, used in indexical ways, at multiple levels and in mul-tiple contexts, for the same purposes and in the same way as are the orienting dichotomies of chapter 1. Arguments about freedom and determinism (or more commonly about the practical judgments that follow from that distinction) are the means by which social scientists identify their tribal ancestries in the world of political ac-ademe. As I argued in the preceding chapter, the complexity of such distinctions, along with the inevitability of our taking each side at some level, provides an extensive if precarious solidarity. Oddly enough, our arguments and battles unify us because they reinforce the fundamental moral symbols with which we all function.

This particular complex of fractal structure proliferates and in-tensifies because of another aspect of the fractal value structure of

---

7. "Agency" sounds less liberal than "freedom," which no doubt explains the Poli-ticians' choice of the word.

academic life. The interpenetration of moral and cognitive arguments occurs not merely in academic writing, but also in the routine practices of academic life. A linguist may well believe that language shift is perpetual and that languages lack archimedean points; that there is no "true basis" for canonical languages; and that grammarians are petty hegemons. But he will still correct the grammar of his students, even if hedging those corrections with the qualification that "this is the dialect you have to write to make a career." Here there seems to be a contradiction between cognitive understandings based on one set of judgments and teaching practices rooted in quite another.

But two fractal themes are mixed in this example. The first is the fractal distinction of freedom and determination. Such a linguist takes a particular cognitive stand about the determined nature of language, because he teaches students that the high dialect of English has no intrinsically authoritative standing but must be mastered because of its (current) imperial power. This is more or less the resisters' position: social inequality is determined and unjust, but can and should be manipulated by the oppressed. But the linguist not only offers this cognitive analysis, but also uses that analysis as a prescription for action. Thus emerges a second aspect of this fractal distinction, the opposition of thinking and doing. This can be seen as the conative aspect of the fractal whose cognitive aspect is the distinction of determinism and freedom.

The dilemma of thought and action is central for every social scientist. By and large, social scientists are people who have chosen what used to be called the contemplative life. They are thinkers rather than doers, in part because they believe social life has discoverable, determining patterns. But within social science, much research works with morally freighted categories, and implicitly or explicitly urges certain kinds of action. Indeed, the generation of social scientists now in its prime—the generation of the 1960s—has woven such moral "action" into its scholarship much more frankly than did its predecessors. Having decided on careers as thinkers, modern social scientists fill their scholarship with explicit attempts to act—to right wrongs by identifying them and labeling them as such. And of course the fact of employment as college teachers entails the necessity of daily "action" in classroom and office in addition to the research work of thinking. To be sure, the 1960s generation has reinterpreted this daily "doing" with the argument that academic writing and classroom work have always been political; in that sense, they say, academic "action" is hardly new. But as in the example of men's selfishness, there is little question that an empirical analysis of current sociological writing and teaching would find a level of explicitly moral statements—on any reasonable coding of moral versus nonmoral statements—much higher than that in the scholarship of the 1950s.[8]

The distinction of thought versus action thus seems itself more or less fractal, at least within academia. Academia is, ex ante, the realm of those who spend more of their lives thinking than doing; their main doing is teaching others how to think. Yet within faculty there are clearly those who are active and those who are not. Now to be sure, there are many spheres of potential activity—not only politics, but also teaching, departmental or university affairs, hobbies, and so on; yet political activity is a useful single dimension and does have a fractal character. Academics are in the first instance not practical politicians, but within academia we see a clear division into those who have strong political interests and those who do not. Those who do have such interests divide loosely into those who pursue them in the classroom and those who merely support external political organizations. And those who pursue political interests in the classroom divide into those who undertake such action through direct political content and those who emphasize changes in style of pedagogy. These divisions are not by any means clear or definite. But it is plain that the debate over spheres and means of political activity serves to organize the political structure of a large sector of academic life and that it does so not by being a linear scale from active to inactive, but by being an indexical debate that can be set to whatever scale and group necessary. At each level we have the committed activists and the cautious thinkers. Moreover, arguments tend to be strongest within a given level, following the familiar pattern of fractionation. No debates of academic politics are stronger than those that take place completely within the group that is politically committed.

---

8. Of course my Politician colleagues will not accept this argument, for reasons that are important to understand. As I noted in chapter 1, a central fact about fractal proliferation in time is that new generations always define the remnants of the preexisting line of descent as partisan, rather than as eclectic or consensual. In response, the preexisting ("orthodox") line always takes a position that it is *not* partisan, has no politics, represents the broad consensus, or whatever. The older generation has won its own fractal battles and enjoyed the fruits of victory—the seizure through remapping of its own opponents' turf. But the very move through which a younger generation emerges is to replicate fractal subdivision, which inevitably creates a partisan environment. Such a phenomenon is so common in political systems as to require no comment. (See, e.g., Dahl 1961, chap. 2, on the patricians' denials of a partisan position. See also the discussion of the pleasures of politics in chapter 3.) In any case, what is important here is that accepting or not accepting this particular empirical assertion is of less importance than is the fact that disagreement about it simply testifies further to the utility of a fractal analysis of how such debates unfold.

Thus we find the political debates of academia loosely organized around two fractal or at least indexical distinctions, the cognitive one of freedom versus determination and the conative one of thought versus action.[9] These are in some ways different aspects of one distinction. We see this easily when we look at the histories of certain crucial concepts in social science.

2. Power and Equality

The complex mixture of freedom/determinism and thought/action produces extraordinary results within the major conceptual concerns of social science. A clear example of this mixture is the long-standing social scientific debate over whether or not there can be a concept of power that is not fundamentally based on a moral judgment.

A number of writers have tried to escape this normative sense of power through scientizing moves. Under the leadership of Robert Dahl, the pluralist school emphasized power in action. Power lay in getting people to do something against their own wills. One measured this power simply by measuring proposals, opposition, and success. This definition harked back to Weber's "probability that one actor within a social relationship will be in a position to carry out his own will despite resistance, regardless of the basis on which this probability rests." But for Dahl, Weber's definition underplayed the independent actor; in it the politician was "merely an agent" of larger interests. Dahl was thus arguing for the individual freedom of the strong actor in the same way as the resistance theorists later argued for that of the weak actor. His position of course rested solidly on classical liberalism. It presumed equality in freedom of action and left right and wrong out of the picture altogether.[10]

The pluralists' behaviorism escaped from a moral concept of power by defining power operationally. Another escape lay in defining power as inhering in systems rather than individuals. In a celebrated essay Talcott Parsons pushed the Weberian argument to its ultimate limit, holding power to reside not in even larger interests, but rather beyond them, in the general resources of a collectivity.

---

9. The reader should note that I will be using "freedom" in two different senses in this chapter. Here, in the pairing "determination versus freedom," we are concerned with freedom as an empirical property. Later, in talking of "justice versus freedom," we are concerned with judging a political system by either its overall substantive results or its level of constraint upon the actions of particular individuals. In this latter pairing, "freedom" is a shorthand for placing a high value on the absence of constraints on personal action.

10. Dahl 1961:6. Weber's famous definition of power is at Weber 1978:53.

For him power functioned like money, as a medium of exchange for the "trade" in political goals. There were bankers of power, creditors and debtors of power, and so on. But Parsons perversely limited the notion of "power proper" to more or less consensual systems, using the word "force" to denote what most people call "naked power." (In Parsons's analogy, force was the "gold" of the power system.) Even in his explicit analysis of force he studied the operation of force only *within* a system, not between actors in overt conflict between separate systems, and at the same time squeezed the exercise of force into the analogically conceived concept of "power deflation." But while Parsons drew subtle analogies from neoclassical and Keynesian economics, he drew none whatever from Marxian economics. By looking only at the circulation of power, he could ignore its association with particular actors and groups—the political analogue of what economists would have called capital and capitalism. Thus, while his attribution of power to the system as a whole seemed amoral, in fact Parsons took an implicit moral stand by accepting the life world's definitions of what are the "existing" systems. He thereby also assumed an answer to the very problem of social order that his entire oeuvre aimed to explain.[11]

The radical critique of both of these nonnormative concepts of power rested on their obvious inability to account for long-run inequality. Although powered by the radicals' moral concern with inequality, the critique can be (and often was) phrased in scientific language. If power is more or less equally available systemwide, how are we to explain why some people remain in completely subordinate positions? If we measure power only when it is directly exercised, how are we to account for the effects it has by the mere threat of its existence? Thus generations of radicals have emphasized the importance of the mere being of power, its ability to keep important issues from ever entering the public debates so central to the liberal concept of politics.

To be sure, such challenges to nonnormative accounts of power

---

11. The basic power analysis is Parsons 1967, chap. 10. The analysis of force is Parsons 1967, chap. 9. With respect to my ongoing fractal analysis, Parsons's position was a peculiar one. Although his "theory of action" was ostensibly liberal, his extreme functionalism and identification of structure with functional imperatives implied a strong social determinism. Indeed, his whole focus on the "problem of order" suggested that he found the liberals' absolute freedom a rather fearsome thing. Yet he did not share the political program of the Marxists: quite the reverse. The reason for this was his different stand on inequality, which, like everything else in social life, he thought must serve some function. Unlike everyone I have so far discussed (except the classical economists), Parsons was not particularly upset about social inequality. In short, his rather different affiliation of fractal positions leaves him somewhat off the path of current debates.

all rested on the moral presupposition that social equality is somehow the natural state of human affairs. If we believe that people are
free to act and find that they are not acting so as to right the inequalities from which they suffer, we must then presume something
called power that prevents their doing so. But to make again a
simple empirical assertion, in many social systems the exercise of
this power is obvious enough, quite without the necessity of assumptions about the existence of inequality. Poll taxes and other
franchise qualifications, fellow servant laws, settlement laws: these
and their cousins are the obvious apparatus of legally exercised
power against various groups.[12]

But the moral fervor of the radical position has been so great that
it requires not only an account of why people do not rebel when
their interests are threatened, but also why they often do not seem
to recognize that threat in the first place. The concepts of false consciousness and hegemony were designed to provide this explanation.
Those concepts hold that under many circumstances social actors
cannot perceive their own best interests, a fact that explains why
subordinate groups don't rebel against the inequality that seems so
plain to outside analysts. Logically, false consciousness and hegemony are a supplement that for structural determinists play the
same role as resistance does for the next more general level of determinists. They are the return of agency conceptions within structural
determinism itself, for they would not be necessary were it not that
rebellious agency was expected but unobserved.

On the one hand, the concepts of false consciousness and hegemony seem sensible enough. Superordinate groups can not only cir-
cumscribe the information available to their subordinates, but can
also shape the way those subordinates actually understand their subordinate positions. But on the other hand, to a serious Moralist it is
an act of extraordinary arrogance to tell any human being that we
know his interests—indeed the meaning of his life—better than he
does. This is precisely the "enormous condescension of posterity"
in E. P. Thompson's wonderful phrase.[13] In his great work, Thompson was at pains to show how a real class consciousness was con-

---

12. My friends the Politicians will undoubtedly accept the kicking of this John-
sonian stone, where they didn't accept the previous one. Note that there is, at any
given time, a standing set of judgments about "how extreme" such an assertion is, a
standing belief in what is and is not empirical common sense. It is this set of beliefs
that Marx (and following him Gramsci) meant by a dominant ideology, although of
course there is a nonradical conception of the same in the ideas of weltanschauung,
paradigm, and so on.

13. Thompson notes this condescension both on the left and on the right
(1966:12).

densed in England from shreds of experience, religious doctrine, and local organization. The English laborer was neither Marx's oppressed dope nor the modernizers' reluctant peasant.

The great danger of concepts like false consciousness and hegemony lies precisely in their condescension. This is a quality they share with teleological and presentist history, which treats the past merely as prelude to the present and which has been the mode both for Whig historians and for the radicals who would displace them. Indeed, this quality generalizes even further, for such condescension can infect a relation with any other: a friend, a spouse, an oppressed group, a long-dead collectivity. Condescension lies in understanding the other only on our own turf; it is a disease of both left and right, for like all great falsehoods, it conceals a half-truth—that the other may not know itself well. It is undoubtedly because of this half-truth that Gramsci's writings on power, which rest on a solid theory of hegemony, read surprisingly like those of Parsons, with their purportedly apolitical concept of central values. The politics are different, but the assignment of authority to a narrow center is quite similar. Again, we find ourselves climbing up four Escher staircases and ending up exactly where we started.

In the social science concept of power, then, we see the complexities induced by the fractal relation between social science and value-laden moral activity. The attempt to define power *without* reference to our personal values not only ignores obvious facts, but also conduces to an ugly moral complacency. On the other hand, definitions rooted in our moral values lead ineluctably to condescension and its first cousin hypocrisy. We can't do with a moral definition of power and we can't do without it.

Things only get worse when we turn to what is arguably the most heavily used concept in current social science: equality. I noted at the outset that the Political position rests in important ways on a hidden value assumption that inequality is something to be explained. Not surprisingly, the concept of inequality has its own fractal vicissitudes. Another way to read the disagreement between the Politicians and the Moralists is not as a conflict between freedom and determination but as a debate over how much inequality is too much. Indeed, this rendition of the conflict captures a much more general debate, one that goes well beyond social science.

The phrase "how much inequality" suggests that the formal structure of the debate concerns a linear scale, ranging from a little inequality to a lot. Certainly, we often reflect about inequality using linear scales of income, wealth, and the like. Actual measures of inequality, however, must capture the *distribution* of values on such scales, not the values themselves. Such measures are inevitably more complicated.[14]

But despite these continuous measures of inequality—the Gini index being the most famous—it is plain that in actual social interaction the concept of inequality functions as a fractal dichotomy. Debates about inequality seldom involve disputes about values of continuous coefficients. Social scientists and some of their elite audiences may fulminate about increases in Gini-measured income dispersion in the 1980s, but most public writers (outside the *Wall Street Journal*) conceived of the Reagan years as the rich getting richer and the poor (of whom the writer was always a member or sympathizer, income irrespective) getting poorer. That is, inequality is nearly always conceived, culturally, as a matter of discontinuous and opposed groups, not as a complex continuous attribute of systems. More important, the concept has the reparameterization capabilities of any fractal. Just as electricians switch a voltmeter to the appropriate scale before measuring any circuit, so two debaters about inequality pitch their arguments to fit precisely the available space for disagreement. It is as if there were a ritual requirement in public debate that for any social situation there be a full scale of arguments from those seeing full inequality in a situation to those seeing equality in the same situation. Whether the scale ranges across the entire population, or a corporation, or a university, or even a family there are always those who see the one and those who see the other.[15]

Now this could occur because issues on which people agree don't make much of an appearance in public debate; hence what we see publicly are disagreements. But this agreement "at one level" is a

---

14. In logical terms, to be sure, inequality is a simple dichotomy. A set of equal things is a single equivalence class, and elements are either in that class or out of it. But one can think about scales measuring closeness to that class, and, in fact, one can easily imagine "real equality" as the limit point of a continuous set of levels of inequality. Conceptualizing this limit point is a major difficulty, as we shall see below. But for the moment, we must simply recognize that social scientists have come up with continuous measures of inequality, even though logically inequality is a dichotomous concept.

It is not clear what "linear" would mean for such scales, so I have omitted the word. Income measures constitute, by definition, a linear scale. But measures of distribution of income are not linear, at least in terms of that scale. They might, however, be linear within some other, direct conceptualization of inequality.

15. Perhaps the best illustration of this is that even the editorial pages of the *Wall Street Journal*—a central site for American capitalist ideology—sometimes accept this opposition of rich and poor. Even the political apologists of the Reagan years talked in terms of "trickle down," a concept that presumes the same opposition of haves and have-nots, but that assures the reader that what's good for one is good for the other. Thus, even the economic conservatives talked in exactly the same terms, using a fractal, scalable dichotomy distinguishing between two groups.

mirage. For those who appear to agree in one context disagree in smaller ones. What underscores the fractal character of the equality concept is precisely this concentric character of arguments about it. In the national context, the feminist movement may agree on the degree of women's inequality with men, but within the movement itself, precisely the same debates about equality and inequality re-emerge, conducted in the same language as the larger debate, invoking the same transcendent principles, seeking the same kinds of changes. These are not necessarily debates about internal matters, but about precisely the degrees of inequality on which the movement appears to agree when arguing in a larger context.

Another interesting indication of the fractal character of the equality/inequality judgment is the complete absence, both within the social sciences and beyond them, of any absolute substantive concept of equality. There are absolute nonsubstantive concepts; equality before the law is an example. That is, there are absolute concepts involving equality of some form of process. But there is no vision of what a "truly equal" society might be beyond concepts of equality of process. There is no *substantive* concept of equality.[16]

Consider the usual terms for true equality—for example. "A society in which everyone can reach his highest level of functioning" (or "his potential"). This concept rests on the hoary constitutional concept of due process. But while reaching one's potential may look like a process concept, but it is quite obvious that most of those urging it—other than the free-marketers—expect to see a result of substantive equality on important dimensions like wealth, social resources, and so on. Logically, then, they are assuming that everyone envisions personal aims of "equal" size in some sense, even though in what sense they do not specify. Thus, like most equality concepts, this one is not positive but negative. What is really referred to is the absence of blockage, not the achievement of some substantive result.[17]

---

16. As we shall see below, this is related to the problem of a substantive definition of the good life. As I noted in discussing the stress literature's problems with "positive mental health," developing conceptions of the positive good is a major problem for people functioning in fractal symbolic systems. It is easier to think of the good in terms of removal of the bad as, in many ways, did Marx. Oddly enough, this is the precise reverse of Augustine's classical conception of bad as simply the absence of good. Note that neither version wants to live with the moral Manichaeanism that admits two truly substantive principles—good and evil. Perhaps, underneath the universal tendency to understand things in fractals, and in particular in dichotomous fractal lineages, there is a human desire for singleness.

17. There is a small literature on "incommensurability" that thinks about this problem somewhat (see Espeland and Stevens 1998). It is logically clear that to accept

"Inclusiveness" has hardly more real content. The standard inclusionist rhetoric begins with the belief that the current "center" of society is in fact not really a center, but only a center for certain people. Thus, what had been regarded as "universal" predicates (maleness, whiteness, etc.) are in fact falsely so. They are "unmarked categories," in that they are taken to typify a larger category (humanity, Americans, poets) without further specification. In order to decrease inequality (again the definition is basically negative), such unmarked qualities must be defined as marked and all the arguments of their holders must be defined as sectarian arguments rather than universal ones. Hence, in much feminist writing, universalism itself is treated in its character as an argument often made by these unmarked groups and hence as sectarian (see note 8 above).

A straightforward logic leads from this view of inclusion to the concept of multiculturalism. That is, the destruction of *any* typificatory groups implies a situation in which there are a number of groups, absolutely equal with respect to some unspecified set of criteria. There is no logical or substantive source for these criteria, certainly in the context of a company of equal groups with "truly different" values. The result is a simple collection of groups. Like equality, multiculturalism has in practice hardly any positive content. Like "reaching one's potential," it is actually embodied negatively, as a set of practices asserting that dominant groups are not better and that subordinate groups are not worse, and indeed that dominant groups are not dominant and subordinate groups not subordinate. At its best, multiculturalism is, like the Moralists' equivalent concept ("due process"), a concept of earnest vagueness. It envisions a world in which there are real differences, not the phony ones embodied in ethnic restaurants, and yet there is no subordination.[18]

In classical political theory such a world was imagined only by theories of imperium, in which a single overarching and authoritative power regulated the intercourse of diverse groups. I cited in chapter 1 the classic example of such theory, the Roman system of

most concepts of equality (or of inequality) is to assent to the commensurability of values.

18. At its worst multiculturalism degenerates into teaching students that there is good food from many different ethnicities and more broadly inducting them into a kind of consumptive tourism of cultures. Anyone who knows the heartbreaking difficulty of real contact across cultural differences knows how absurd such a concept is. But the concept at least raises what is the crucial problem of current political theory: whether one can envision an idea of difference that does not entail subordination. I argue in sections 4 and 5 of this chapter that fractal reasoning provides some possibility of that.

ius gentium, which regulated interactions in cases where one of the parties lacked status under the Roman law of citizens. Of course this system presupposed the military authority of the legions, an explicit final arbiter of differences. And there is no equivalent force in the "multicultural world," other than the global corporations and their pax Americana. Like Parsons, the multicultural argument in fact presupposes what it sets out to provide: an arbiter of foundational differences.[19]

One of the central problems of the whole debate over power and inequality is that its conceptual machinery—the particular fractal that it involves—seems so well understood and so inescapable. It is the terrifying balance that makes the whole thing so inevitable: the same values repeated at dozens of levels, the same arguments of inclusion versus independence, of difference and equality, of freedom and determination. Even the vices seem oddly complementary—liberals' complacency versus radicals' hypocrisy. Perhaps the problem comes from the inevitable mixture of the moral and the academic. Perhaps the moral world itself will prove free from such problems.

3. Levels of Moral Argument

But hardly so. To begin at the beginning: as acting people we are used to the concept of absolute moral rules, but as social scientists we see easily that there are no such things. Moral life in general is subject to a fractality that provides for continuously changing balances in moral arguments. A simple illustration of this is the phenomenon of exposés.

Exposés take the form of changing levels in a fractal judgmental system. An exposé works by bringing knowledge of a particular activity to a much wider public than previously knew it. Generally, those concerned with its original venue know all about it and are more or less inured to it, whether they be participants in it or local opponents of it.

For example, when I worked in a large mental hospital during my graduate years, it was openly acknowledged that the moral life of the hospital was often revolting. Staff sometimes threatened and beat patients, and patients beat, robbed, and occasionally raped each other. These activities were taken for granted by all staff and

---

19. It is a somewhat disconcerting fact that associations of full equals have existed under Western law for centuries (under the law of partnership, *societas*) but that associations with internal hierarchical structures (under the law of incorporation, *universitas*) have always eventually proved more effective in changing (and ultimately in dominating) their world.

patients. Of course there were ritualistic efforts to curtail them and ritualistic denials of them by hospital officials in any formal context; if real knowledge of these activities were to reach the outside world with its higher standards, there would be an exposé and consequent internal troubles. But in their everyday world, even those hospital staff members who were fully engaged in the outside world of reformist politics (this was the heyday of community mental health and the "myth of mental illness") regarded the background level of inhumanity in the hospital as something more or less routine, something to worry about occasionally and to laugh about often. They told themselves that the social order of the hospital was probably as moral as it could be given the minimal human, material, and monetary resources that the larger society was willing to dedicate to those of us who lived and worked there.[20]

Yet there *were* offenses that breached this local consensus. Once some people tried to run a brothel off-grounds using female patients as tricks, smuggling them to a motel in the trunks of cars. Most locals found this episode morally outrageous. To the outside world, of course, it would have seemed pretty much the same as beating up the patients or leaving them alone in the dormitories long enough to rape and beat each other. But to the locals, there was a world of difference.

There are myriad examples of this phenomenon.[21] When I read in the *Wall Street Journal* about instances of insider trading, I am bewildered by what seem to me to be arbitrary definitions of that phenomenon. Virtually everything that goes on in the immediate Wall Street world seems like insider trading to me. Anyone who knows the theory and empirical data on simple friendship networks knows that tracing two or three acquaintanceship links sequentially out from the inside of any particular company takes one well out across the entire U.S. population. It seems then a theoretically expected fact that all nontechnical information on Wall Street derives in one way or another from personal connections traceable to inside sources. Yet Wall Street denizens and regulators seem to have quite clear notions about which leaked information is and which is not legitimate. These are seemingly well-formed moral judgments. In form, they seem no different from, say, my own judgments of what is and is not plagiarism, judgments that I take with deadly seri-

---

20. The phrase "myth of mental illness" is from Szasz 1961.

21. I cannot resist retelling the wonderful example of the socialist who stole a jeep from his factory intending to sell it and make a little much-needed cash. The jeep was stolen from his house overnight, much to his shock and chagrin. One can't trust anyone! (Wedel 1986:15).

ousness and believe I perform accurately. I think it is OK to reuse
someone else's ideas in my own words, as long as I cite that use, but
that using their words without a citation constitutes plagiarism for
which I should be fired. Yet to an outsider, both of these cases may
very well seem to constitute a direct borrowing of others' ideas,
equally justifiable or unjustifiable depending on the outsider's own
beliefs.

Here then we have the moral equivalent of the New Yorker's map.
Local groups make fine moral distinctions that nonlocals refuse to
recognize. Morals are thus themselves a fractal system. As I have
said before, we sometimes think of such systems as linear. But I
have already rejected this argument throughout. All linear scales are
approximatable by a certain kind of fractal, but very few fractals
are approximatable by linear scales. Fractals are therefore the more
general conception. The reality is that our moral systems do function fractally. A single distinction of moral and immoral action is
imported to various levels and applied locally as a way of making
sense of local conditions. Even in one of society's most morally
questionable organizations—the traditional mental hospital—
people applied the same kinds of comparisons to make their local
moral judgments as people do elsewhere. The substance was different, but the means of judgment the same. Morals are in that sense
fully indexical.

The obverse of the exposé phenomenon is quite similar to what I
earlier called reparameterization. Again, let me begin with an example. Social science—as opposed to everyday knowledge of the social world—consists at least in part in a willingness to change one's
judgments based on new facts about the social world. But a very
familiar sight in social science today is the scholar whose moral
judgments cannot be changed by any set of facts. The moral versions
of the gender arguments reviewed in the last chapter exemplify this.
In the 1970s there arose in sociology serious concern about the balance of men and women in the discipline. Then people noticed that
men and women were about equal in undergraduate programs. But
though men and women were equally represented in undergraduate
school, some scholars began to focus on the discrimination that persisted at the graduate level. When there was graduate equality, then
they decried discrimination in the professorial ranks. As gender
equality emerged among assistant professors, the concern turned to
the tenured level. Now, as equality may be emerging at that level
too, concern begins to turn to the tenured level in elite departments.
But these elite departments are in fact a tiny, tiny fraction of socio-

logical employment. An outsider would feel that sociology as a discipline does not suffer from major gender discrimination. Yet many in the discipline remain honestly persuaded that women are in a precarious position throughout it.[22]

Thus, in order to maintain their outrage if actual discrimination lessens, those who take what I earlier called a Political view must focus on a smaller and smaller turf, much as those who accept the Achilles paradox focus on smaller and smaller slices of time in order to avoid recognizing the moment when Achilles does in fact pass the tortoise. It is plain that the eventual outcome of such a process is to push the definition of discrimination to new levels altogether.

It is also plain that this process of moral reparameterization is extremely general. It is nowise restricted to the left. If we consider the development of capitalism, we can see that it consists to a large extent in the relaxation of certain rules—about property, about human relations, about exploitation—that were essentially moral rules. The relaxation arose from a fractal process. At any given time, those who violated existing rules were indeed punished (at least in theory), but, at the same time, those who came closest to violating them *without* going over the line did much better than those who followed them unthinkingly. Those who pushed the limits were able, as the rational choice argument has it, to free ride on the common resources developed by the strict law abiders. For example, those who enclosed the English commons made their fortunes by inventing the concept of alienability and allowing peasants to alienate the rights of future generations for a mere fraction of what those rights were actually worth, in terms of long-run payoff. That is, the enclosers, like those who destroyed the law of entail, managed to obliterate the previously accepted rights of the future in the present. Note that the peasants didn't think in such a cost calculus; that's why they fell for the arguments of the capitalist landlords who did. To an outsider, enclosure seems like a pretty obvious moral swindle, but it was just barely legitimate within the rules conceived by the English legal system. And the economic success of those who enclosed and capitalized of course drove the other aristocrats—buried in their somnolent traditions—off the land entirely, just as drivers who race ahead in construction lanes inevitably pass the strict rule abiders who move over as soon as they see the signs warning of lane closure. If there is a distribution of behaviors, the establishment of

---

22. On feminization and the position of women in sociology, see Roos and Jones 1993.

rules truncating that distribution at a point (of illegality or other forbiddenness) does not prevent the dynamics whereby those adjacent to the truncation point can take advantage of the others.

The same story has been repeated dozens of times over. The development of capitalism always includes, among many other things, this pushing of rules to the utmost so that the majority of the economic population can be treated as providing a free ride for insiders. Michael Milken was undoubtedly a swindler, but what he did seemed to many of us little different from the generations of legalized tax dodges and Ponzi schemes that litter the landscape of capitalism. Indeed the biggest swindles—witness the Chrysler and savings and loan bailouts—constitute straightforward free-riding off the state itself, taking the well-being of thousands of little people hostage and using the threat of general economic damage as a grand form of blackmail. This has been extremely common in the history of capitalism.

Thus we see that moral systems are indeed characterized by a kind of reparameterization that we have seen in other fractal systems. The result can be something like the fractionation of chapter 3. Things get more and more extreme as each succeeding position moves closer and closer to a moral edge of some sort. But unlike academia, which has the relatively fixed underlying social structure discussed in chapter 5, the real world lacks a fixed substrate. Hence, the result of reparameterization in the general social world, unlike its result in academia, is drift in the position of the edge, the moral standard itself. For the gender discriminationists of my first example, this drift is deliberate; without it they would have to acknowledge the overwhelmingly rapid decline of gender discrimination in sociology. For the capitalists, enmeshed in a much larger process, the drift is no doubt much more complex and partly unintentional, but it has had the end result of creating a world that would be morally unrecognizable to any denizen of the middle nineteenth century other than a hardened adventurer. It is a world in which a vast increase of trust and legal organization has gone hand in hand with an equally vast increase in the size and systematic nature of potential and actual swindles.

An obvious result of all this drift is a steady redefinition of central moral terms, much as we saw for intellectual ones in chapter 1. This too permits the maintenance of the left's outrage and of the right's self-righteousness. On the left we see this extraordinary drift in the usage of words like "patriarchy" and "oppression" to describe relations in upper-class American households and American industry, as if these closely resembled the families of nomadic tribes or the class relations of mid-Victorian England. Just so we see it on the right in the use of the phrase "free market" to describe the most elaborately constructed and regulated social structure in the history of humankind.

Rhetorics of inclusion provide further examples. Since the nineteenth century, a standard rhetoric of reform has urged the "inclusion" of groups excluded from the core of society. But the inclusion of any one group in the societal core simply rearranges the location of the edge, creating new forms of exclusion for others. As more and more groups are included, inclusionists are forced to turn to smaller and smaller excluded groups. The inclusionist argument started by urging the redemption of the nineteenth-century workers who made up probably 80 percent of their society, but is now adduced with equal fervor on behalf of groups like gays and the handicapped, each of whom makes up a tiny fraction of contemporary society. In the process, one period's inclusion/reward—workers getting subsistence wages and a ten-hour day—is redefined as another period's exclusion/oppression. It was with much trepidation that small support payments for the blind were added to the obligations paid from Social Security funds (in the creation of the SSI program), while today the Americans with Disabilities Act requires a substantial surcharge on the price of every public building built in the United States.

Interestingly, there is an absolute limit to inclusionist rhetorics. The Achilles-tortoise logic drives one eventually to the position of defending the interests of a single individual against the rest of society. Oddly enough, therefore, the strong inclusionist arguments used by the left lead ultimately, via another Escheresque arrangement of staircases, back to the very beginning position of the entire debate—extreme individualistic liberalism. To be sure this limit is in practice not reached. Since there are pulls on both sides of most issues and since these drifts of moral judgment move in diverse directions, not one, we never quite arrive back at Lockean individualism. But there is in the process a steady but unpredictable redefinition of the basic language of morality over time. Fractal moral structures conduce to an intrinsic mutability in the definitions of our moral life.

And we see this drift even in moral systems that are not explicitly political. One functional account of modern sports, for example, is as a surrogate for overtly violent activity; we have sports to give young men a way to be aggressive without killing each other. As a result, there arises a fractal structure in which the violent world of war is opposed to the nonviolent world of peace, with sports as the "return" incarnation of violence within the nonviolent world. Yet even if sports does substitute to some extent for the random armed raid, it too becomes saturated with real violence, which always threatens to burst its bounds. Indeed, our attempts to contain the "bad" through the production of surrogates within the good seems, almost inevitably, to fail. To fight fascists, the liberal democracies raised citizen armies. But within those "democratic" armies behavior was quite fascistic, as Mailer so unforgettably told us in *The Naked and the Dead*[23] and as those of us who have served in armed forces can readily attest. The fractal other side of a moral dichotomy always reappears and is seldom fully controlled.

This inevitable failure of moral systems—implied by fractal drift—is deeply problematic. Our political debates implicitly (but never explicitly) invoke an imagined good world, one in which evil does not appear. And yet it seems that the fractal character of our moral judgments condemns us to re-create the evil or the immoral within our very citadels of justice. When we create good things, we find bad ones within them, just as, on the other end, we find good things emerging within evil (the *Schindler's List* phenomenon). These recurrences suggest that it is of the nature of our perception of moral and political affairs to see—in any social system whatsoever—a dialogue of good and bad, or inclusion and exclusion, or whatever. Our very mode of judgment dooms us to perpetual dissatisfaction.[24]

That morality appears to function fractally is profoundly disturbing. Most of us want to retain at least a few absolute ethical rules (e.g., people should not be exterminated for their religion). Even granted those, we are frightened of the welter of relativistic moral and political judgment in the world. But fractal moral structures are not the same as relativistic ones. To speak of relativistic ethics is to believe that judgments of the good derive simply from group membership and arbitrary interests. Noting the fractal character of moral judgment focuses us rather on *how* people make moral judgments. And the fact seems to be that the same kinds of moral tools are used to make judgments even in the vastly different worlds of the mental hospital, the academic discipline, and the capitalist's office. All these moral decisions are recognizable to an outsider as borrowing a single common vocabulary, which is scaled to fit the situation, and, indeed, to provide actors in the situation with options for right and wrong action. What is of interest scientifically, then, is how the scaling of moral rules actually works. What is of

23. Mailer 1948.
24. The Schindler phenomenon was described by Keneally (1982).

interest morally is the fact that we aren't really as divided by moral and political differences as we often think.[25]

4. Some Articles of a Fractal Morality

Let me summarize. I began the chapter with the empirical argument that mixing of moral/political and cognitive judgments seems to be endemic in social science. My initial example hinged on several fractal distinctions that are commonly combined in the moral debates of academia. The first of these was the dichotomy of individual freedom and social determinism, which produces my Politicians (subdividing into true structural determinists and resisters) and my Moralists (subdividing into guilty liberals and free-marketers). The second was the division of thought and action, illustrated in the first instance by academics versus other social actors, and within academics by numerous internal subdivisions. These two fractals undergirded my analysis of the value complexities involved in social scientific analyses of power and equality. My third fractal structure was the judgment of right and wrong itself, with its indexicality, reparameterization, and fractionation. This I pursued into the real world beyond academia.

These arguments have moved the fractal concept from the intellectual and empirical world to the moral one. But taken together with the arguments of earlier chapters, they contain the ideas with which I have tried to answer the very personal question posed in the opening pages of the preface: how can one theorize comprehensive intellectual eclecticism? More practically, how can one understand the very common academic experience of having had so many arguments, both intellectual and political, about so many things, with

---

25. It is apparently possible to read this sentence, and more broadly this chapter, as an exercise in hegemonic universalism. One commenter on it said exactly that: that the chapter attempts to make "real difference" disappear, to position the author as an outsider "above the fray," and to use the fractal argument to appropriate—while at the same time denying—others' experience. I was bewildered by that comment and remain so. But I report it to indicate that at least I heard it. My intent in the chapter is meliorative. It tries to make sense of my own and others' experience and to do so by searching for a via media—or perhaps we should say a mutually defining relationship—between universalism and particularism. Of course I have plenty of moral judgments of my own and have made no secret of them. If I did not think that moral judgments were worth having, I would not have written about them at all (nor would I be a human being in the full sense of the term). But it is also true that I would not have written anything like this argument were I the smugly condescending universalist this reader saw. Quite the contrary, then indeed I would have blown off the many views with which I disagree and set out an axiomatic argument from first principles. But I gave such things up years ago. I may have failed to get beyond universalism as a hegemonic discourse—but for want of ability, not of effort.

people with so manifestly close to oneself? How can one understand the diversity of academic inquiry?

But having answered these questions as intellectual ones—or at least having shown the materials with which one could begin to answer them—I must address the prescriptive issues beyond. What are the prospects for making those arguments more productive and helpful, less wasteful and hurtful, in a way that does not simply avoid the complexities involved? In particular, what implications do these arguments have for organizing intellectual life and, beyond the ivory tower, for the organization of morality and politics in general? I begin with the latter question, about general morality, and work toward the question of intellectual life, with which I am both more familiar and more comfortable.

I begin with the basic question of whether fractal thinking tells us anything about the exact nature of what is good. It doesn't. I don't for a second imagine that I know the content of human good—that the good society is everyone's having lots of modern consumption goods, or full life spans, or successful vision quests, or proper relations with cross-cousins, or whatever. Nor do I know the content of the bad, nor do I imagine that the good life constitutes—as meliorism would have it—any life from which the bad has been eradicated. On the other hand, if I don't know the specific content of the good, I think I have an idea of the good—how shall I say it?—as a direction. It seems to me that destroying things human is bad and that creating new things that humans can be is good. Indeed, this is what makes us human. Ant society may be empirically successful as a social system, but it is repulsive precisely for its uniformity.

To me it seems that fractal thinking helps us navigate morally in this welter of creation that is the human social process. What do we want a system of moral thinking to do? We want it, first, to rule out some things absolutely, things involving the absolute destruction of the human: human sacrifice, extermination, wanton destruction of culture; a functioning moral system has to have some absolute places. Beyond those few absolute things, we want a moral system, second, to be able to function in the face of the sea of differences that is the social world, even differences that seem to burst the limits of the humane. A moral system is no use unless it works anywhere, anytime. It has to be both *ius civile*, a law for relations with people like oneself, and *ius gentium*, law for relations with those who are different. We want it, third, to give us practical guidance. A moral system has to be usable, not so ideal as to be irrelevant.

It was the Enlightenment's virtue to see that these points required a certain kind of universality. This was simple enough in the case of the proscriptions (the first purpose above), but less so in the case of morality in the face of difference (the second and third purposes above). It was the Enlightenment's mistake to think that the only way to find morality among differences was to conceive of moral action as purely formal, involving only the contentless shape of action. Only if we conceived of moral action as having the same shape in all places and times could we imagine it with sufficient universality to function in the face of difference.[26]

Fractal thinking offers a way to think about that "similar shape" that evades the by-now-traditional postmodern critique of universalism, which is that either it is contentless and hence unlike any form of actual experience or it is not really universal at all but simply the local morality of some dominant group. If we imagine moral action as action within a fractal social structure then we can imagine Kant's "So act that the maxim of your will could always hold at the same time as a principle establishing universal law" in a new way.[27] Think again of my investigators in a city, back in chapter 1, elaborating a simple branching fractal, and imagine moral action as a way of choosing where to go next, given where one is. The absolutist moral rules of the Puritans would tell everyone to go, say, to the upper left corner. The contentless moral rule of the Enlightenment would tell them all to turn left *with respect to the entire city diagram*. (That is contentless universalism.) But a fractal rule might tell them all to turn left *with respect to their current trajectory*. Note that the fractal rule has vastly different consequences for the overall distribution of moral actors in the space than the Enlightenment rule, because it conceives of morality as fundamentally local, as being about the actor, the time, the place—in short as being grounded in the real content of actual social relations. But by assuming a certain self-similarity to moral action it retains the Enlightenment's concept of a universal *shape* to moral action.[28]

---

26. The locus classicus for this argument was of course Kant's *Critique of Practical Reason* (Kant 1956), esp. pt. 1, bk. 1, chap. 1, "Principles of Pure Practical Reason," secs. 1–8.

27. The categorical imperative appears in *Critique of Practical Reason*, pt. 1, bk. 1, chap. 1, sec. 7 (Kant 1956:30).

28. For the moment let us not try to imagine what the dimensions of the city mean in this particular analogy. Note that I am leaving unanswered the question of exactly how a fractal conception invokes real content where the Enlightenment conception does not. Perhaps a way of thinking about it is to borrow the conception of reenactment from Collingwood (1946:282–302). In this translation, the categorical imperative becomes "so act that the maxim of your will could always hold as a law for a reasonable human reenacting your experience in your time and place." That chases a lot of difficult problems off into the definition of reenactment and the question of how much of "your experience" is required for a legitimate reenactment. But it points in the direction I am thinking. It is this concept of reenactment that lies

Consider an example. There are people starving to death all over
the world. Why don't I give away everything I have to feed them? Of
course we can all spin various stories in response to this: the money
would get wasted, it would encourage behaviors that would make
people worse off, one should fight the system that makes them
starve, etc. Left, right, center: we can all explain quite legitimately
why we don't do this. The explanations are all rationalizations, of
course; virtually all of us believe it to be our obligation to prevent
another human starving to death, yet almost none of us does it. The
easy question is to explain why we don't. But the harder question
is whether there might be rules under which our behavior in this
particular moral dilemma might be judged—how shall we say it?—
more realistically. In fact, virtually none of us is going to give away
everything that he has. Yet just the same, we need ways of making
real moral judgments about the real possibilities, such that there *are*
right actions that we can realistically envision (like giving away
some part of what we have). Nor need we choose so extravagant an
example. To what extent can I ignore my children before becoming
morally culpable? What is right behavior as an editor? a colleague?
a tenure referee?

As the example shows, in reality the issue about morality lies less
in the proper shape of our actions—that seems to be well comprehended by the idea of a fractal "shape" that is our scalable model of
thinking about morals in a situation—than in deciding the proper
size of our moral zone of relevance, the size of the situation. Put in
the city fractal framework, how much of the past trajectory do we
consider in deciding what we are turning left from? In practice, most
of the moral debates of modern politics take the form precisely of
this issue of zones of relevance; for example, this is the issue in all
the various "complicity" debates—slavery, the extermination of the
Jews, capitalist oppression, and so on.

Not only does a fractal conception allow us to have universality
without uniformity, and to develop a concept of the zone of moral
relevance, it also enables us to think about issues like the relative
importance of justice and freedom in new ways.[29] By justice, I mean
the overall result of moral action in a society. Clearly any system of
justice ought not to repress human differences, since the production

---

behind the moral stance of classical ethnography: one can't succeed in really understanding the other, but it is the only thing worth trying to do. Universalism may not
be possible, but nothing else is worthy of the human project. Again, as Terence put
it: "I am human, therefore let nothing human be alien to me" (see chapter 1, note 6).

29. Note that freedom here means not freedom the empirical property (as in the
fractal described in the first section of the chapter) but rather freedom as a positively
valued aspect of personal experience.

of different ways to be human is the glory of human social life as opposed to insect social life. Indeed, the evil of puritanism, and of all fundamentalist ethical systems, is that by vastly extending the realm of the absolute in moral life they repress the creation of new ways of being human and, thereby, the human itself. Now Kant escapes from puritanism by removing the content from morality and replacing it with a form, although perhaps still insisting on a uniform direction within that form. So while in the puritan world moral action takes the form of everyone doing the same things, in a Kantian world moral action takes the form of everyone turning in the same universal direction, as I have noted. Obviously, the results of these—the overall distribution of moral action in the whole social space or what I am calling justice—are very different. Different still are the overall results of a *fractal* action rule, which separates out three things: the contents (which both the fractal and Kantian conceptions treat as varying), the form of moral action (for which we might consider something different from the Kantian rule), and the zone of relevance (which Kant has ignored). Thus in undertaking to reflect about justice in fractal terms, we have a much more differentiated and conceptualized terrain of discussion than in either of the other views.[30]

These distinctions enable us to take a new view of the traditional debate between justice and freedom. In the usual argument justice and freedom are contrasting, even antithetical terms (and thus one might expect me to view them as a straightforward fractal pair, as I earlier did freedom [in a different sense] and determination). Freedom is a property of individuals and of individual decisions, while justice is property of social systems as a whole. Most political theories believe in some kind of trade-off between them such that the more individual freedom a society has, the more general social justice is at risk and vice versa. But in a fractal view the two are related differently. Justice remains an emergent property that results from the ensemble of moral action (corporate and personal) in a society. But since we now allow for moral action at many scales, even if always following the same formal rule, the overall results are not

---

30. I am well aware that I am caricaturing Kant to some extent. His view *is* in many ways fractal, in the sense that he specifically aimed to transcend content limitations (i.e., localism) by the move to a formal morality. As one reflects about the Kantian view, one can see that there is something suspicious in the fractal view, because the notion of fractals as contraction mappings implies that local (personal?) moral action is somehow a small version of translocal (social? societal?) moral action, and that seems worrisome. In fact, my response to this has to do with the notion that social life is *always* local, even when we think about grand processes like "the rise of capitalism." But that must await another book.

immediately obvious. The consequences of more or less freedom of action become an empirical issue, a function of the pattern of zones of relevance and the actual form of the moral rule generating the local decisions (the fractal generator—which doesn't have to be Kant's categorical imperative, but could be some other reenactment rule).

The aim therefore of a fractal approach to morality is to extend the Enlightenment view by giving us a way to have *both* a universal aspect *and* a particular aspect to moral action. This happens via the reproduction of a universally construed "shape" of moral action in varying places and times and at varying scales. As the previous chapter argued, this gives us a solidarity that does not require sameness. Like the Kantian view, then, this fractal conception lies between absolute moral rules and absolute moral relativity. But by admitting the local and the concrete, it escapes the contentless universality of the Enlightenment. Thinking about morality this way also prepares us better to understand some of the ongoing processes of moral debates: the play of reparameterization and the impetus of fundamentalism (the moral equivalent of fractionation). It also gives us new ways to think about rearranging moral action—by changing the valued zone of relevance or by changing the fundamental shape in which we envision moral action. It even gives us a new approach to traditional problems like the trade-off of freedom and justice.

But all this has come through reasoning at the level of moral action. Moralist that I am, I have slid away from the Politicians' problem of value conflict itself. The fractal approach to morality allows for real content, but what happens when the values that make up that content conflict directly?

5. Difference without Hierarchy

Posed in its barest form, the central question about value conflict is whether it is possible to have difference of values without conflating that difference with preferability. Can there be difference without better and worse? It was of course the great dream of liberalism that this was possible, and those who urge the politics of difference on us are, ironically enough, in that sense the most obvious inheritors of classical liberalism.

Liberalism aimed to accomplish this miracle by positing a foreground realm of absolute equality—citizenship—in which everyone would be equal in principle and insisting that that realm be purely processual, that is, that it lack substantive content, but merely consist of legitimate processes. On this view, value difference could safely exist in the personal background—the private sphere—without compromising the foreground of equality. The problem with this strategy was simple. As the nineteenth century showed, the empirical result was that the public sphere merely helped to reproduce, even to further, the substantive inequalities of the private sphere. Although elites long pretended that these inequalities were due to value differences, and hence legitimate, large-scale resistance forced them to change their minds. The solution to this problem was the welfare state, an absolute floor comparable to my absolute proscriptions in the preceding section.[31]

The welfare state was itself organized in terms of certain social expectations (about families, for example), an organization that at first left other substantive inequalities (e.g., of gender) completely outside the realm of the political. Of course, social change made its own short work of some of those inequalities—married women flooded the American labor force from the mid-1930s on. And eventually liberalism in the United States has resulted in a gradual and steady expansion of the realm of the political, in all senses, throughout the twentieth century. But to notice the changing boundary of the political and the nonpolitical continues to evade the problem of whether liberalism can really provide a way to have value difference without hierarchy.[32]

As I have several times noted, the other classical approach to handling value differences flows from the political theory of imperium. If we imagine the social world as a series of separate, equal groupings, with a more or less unchanging selfhood, these can coexist despite their differences if there is some outside authority to decide their disputes. This is hardly a solution, of course, for it simply assumes the existence of the outside referee and provides no constraints on that referee, and hence no answer to value conflicts with that referee. It is true, historically, that the great imperial cities of the past were often for their time astonishingly tolerant places; one

31. The nonregulation of the private was in fact a mirage, as Novak (1996) and many others have shown. Liberal society only lessened somewhat—it did not stop—the regulation of private life. See also Dewey 1954, chap. 3, on the question of "freedom" from institutions.

32. Note that the common postmodern position that "everything is political" is exactly the same as the position of the sixteenth- and seventeenth-century Puritans that the state's unwillingness to tolerate their intolerance constituted state interference with religion. For the puritans too, everything was political, that is, everything was a part of religion, a view they put into active practice in Massachusetts. See Walzer 1965.

thinks of the religious toleration policies of the early caliphates, for example. But the equality of such a system boils down to equality of subjugation.[33]

In short, neither of these views really offers us a way of thinking about difference that doesn't become hierarchy. One view boils down to saying that we should create a dream world in which we pretend difference doesn't exist, the other says we should find a big brother to settle our problems for us.

In the last thirty years, the most important example used to reflect about difference without hierarchy is gender relations. Let us set aside for a moment the social transformation of gender relations in the twentieth century, with all its real changes and its fractal reparameterizations that recast the standards so that "patriarchy" is believed to endure. Let us reflect about how one could imagine a gender relations system in which real gender differences persisted but did not become linked up with any form of hierarchy. It is obvious that gender relations are fractally driven, as I have noted again and again. Are there ways of understanding that fractal structure that don't end up implying subordination?

There seem to be two possibilities. Throughout this book, I have a number of times spoken of curious systems where some kind of distinction, taken to a limit, ends up turning into its opposite. I have usually used referred to these as Escher staircases, referring to the famous M. C. Escher engraving in which four rising staircases march around the four sides of the picture to end up where they started. Examples are the turning of extreme constructionism into absolute realism, in chapter 3, and the turning of extreme inclusionism into individualistic liberalism, mentioned earlier in this chapter. Thus, fractal systems can develop a kind of circularity, which gives them order without hierarchy.[34]

Another concept for order without hierarchy comes from the idea

---

33. See Hodgson 1974, bk. 2, chap. 2, "Absolutism in Flower."

34. Actually, it is in the first instance the circularity that matters here, not the fractality. For the quality of having order but no absolute top or bottom is a property of any circular system. Indeed, recalling the discussion of gender differentiation as a prestige hierarchy in the preceding chapter, one could speculate what the results for gender hierarchies would be if one thought of them as embedded in a positively curved space such as a circle. In that case the hierarchies flow into one another and they have no top or bottom. But it is not clear what it would mean substantively to say that "gender hierarchy could be embedded in a circle," like the Escher staircases. It seems to imply two separate lineages, perhaps with different values. This begins in turn to suggest the nineteenth-century conception in which men were superior to women in some systems (the secondary sphere of public life) and women to men in others (the primary sphere of home life). This system would not be thought by many writers today to embody difference without hierarchy.

of rootless fractals. I have usually expressed fractals as starting from a single root, which divides and subdivides and so on. What if, as in the classic case of the Nuer lineages, there isn't any original root, but just an infinite regress? In such an image, say of the gender division of labor discussed in the preceding chapter, there isn't any "place where it all starts." There is simply the currently known bit of the proliferating system. We lose the idea of whether the current master root used to be one thing or the other. This is historically true with gender relations. It is only via fractal reparameterization that the current male role in society has much in common with the masterful male roles of some earlier times; even by Victorian standards today's men have had their fangs drawn. At least, under this conception, one models how the actual content of subordination has been vastly reduced, even if the form of relation remains.

But that transposition still leaves us with that form, a difference that is subordination. Women may have acquired property rights, the vote, near equality in the labor market, and many other things, but one still finds the curious self-similar gender structure described in the last chapter. Perhaps a better image of a rootless fractal is one of simple concentric structures in which maleness is, say, the inside of any layer and femaleness the outside. Like an onion, this concentric system is fractal in the sense of being self-similar, but it also has a noncircular order property (and hence real "difference"), and if we assume it can become as large or as small as we want, no type can identified as the ultimate top or bottom of the system. (Such a system of concentric differences appears to have been what Doris Lessing had in mind in one of her science fiction novels.)[35]

The fractal metaphor thus does provide us with some ways to begin thinking of difference without hierarchy. They are only a beginning, but they suggest that thinking about difference in fractal terms does not automatically imply imposition of value differences.

For the time being, however, such ideals are not at issue. We have rather the spectacle of a politics that operates on the assumption of a fractal social structure, which it then attempts to manipulate. As we have seen in the Achilles arguments mentioned earlier, these manipulations often take the form of looking only at certain things or in certain fractal directions rather than seeing the broad sweep of human creation.

Thus, as I have mentioned, the meliorists game the system of liberalism by trying to push things from the private into the public,

---

35. Lessing discusses a set of endless zones in *The Marriages between Zones Three, Four, and Five* (Lessing 1981). Onions are a good metaphor for gender relations. Like them, they make us cry.

ultimately reinventing a monist world. By their opponents they are labeled politicizers, a label they welcome. Against them fight the conservatives, who try to push things the other way and are hence seen as those who "erase" the political, those who hide things. The contests take place, as I have said, most often through fights over the zones of fractal relevance. The actual form of moral decisions, or as I have put it, of reenactment, attracts less attention.

It may be that this problem of zones is insoluble and that we should focus more on rethinking the form and character of our moral choices, developing a clearer concept of reenactment. We have before us very clear examples of the futility of trying to solve our value conflicts via manipulations of moral zones. The saddest of these is the problem of nationalism. Throughout the twentieth century men have tried to solve the problem of nationalism by self-determination. But if people are mixed seriously in geographical space, drawing a line around a nation just creates more minorities within. If one then draws lines around *them*, that just creates more minorities—perhaps of the "larger" majority—within the enclave, and so on. The logical impossibility of "national self-determination"in an interpenetrating world is a sad metaphor for the attempt to solve moral conflict through recasting our sense of moral zones. For whether the turf involved be nation or school or church or profession the endless interpenetration of differences will be the same.

Yet I would not end this analysis on such terms. In many ways, our optimism or pessimism arises from the arbitrary choice to look in a certain direction. Let me then close this moral discussion with a few words about the moral future of the division of labor.

As the classical writers all recognized, the division of labor itself has two aspects: the division of products and the division of tasks. It is the latter, of course, that kindled Smith's admiration and Marx's ire. But the two are not, in fact, qualitatively different. A Marxian artisan who makes a complete product for exchange with an agriculturalist is a specialist in logically the same sense as an assembly-line operator or an operating room nurse. A true subsistence society would find both the artisan's and the agriculturalist's lives to be as woefully incomplete as Marx was to find the shop worker's and current critics do the nurse's. The division of labor, that is, is a self-similar social structure. We call that portion of the structure that we find culturally acceptable the division of products and tolerate or admire it. We call that portion of the fine structure that undercuts our own sense of being the division of tasks and detest it. The two aspects of the division of labor, that is, really refer to two directions we can look from our position in the social structure.

Thus it is that even values are not absolute scales, but ultimately nested ones, generated by endless fractal reproduction. In the concentration camps, Primo Levi tells us, freedom consisted in the tiniest acts of selfhood. In China, democracy is hardly the conformist anarchy that Americans imagine democracy to be, any more than the good life for an African peasant consists in malls and traffic lights. In any particular human situation, a value is a direction, a way of ordering that situation on its own moral terms, not a way of imposing a content.

The fractal conception of social structure and with it the fractal conception of values imply a fairly complete rethinking of our attempts to create the good society. They imply that there is no one good society, but rather a universal straining after justice in any situation. That may not appeal to the absolutist sensibility, either conservative or radical. But it is the only foundation for a truly humane sensibility.

Fortunately for those of us who fear that the world will end up as an "American democracy" with only one language, one suburban life zone, and one culture, the fractal character of social structure provides for infinite divisibility within the most conformist of societies. Even in the holy confines of the Bruderhof, where every individual meets standards of selflessness and sacrifice far exceeding what one could imagine on the outside, the members yet manage to find deviants, those who are not selfless enough. No matter how uniform the mass society might become, to those of us who can remember or have lived alternatives to it, there will always be the fractal possibility of re-creating a million distinctions within its conformity. They will not be divisions we care about or can even imagine, any more than an Elizabethan could care about or imagine the difference between the Rotary Club and a professional association. To those of us who went before they might seem mind-chilling splitting of hairs. But for those in the situation they will provide all the differences required to exercise and argue the ancient human problems of freedom and tolerance, justice and equity.

6. The Future of Social Science

I finish this chapter with a few words about academic values. Throughout the earlier chapters I argued that the fractal processes I saw in social science were not only a model for what happened there, but also a model for how to proceed. Now that we have reflected a bit about how fractal value systems work—that is, about what it means to have a fractal understanding of right action—we are ready to think about academic values, about how we ought to act as social scientists.

In some senses, of course, this analysis is apologetic. To say that one has a model for inquiry and that one's model is not only descriptive but also prescriptive is to say, putting it in the most ugly form, that what is is right. Seen at its best, however, as a version of the Moralist position, to make this dual claim is to say that one accepts the broad humanity of the social science enterprise and that one would not say to anyone in it that she doesn't understand what it is to *really* know society. In that sense, then, I take a Moralist position. And further, I take with it the stand that scientific thinking consists, just as my fractal action argument has held for moral action, in a form of activity that is universal, but reenacted in ways proper to the localities in which social scientists work. Thus, for me to make recommendations about social science practice is essentially to talk about the best versions of that form of activity.

As we have just seen, it is also to talk about the issues of zone definition. As with ethnicity, however, I feel that the attempt to mend social science by broadening its zones of relevance is a failure. Interdisciplinarity for its own sake is a failure. Bott was right when she said that what mattered about interdisciplinarity was that interdisciplinary contact modified each researcher individually, not that it created grand new zones of endeavor (see chapter 5, section 2). It is the form of scientific enactment that matters, not the size of the zone within which a social scientist tries to define the goodness of his or her work.

Now the aim of social science is to know things about society, things without number, things interesting, systematic, curious, unbelievable, obvious, complex. And no reader can doubt at this point that I see two sides to that knowing: the imagining of possible things to know and the application of those imaginings to the social world as it confronts us. What the fractal model shows us is exactly how we go about finding new areas of things to know; we rearrange our fractal allegiances. We disassemble traditional conflations. We get ourselves out of blind alleys by flipping our position on one little fractal choice. Perhaps we suddenly decide to invoke the context; perhaps, quite the contrary, we decide to consider our problem in abstract isolation. Perhaps we make a rash assumption and see where it will take us; perhaps, quite the contrary, we rule out all but the safest assumptions. Wherever we are, the way of creativity lies in playing with the system of fractal ideas that we use to generate our concepts about social life. It is this process, in fact, for which interdisciplinarity is a proxy. The real utility of contacting others is in the way it opens up new choices for us—not to become *like* them, or even to steal their methodologies directly—but rather to enact what they enact but in our own place and time, on our own materials and in our own tradition; in short, to make a translation.

There is something deeply exciting about making these methodological moves. And there is something very beautiful about the way social science circles around them. It is an emotional business, this work of ours. I have mentioned those emotions from time to time: the stolid virtue of scientism in chapter 2, the heady pleasures of opposition and theoretical consistency in chapter 3, and in the present chapter the thrill of self-righteousness as well as the grayer enjoyments of complacency. For me, the chief emotion is a sense of wonder at all the possible ways to know social life. That is what it is to be an eclectic, and that is why it has been necessary for me to think up a way of imagining social scientific knowledge that would give me a way of embracing all the best of it. As I said at the outset, social science is progressive, but not cumulative. It can and does forget. But its evolutions are wonderful to watch. And the ever-growing complexity that grows out of the endless permutations of its fundamental ideas is a fulfillment in itself.

Epilogue

THIS BOOK began with an attempt to take a large, complex, and contingent set of phenomena and to locate them as avatars of a single process. My aim was not so much to explain intellectual life in academia as it was to give an abstract description of it. There was no claim that this or that development *had* to happen in intellectual life, but rather an account of the typical moves and patterns—limited in number—that in fact do happen. The first part of the book thus lies in the same tradition as did my earlier book about professions,[1] which also offered not an explanation of why professions developed in this or that direction, but a comprehensive theoretical description of the various contingencies professions faced and the main interacting forces governing those contingencies.

Like the earlier book too, this one grows out of a single metaphor, here the proliferation of fractals, there the structures of ecology. Indeed, in both cases the underlying strategy has been to take a single metaphor and work it out in endless detail. Now, in these last two chapters I have left the detail behind and simply pushed the metaphor as far as I can to see what comes out.

These strategies may leave some readers with important questions. For example, once we move off into general social structure or morals, the compelling quality of the careful examples is gone and one begins to wonder whether the fractals are really there or whether I am simply imposing a fractal logic on whatever I study. Even for the earlier argument about intellectual systems, one might wonder whether I shouldn't be testing these ideas or proposing formal counterhypotheses. One might wonder whether fractal distinc-

---

1. Abbott 1988a.

tions really do provide a model for what goes on or whether they are just a compact way to describe what goes on. If so, why not some other description?

This is not the place to consider these questions in detail. I wish merely to point out that these are general questions, questions that can be posed to any sustained theoretical enterprise. There is nothing particular about the present argument that makes these questions especially salient here: neither the metaphorical nature of the basic theoretical construct nor the theoretical strategy of abstract description.[2] The first duty of the theorist is to present a plausible argument, and it requires not only much theoretical discussion but also careful analysis of cases to establish the plausibility of an argument. That seems enough for one book; testing and counterarguments can wait.

But perhaps a more frank avowal is necessary on the matter of why I should think that complex fractals are better and that richness of exploration of the potential field of knowledge is better than poverty. I don't know why I think complex exploration is more beautiful. I just do. I think knowledge is improved by making it more complex and deep, more comprehensive and multiple. This doesn't mean a bias against simplicity. After all, I have just tried to bring a whole range of facts about intellectual life under a single idea. But it means my bias is toward comprehensiveness, both in the common metaphorical sense of wide coverage and in the older, literal sense of depth of understanding. And it also means that for me the more important side of knowledge is envisioning new things that could be known, not the routine discovery of things that are there.[3]

But it is also true that this leaning toward complexity drives my love of eclecticism, makes it an aesthetic of intellectual life. For if one knowledge of something is good, two are better, and three better still. There is to be sure something very beautiful, something severely elegant, about single-minded disciplines like economics or psychoanalysis, where there is a right way and a wrong way. But I would rather be Miranda with all those brave new knowledges ahead of me, or, more realistically, I would rather be a Conradian skipper piloting my old tramp steamer from island to island and picking up odd facts and methodologies like so many castaways. It might be

---

2. I have dealt with the issue of causal explanation versus description at some length in Abbott 1998.

3. In reflecting about this personal preference for complexity I was reminded that Teilhard's *Phenomenon of Man* (1961) was one of the influential books of my youth. I have no idea what I would think of this book today—I'm afraid to read it lest my memory turn to dust—but it seemed glorious when I was sixteen.

nice to captain a fancy boat for a well-kept imperial fleet. But it's not for me.

The power of theorizing in fractals makes one want to push further and further. It is tantalizing to speculate, for example, whether the concept of self-similarity might not be useful in the analysis of personality. There are beguiling possibilities.

Many personality characteristics operate in ways similar to the fractal distinctions discussed in chapter one. Indeed, enduring qualities of temperament work themselves out in self-similar fashion over the life course as an individual enters differing circumstances, a sort of fractal cycle within the individual. The quality of tending to disagree with everyone in one's environment can be useful or not depending on the circumstances. In some school settings such a quality might conduce to delinquency, in others it might become a mark of creativity, in still others a grounds for social isolation. At one point, it might be helpful, at another harmful. All professors are familiar with this quandary. Having a tendency to see things in a unique way is quite useful for an undergraduate. Such students seem special both to their own teachers and to those who read their graduate school applications. But such a tendency is not very helpful once one enters the much smaller group of beginning graduate students, or even among the still smaller cadre of assistant professors. In both those career phases, uniqueness can be problematic indeed. Yet later, independence and personal vision turn out to be the chief foundation for eminent work at middle age, among the few who have managed to remain active in the discipline to that point. Thus after training vision out of our students, we bemoan its absence in ourselves and our colleagues. Morris Janowitz saw the same pattern in the elite military; the true leaders were not from the central elite, but from its periphery—the strangest, most unusual members of that elite.[4] Indeed, it is this self-similarity of personal qualities over the life course that lies at the foundation of the Freudian theory of the personality, in which emotional patterns established at early ages become templates for later life experiences. Fractals are laid over earlier fractals.

The fractal argument could thus take us yet further. But when we come to the nature of personality and, more puzzling still, to the question of the temporal nature of personality, we have reached a logical resting place. After what I have argued in this book, to stop and rest may seem an odd conclusion. Within the fractal view of social science there are no resting places, only the endless city of

4. Janowitz 1960, chap. 8.

things to know about society, which is really the city of things to dream up about society. But temporality and personality are accessible from here only by taking a detour that starts in that unappetizing alley across the way. Over the wall, we can hear the noisy buses rushing to Regression Square and Postmodern Park, where the seasoned tour guides are shouting at visitors about the date of this or that citation and perhaps arguing among themselves over whether intellectual architraves should be more or less pronounced, and whether one can, by some back passage dating from an early paradigm, reach the subtle lane along the old city wall. It is a city of bustle, this town of knowledge, with its tourist traps and museums, its shops and coffeehouses, its money changers turning the diverse talents of the tourists into the single coin of the mind. And the undergraduates and visitors will buy with that coin souvenirs to show themselves and their friends in twenty years' time, telling how this or that vista of ideas or perhaps even a particular tour guide seemed quite amazing and important, while they smile across their drinks at the shelf of half-forgotten college texts.

But just now, let us rest in this sudden sunlit courtyard, empty save for ourselves and the marks of a few earlier visitors. There will be time enough for personality and temporality this afternoon. Just now, let us quietly remember the sights of the morning.

References

Abbott, A. 1980. "Religion, Psychiatry, and the Problems of Everyday Life." *Sociological Analysis* 41:164–71.

———. 1981. "Status and Status Strain in the Professions." *American Journal of Sociology* 86:815–35.

———. 1982. "The Emergence of American Psychiatry." Ph.D. diss., University of Chicago.

———. 1983. "Sequences of Social Events." *Historical Methods* 16:129–47.

———. 1986. "Notes for a Theory of Disciplines." Unpublished paper, presented 25 September 1986, Center for the Critical Analysis of Contemporary Culture, Rutgers University.

———. 1988a. *The System of Professions.* Chicago: University of Chicago Press.

———. 1988b. "Transcending General Linear Reality." *Sociological Theory.* 6:169–86.

———. 1990a. "Conceptions of Time and Events in Social Science Methods." *Historical Methods,* 23:140–50.

———. 1990b. "Positivism and Interpretation in Sociology." *Sociological Forum* 5:435–58.

———. 1990c. "Vacancy Methods for Historical Data." In *Social Mobility and Social Structure.* Ed. R. Breiger, 80–102. Cambridge: Cambridge University Press.

———. 1992a. "From Causes to Events." *Sociological Methods and Research* 20:428–55.

———. 1992b. "What Do Cases Do?" In *What is a Case?* Ed. C. Ragin and H. S. Becker, 53–82. Cambridge: Cambridge University Press.

———. 1995a. "Sequence Analysis." *Annual Review of Sociology* 21:93–113.

———. 1995b. "Things of Boundaries." *Social Research* 62:857–82.

———. 1996. "La sintesis de otros tiempos y la del futuro" (The once and future synthesis). Trans. E. A. Scholz. *Historia, antropologia y fuentes orales* 1:31–39.

————. 1998. "The Causal Devolution." *Sociological Methods and Research* 27:148–181.

————. 1999a. *Department and Discipline.* Chicago: University of Chicago Press.

————. 1999b. "Temporality and Process in Social Life." In *Social Time and Social Change.* Ed. F. Engelstad and R. Kalleberg, 28–61. Oslo: Scandinavian University Press.

Abbott, A., and A. Hrycak. 1990. "Measuring Resemblance in Social Sequences." *American Journal of Sociology* 96:144–85.

Abbott, E. A. [1884] 1956. *Flatland.* New York: Dover.

Abell, P. 1987. *The Syntax of Social Life.* Oxford: Oxford University Press.

Abrams, P. 1982. *Historical Sociology.* Ithaca: Cornell University Press.

Ad Hoc Committee on ASA Future Organization Trends. 1989. "The Future Organizational Trends of the ASA." *Footnotes* 17:6:1–6.

Aiken, L. R. 1961."Stress and Anxiety as Homomorphisms." *Psychological Record* 11:365–72.

Alter, G. 1981. "History and Quantitative Data." *Historical Methods* 14: 145–48.

Aminzade, R. 1992. "Historical Sociology and Time." *Sociological Methodology and Research* 20:456–80.

Atkinson, P. 1988. "Ethnomethodology." *Annual Review of Sociology* 14: 441–65.

Bakwin, H. 1945. "Pseudodoxia Pediatrica." *New England Journal of Medicine* 232:691–97.

Barnard, D. S. 1985. "Psychosomatic Medicine and the Problem of Meaning." *Bulletin of the Menninger Clinic* 49:10–28.

Barnes, B. 1974. *Scientific Knowledge and Social Theory.* London: Routledge.

————. 1981. "On the 'Hows' and 'Whys' of Cultural Change." *Social Studies of Science* 11:481–498.

Barnsley, M. 1988. *Fractals Everywhere.* San Diego: Academic Press.

Barthes, R. 1967. *Systeme de la mode.* Paris: Seuil.

————. 1974. *S/Z.* Trans. R. Miller. New York: Hill and Wang.

Bateson, G. [1936] 1958. *Naven.* Stanford: Stanford University Press.

Baum, A., N. E. Gomberg, and J. E. Singer. 1982. "The Use of Psychological and Neuroendocrinological Measurements in the Study of Stress." *Health Psychology* 1:217–36.

Becher, T. 1987. "The Disciplinary Shaping of the Profession." In *The Academic Profession.* Ed. B. R. Clark, 271–303. Berkeley and Los Angeles: University of California Press.

Becker, H. S. 1963. *Outsiders.* New York: Free Press.

————, ed. 1964. *The Other Side.* New York: Free Press.

————. 1974. "Labelling Theory Reconsidered." *Deviance and Social Control.* Ed. P. Rock and M. McIntosh, 41–66. London: Tavistock.

Ben-David, J., and R. Collins. 1966. "Social Factors in the Origin of a New Science." *American Sociological Review* 31: 451–65.

Benedict, R. [1946] 1989. *The Chrysanthemum and the Sword.* Boston: Houghton Mifflin.

Berger, P. and T. Luckmann. 1967. *The Social Construction of Reality.* New York: Doubleday.

Berkhofer, R. F. 1983. "The Two New Histories." *OAH Newsletter* 11, no. 2: 9–12.

Bernal, J. D. 1953. *Science and Industry in the Nineteeenth Century.* London: Routledge.

Bernert, C. 1983. "The Career of Causal Analysis in American Sociology." *British Journal of Sociology* 34:230–54.

Bernstein, M. H. 1955. *Regulating Business by Independent Commission.* Princeton: Princeton University Press.

Bhaskar, R. 1986. *Scientific Realism and Human Emancipation.* London: Verso.

Biderman, A. 1966. "Social Indicators and Goals." *Social Indicators.* Ed. R. Bauer, 68–153. Cambridge: MIT Press.

Biderman, A., A. Johnson, J. McIntyre, and A. W. Weir. 1967. "Report on a Pilot Study." U.S. President's Commission on Law Enforcement and the Administration of Justice, Survey #1. Chicago: National Opinion Research Center.

Biderman, A., and A. Reiss. 1967. "On Exploring the Dark Figure of Crime." *The Annals* 374:1–15.

Black, D. 1984. "Social Control as a Dependent Variable." In *Toward a General Theory of Social Control.* Ed. D. Black, 1–36. New York: Academic.

Black, J. B. [1936] 1959. *The Reign of Elizabeth.* Oxford: Oxford University Press.

Bloor, D. 1976. *Knowledge and Social Imagery.* London: Routledge.

Blumer, H. 1931. "Science without Concepts." *American Journal of Sociology* 36:515–33.

———. 1956. "Sociological Analysis and the 'Variable.' " *American Sociological Review* 21:683–90.

———. 1971. "Social Problems as Collective Behavior." *Social Problems* 18:298–306.

Blumstein, S. 1990. *The Brown Curriculum Twenty Years Later.* Providence: Brown University.

Bogue, A. G. 1983. *Clio and the Bitch Goddess.* Beverly Hills: Sage.

———. 1990. "The Quest for Numeracy" *Journal of Interdisciplinary History* 21:89–116.

Bonnell, V. E. 1980. "The Uses of Theory, Concepts, and Comparison in Historical Sociology." *Comparative Studies in Society and History* 22:156–73.

Bott, E. [1957] 1971. *Family and Social Network.* New York: Free Press.

Bourdelais, P. 1984. "French Quantitative History." *Social Science History* 8:179–92.

Brown, G. W., and T. O. Harris. 1978. *Social Origins of Depression.* New York: Free Press.

Burawoy, M. 1989. "Two Methods in Search of Science." *Theory and Society* 18:759–805.

Burke, K. 1969. *A Grammar of Motives.* Berkeley and Los Angeles: University of California Press.

Burrage, M. C., and D. Corry. 1981. "At Sixes and Sevens." *American Sociological Review* 46:375–93.

Burridge, K. 1989. "The Subject and the Profession." *Culture* 9:89–96.

Calhoun, D. W. 1950. "The Reception of Marxist Sociological Theory by American Academic Social Scientists." Ph.D. diss., University of Chicago.

Campbell, D. T. 1969. "Ethnocentrism of Disciplines and the Fish-Scale Model of Omniscience." In Sherif and Sherif 1969, 328–48.

Cannon, W. B. 1914. "The Interrelations of Emotions as Suggested by Recent Physiological Researches." *American Journal of Psychology* 25: 256–82.

———. 1929. *Bodily Change in Pain, Hunger, Fear, and Rage.* New York: Appleton.

Cappell, C. L., and T. M. Guterbock. 1986. "Dimensions of Association in Sociology." *Bulletin de methode sociologique* 9:23–29.

Chalmers, B. E. 1981. "A Selective Review of Stress." *Current Psychological Reviews* 1:325–43.

Chatman, S. 1978. *Story and Discourse.* Ithaca: Cornell University Press.

Chirot, D. 1976. "Thematic Controversies and New Developments in the Uses of Historical Materials by Sociologists." *Social Forces* 55:232–41.

Cicourel, A. 1968. *The Social Organization of Juvenile Justice.* New York: Wiley.

Clark, T. N. 1973. *The French University and the Emergence of the Social Sciences.* Cambridge: Harvard University Press.

Cobban, A. 1957. *A History of Modern France.* Vol. 1:1715–1799. Harmondsworth: Penguin.

Cohen, S., and S. L. Syme. 1985. *Social Support and Health.* Orlando: Academic Press.

Cole, S. 1975. "The Growth of Scientific Knowledge." In *The Idea of Social Structure.* Ed. L. A. Coser, 175–220. New York: Harcourt Brace.

Collingwood, R. G. 1946. *The Idea of History.* London: Oxford University Press.

Collins, H. M. 1981. "Stages in the Empirical Programme of Relativism." *Social Studies of Science* 11:3–10.

Collins, R. 1998. *The Sociology of Philosophies.* Cambridge: Harvard University Press.

Comfort, A. 1970. *The Anxiety Makers.* New York: Delta.

Conk, M. 1980. *The United States Census and Labor Force Change.* Ann Arbor: UMI Research Press.

Cooper, C. L., and J. Marshall. 1976. "Occupational Sources of Stress." *Journal of Occupational Psychology* 49:11–28.

Cornell, L. L. 1987. "Reproduction, Production, Social Science, and the Past." *Social Science History* 11:43–52.

Coxon, A. P. M., and C. L. Jones. 1978. *The Images of Occupational Prestige.* London: Macmillan.

———. 1979. *Class and Hierarchy.* New York: St. Martins.

Crozier, M. 1964. *The Bureaucratic Phenomenon.* Chicago: University of Chicago Press.

Dahl, R. 1961. *Who Governs*. Yale: Yale University Press.

Dain, N. 1964. *Concepts of Insanity in the United States, 1789–1865*. New Brunswick: Rutgers University Press.

———. 1980. *Clifford W. Beers*. Pittsburgh: University of Pittsburgh Press.

Daipha, P. 1999. "The Intellectual and Social Organization of the ASA." MA paper, Department of Sociology, University of Chicago.

Davies, G. [1937] 1959. *The Early Stuarts*. Oxford: Oxford University Press.

Davis, A., B. Gardner, and M. R. Gardner 1941. *Deep South*. Chicago: University of Chicago Press.

Dean, A., and N. Lin. 1977. "The Stress-Buffering Role of Social Support." *Journal of Nervous and Mental Disease* 165:403–17.

Desrosières, A., and L. Thévenot. 1988. *Les catégories socioprofessionnelles*. Paris: Éditions la Découverte.

Dewey, J. [1927] 1954. *The Public and Its Problems*. Athens: Swallow Press.

Dix, G. 1945. *The Shape of the Liturgy*. London: Dacre.

Dogan, M., and R. Pahre. 1989. "Fragmentation and Recombination of the Social Sciences." *Studies in Comparative International Development* 24, no. 2: 56–73.

Dohrenwend, B. S., and B. P. Dohrenwend. 1974. *Stressful Life Events*. New York: Wiley.

———. 1978. "Some Issues in Research on Stressful Life Events." *Journal of Nervous and Mental Disease* 166:7–15.

Dumont, L. 1980. *Homo Hierarchicus*. Trans. M. Sainsbury, L. Dumont, and B. Gulati. Chicago: University of Chicago Press.

Ehrenreich, B. 1983. *The Hearts of Men*. Garden City, N.Y.: Doubleday.

Eliot, T. S. 1943. *Four Quartets*. New York: Harcourt Brace and World.

Ellingson, S. 1995. "The Emergence and Institutionalization of the Major-Minor Curriculum, 1870–1910." Unpublished paper, Department of Sociology, University of Chicago.

Elliott, G. R., and D. Eisdorfer, eds. 1982. *Stress and Human Health*. New York: Springer.

Ennis, P. H. 1967. "Criminal Victimization in the United States." U.S. President's Commission on Law Enforcement and the Administration of Justice, Survey #2. Chicago: National Opinion Research Center.

Epstein, S. 1996. *Impure Science*. Berkeley and Los Angeles: University of California Press.

Erikson, K. 1962. "Notes on the Sociology of Deviance. *Social Problems* 9:307–14.

———. 1966. *Wayward Puritans*. New York: Wiley.

Espeland, W. N., and M. L. Stevens. 1998. "Commensuration as a Social Process." *Annual Review of Sociology* 24:313–43.

Evans, M. D. R., J. Kelley, and T. Kolosi. 1992. "Images of Class." *American Sociological Review* 57:461–82.

Evans-Pritchard, E. E. [1940] 1970. *The Nuer*. New York: Oxford University Press.

———. [1937] 1976. *Withcraft, Oracles, and Magic among the Azande*. Oxford: Oxford University Press.

Fisher, D. 1993. *The Fundamental Development of the Social Sciences.* Ann Arbor: University of Michigan Press.

Floud, R. 1984. "Quantitative History and People's History." *Social Science History* 8:151–68.

Fogel, R. W. 1964. *Railroads and American Economic Growth.* Baltimore: Johns Hopkins University Press.

Fogel, R. W., and S. L. Engerman. 1974. *Time on the Cross.* Boston: Little Brown.

Frank, R. H. 1985. *Choosing the Right Pond.* New York: Oxford University Press.

Frazier, E. F. 1965. *Black Bourgeoisie.* New York: Free Press.

Freudenthal, G. 1984. "The Role of Shared Knowledge in Science." *Social Studies of Science* 14:285–95.

Fuchs, S. 1992. *The Professional Quest for Truth.* Albany: SUNY Press.

Gabin, N. F. 1990. *Feminism in the Labor Movement.* Ithaca: Cornell University Press.

Gal, S. 1991. "Bartok's Funeral." *American Ethnologist* 18:440–58.

Gal, S., and J. T. Irvine. 1995. "The Boundaries of Languages and Differences." *Social Research* 62:965–1001.

Gans, H. 1992. "Sociological Amnesia." *Sociological Forum* 7:701–10.

Geertz, C. [1966] 1973. "Religion as a Cultural System." In *The Interpretation of Cultures,* 87–125. New York: Basic.

———. 1980. "Blurred Genres." *American Scholar* 49:165–179.

Genette, G. 1980. *Narrative Discourse.* Ithaca: Cornell University Press.

Gerschenkron, A. 1967. "The Discipline and I." *Journal of Economic History* 27:443–59.

Giddens, A. 1979. *Central Problems in Social Theory.* Berkeley and Los Angeles: University of California Press.

Gieryn, T. 1982. "Relativist/Constructivist Programmes in the Sociology of Science." *Social Studies of Science* 12:279–97.

Gifford, S. 1978. "Medical Psychotherapy and the Emmanuel Movement." In *Psychoanalysis, Psychotherapy, and the New England Medical Scene, 1904–1912.* Ed. G. E. Gifford, 106–18. New York: Science History.

Goffman, E. 1961. *Asylums.* Garden City, N.Y.: Doubleday.

Goldmann, L. 1964. *The Hidden God.* Trans. P. Thody. New York: Humanities Press.

Goldstone, J. A. 1986. "How to Study History." *Historical Methods* 19: 82–84.

Gosling, F. 1976. *American Nervousness.* Ph.D diss., University of Oklahoma.

Gouldner, A. W. 1968. "The Sociologist as Partisan." *American Sociologist* 3:103–16.

———. 1970. *The Coming Crisis of Western Sociology.* New York: Avon.

Gove, W. R. 1970. "Societal Reaction as an Explanation of Mental Illness." *American Sociological Review* 35:873–84.

Graff, G. 1987. *Professing Literature.* Chicago: University of Chicago Press.

Green, V. H. H. 1974. *A History of Oxford University.* London: Basford.

Griffin, L. J. 1993. "Narrative, Event-Structure Analysis, and Causal Interpretation in Historical Sociology." *American Journal of Sociology* 98: 1094–133.

Grimshaw, W. J. 1992. *Bitter Fruit*. Chicago: University of Chicago Press.

Grob, G. N. 1973. *Mental Institutions in America*. New York: Free Press.

———. 1983. *Mental Illness and American Society*. Princeton: Princeton University Press.

Gurin, G., J. Veroff, and S. Feld. 1960. *Americans View Their Mental Health*. New York: Basic.

Gusfield, J. 1981. *The Culture of Public Problems*. Chicago: University of Chicago Press.

Guterbock, T. L., and C. L. Cappell. 1990. "Visible Colleges." Unpublished ms., University of Virginia, Department of Sociology/Northern Illinois University, Department of Sociology.

Hagan, J., and A. Palloni. 1990. "The Social Reproduction of a Criminal Class in Working-Class London, 1950–1980." *American Journal of Sociology* 96:265–99.

Hall, J. A. 1989. "They Do Things Differently Here." *British Journal of Sociology* 40:544–64.

Hall, S. 1978. "Marxism and Culture." *Radical History Review* 18:5–14.

Halliday, T. S., and M. Janowitz. 1992. *Sociology and Its Publics*. Chicago: University of Chicago Press.

Hamilton, G. G., and J. Walton. 1988. "History in Sociology." In *The Future of Sociology*. Ed. E. F. Borgatta and K. Cook, 181–99. Newbury Park, Calif.: Sage.

Hanagan, M., and L. A. Tilly. 1996. "¿Sintesis perdida, sintesis reencontrada?" Trans. E. A. Scholz. *Historia, antropologia y fuentes orales* 1:11–29.

Harris, A. R., and G. D. Hill. 1982. "The Social Psychology of Deviance." *Annual Review of Sociology* 8:161–86.

Hartz, L. 1955. *The Liberal Tradition in America*. New York: Harcourt Brace.

Hauser, A. 1951. *The Social History of Art*. London: Routledge.

Hauser, R. M., and J. R. Warren. 1997. "Socioeconomic Indices for Occupations." *Sociological Methodology* 27:177–298.

Hawkins, N. G., R. Davies, and T. H. Holmes. 1957. "Evidence of Psychosocial Factors in the Development of Pulmonary Tuberculosis." *American Review of Tuberculosis and Pulmonary Diseases* 75:768–80.

Hechter, M. 1987. *Principles of Group Solidarity*. Berkeley and Los Angeles: University of California Press.

Henslin, J. M. and P. M. Roesti. 1976. "Trends and Topics in *Social Problems* 1953–1975." *Social Problems* 24:54–68.

Herd, J. A. 1984. "Cardiovascular Responses to Stress in Man." *Annual Review of Physiology* 46:177–85.

Higham, J. 1989. "Changing Paradigms." *Journal of American History* 76:460–66.

Hinkle, L. E. 1975. "The Concept of Stress in the Biological and Social Sciences." *International Journal of Psychiatric Medicine* 5:335–57.

Hirsch, E. L. 1990. *Urban Revolt*. Berkeley and Los Angeles: University of California Press.

Hodge, R. W., P. M. Siegel, and P. H. Rossi. 1966. "Occupational Prestige in the United States." In *Class, Status, and Power*. Ed. R. Bendix and S. M. Lipset, 322–34. New York: Free Press.

Hodgson, M. G. S. 1974. *The Classical Age of Islam*. Chicago: University of Chicago Press.

Hofstadter, R. 1968. *The Progressive Historians*. New York: Knopf.

Holmes, T. H., and E. M. David. 1984. *Life Change Events Research 1966–1978*. New York: Praeger.

Holmes, T. H., and R. H. Rahe. 1967. "The Social Readjustment Rating Scale." *Journal of Psychosomatic Research* 11:213–18.

Holzner, B. 1968. *Reality Construction in Society*. Cambridge, Mass.: Schenkman.

Honan, W. H. 1994. "Academic Disciplines Increasingly Entwine, Recasting Scholarship." *New York Times*, 23 March, B8.

Honeyman, K., and J. Goodman. 1991. "Women's Work, Gender Conflict, and Labor Markets in Europe." *Economic History Review* 44:608–28.

Hostetler, J. A. 1993. *Amish Society*. Baltimore: Johns Hopkins University Press.

Hummon, D. M. 1990. *Commonplaces*. Albany: SUNY Press.

Irvine, J. T., and S. Gal. 2000. "Language Ideology and Linguistic Differentiation." In *Regimes of Language*. Ed. P. Kroskrity, 35–83. Santa Fe: School of American Research.

Janowitz, M. 1960. *The Professional Soldier*. New York: Free Press.

Jarausch, K. H. 1982. *Students, Society, and Politics in Imperial Germany*. Princeton: Princeton University Press.

———, ed. 1983. *The Transformation of Higher Learning*. Chicago: University of Chicago Press.

Jenkins, C. D. 1971. "Psychological and Social Precursors of Coronary Disease." *New England Journal of Medicine* 284: 244–55, 301–17.

Johnson, H. M. 1929. "The Real Meaning of Fatigue." *Harper's* 158:186–93.

Johnson, R. 1978. "Edward Thompson, Eugene Genovese, and Socialist-Humanist History." *History Workshop Journal*, no. 6: 79–100.

Judt, T. 1979. "A Clown in Regal Purple." *History Workshop Journal*, no. 7: 66–94.

Kammen, M. 1980. "The Historian's Vocation and the State of the Discipline in the United States." In *The Past Before Us*. Ed. M. Kammen, 19–46. Ithaca: Cornell University Press.

Kant, I. [1788] 1956. *Critique of Practical Reason*. Trans. L. W. Beck. Indianapolis: Bobbs Merrill.

———. 1963. *On History*. Trans. L. W. Beck. Indianapolis: Bobbs Merrill.

———. [1790] 1968. *Critique of Judgment*. Trans. J. H. Bernard. New York: Hafner.

———. [1793] 1974. *On the Old Saw: That May Be Right in Theory but It Won't Work in Practice*. Trans. E. B. Ashton. Philadelphia: University of Pennsylvania Press.

Keller, E. F. 1989. "Just What *Is* So Difficult about the Concept of Gender as a Social Category?" *Social Studies of Science* 19:721–24.

Keneally, T. 1982. *Schindler's List*. New York: Simon and Schuster.

Kessler, R. C., R. H. Price, and C. B. Wortman. 1985. "Social Factors in Psychopathology." *Annual Review of Psychology* 36:531–72.

Kimeldorf, H. 1991. "Bringing Unions Back In." *Labor History* 32:91–103.

Kitsuse, J. I., and A. Cicourel. 1963. "A Note on the Use of Official Statistics." *Social Problems* 2:131–39.

Kitsuse, J. I., and M. Spector. 1973. "Toward a Sociology of Social Problems." *Social Problems* 20:407–19.

Knapp, P. 1983. "Can Social Theory Escape from History?" *History and Theory* 23:34–52.

Knorr-Cetina, K. D. 1983. "New Developments in Science Studies." *Canadian Journal of Sociology* 8:153–76.

Kocka, J. 1984. "Theories and Quantification in History." *Social Science History* 8:169–78.

Kohn, M. L. 1976. "Looking Back: A 25-Year Review and Appraisal of Social Problems Research." *Social Problems* 24:94–112.

Kousser, M. J. 1980. "History QUASSHed." *American Behavioral Scientist* 23:885–904.

———. 1989. "The State of Social Science History in the Late 1980s." *Historical Methods* 22:13–20.

Kroeber, A. L., and C. Kluckhohn. [1952] 2000. *Culture*. Westport, Conn.: Greenwood.

Kuklick, H. 1983. "The Sociology of Knowledge." *Annual Review of Sociology* 9:287–310.

Lauer, R. H. 1976. "Defining Social Problems." *Social Problems* 24:122–30.

Lauwerier, H. 1991. *Fractals*. Princeton: Princeton University Press.

Lazarus, R. S., J. Deese, and S. F. Osler. 1952. "The Effects of Psychological Stress upon Performance." *Psychological Bulletin* 49:293–317.

Lazarus, R. S., and S. Folkman. 1984. *Stress, Appraisal, and Coping*. New York: Springer.

Lears, J. 1982. *No Place of Grace*. New York: Pantheon.

Lee, E. B., and A. M. Lee. 1976. "The Society for the Study of Social Problems." *Social Problems* 24:4–14.

Lemert, E. M. 1951. *Social Pathology*. New York: McGraw-Hill.

Leontief, W. 1982. "Academic Economics." *Science* 217:104–7.

Lerner, G. 1989. "A View from the Women's Side." *Journal of American History* 76:446–56.

Lessing, D. 1981. *The Marriages between Zones Three, Four, and Five*. New York: Vintage.

Levin, J., and B. Nalebuff. 1995. "An Introduction to Vote-Counting Schemes." *Journal of Economic Perspectives* 9:3–26.

Lévi-Strauss, C. 1963a. *Structural Anthropology*. New York: Basic.

———. 1963b. *Totemism*. Boston: Beacon.

Licht, W. 1983. *Working for the Railroad*. Princeton: Princeton University Press.

Lloyd, C. 1986. *Explanation in Social History.* Oxford: Basil Blackwell.

Lorrain, F., and H. C. White. 1971. "The Structural Equivalence of Individuals in Networks." *Journal of Mathematical Sociology* 1:49–80.

Lovejoy, A. O. [1936] 1960. *The Great Chain of Being.* New York: Harper and Row.

Luhmann, N. 1982. *The Differentiation of Society.* New York: Columbia University Press.

Lukács, G. 1969. *The Historical Novel.* Harmondsworth: Penguin.

Lundberg, U. 1984. "Human Psychobiology in Scandinavia: II. Psychoneuroendocrinology: Human Stress and Coping Research." *Scandinavian Journal of Psychology* 25:214–26.

Lynch, M. 1993. *Scientific Practice and Ordinary Action.* Cambridge: Cambridge University Press.

MacAloon, J. J. 1992. *General Education in the Social Sciences.* Chicago: University of Chicago Press.

MacDonald, T. J. 1990. "Faiths of Our Fathers." Paper presented at conference, Modes of Inquiry for American City History, 25 October, at Chicago Historical Society.

———. 1996a. *The Historic Turn.* Ann Arbor: University of Michigan Press.

———. 1996b. "What We Talk about When We Talk about History." In MacDonald 1996a, 91–118.

Mackie, J. D. 1952. *The Earlier Tudors.* Oxford: Oxford University Press.

Mailer, N. 1948. *The Naked and the Dead.* New York: Rinehart.

Mannheim, K. 1936. *Ideology and Utopia.* New York: Harcourt, Brace, World.

Marcuse, H. 1964. *One-Dimensional Man.* Boston: Beacon.

Marx, K., and F. Engels. [1846] 1970. *The German Ideology.* New York: International.

Mason, J. W. 1975. "A History of the Stress Field." *Journal of Human Stress* 1:1:6–12, 1:2:22–36.

Mayhew, B. H. 1990. *Researches in Structural Sociology.* Compiled and edited by J. S. Skvoretz. Department of Sociology, University of South Carolina.

McClelland, C. 1980. *State, Society, and University in Germany, 1700–1914.* Cambridge: Cambridge University Press.

McClelland, P. D. 1975. *Causal Explanation and Model Building in History, Economics, and the New Economic History.* Ithaca: Cornell University Press.

McDonald, W. F. 1976. *Criminal Justice and Victimization.* Beverly Hills: Sage.

McLaughlin, N. 1998a. "How to Become a Forgotten Intellectual." *Sociological Forum* 13:215–46.

———. 1998b. "Why Do Schools of Thought Fail?" *Journal of the History of the Behavioral Sciences* 34:113–34.

McMichael, P. 1990. "Incorporating Comparison within a World-Historical Perspective." *American Sociological Review* 55:385–97.

McNeill, W. H. 1991. *Hutchins' University.* Chicago: University of Chicago Press.

Melossi, D. 1985. "Overcoming the Crisis in Critical Criminology." *Criminology* 23:193–208.

Merton, R. K. 1973. *The Sociology of Science.* Chicago: University of Chicago Press.

Meyer, A. [1919] 1948. "The Life Chart." In *The Commonsense Psychiatry of Dr. Adolf Meyer.* Ed. A. Lief, 418–22. New York: McGraw Hill.

Moffatt, M. 1979. *An Untouchable Community in South India.* Princeton: Princeton University Press.

Morland, J. K. 1958. *Millways of Kent.* Chapel Hill: University of North Carolina Press.

Mulkay, M., and N. Gilbert. 1982. "What Is the Ultimate Question?" *Social Studies of Science* 12:309–19.

Mullins, N. C. 1973. *Theories and Theory Groups in Contemporary American Sociology.* New York: Harper.

Novak, W. 1996. *The People's Welfare.* Chapel Hill: University of North Carolina Press.

Novick, P. 1988. *That Noble Dream.* Cambridge: Cambridge University Press.

Ogburn, W. F., and A. Goldenweiser. 1927. *The Social Sciences.* Boston: Houghton Mifflin.

Oleson, A., and J. Voss, eds. 1979. *The Organization of Knowledge in Modern America.* Baltimore: Johns Hopkins University Press.

O'Neill, W. L. 1986. *American High.* New York: Free Press.

Otter, S. 1998. " 'White Trash' as Cultural Image." B.A. paper, Department of Sociology, University of Chicago.

Padgett, J. F. 1981. "Hierarchy and Ecological Control in Federal Budgetary Decision-Making." *American Journal of Sociology* 87:75–129.

Parsons, T. 1967. *Sociological Theory and Modern Society.* New York: Free Press.

Paton, G. W. [1946] 1964. *Jurisprudence.* Oxford: Oxford University Press.

Peitgen, H-O., H. Jürgens, and D. Saupe. *Chaos and Fractals.* New York: Springer.

Pelikan, J. 1971–89. *The Christian Tradition.* 5 vols. Chicago: University of Chicago Press.

Penick, B. K., and M. E. B. Owens. 1976. *Surveying Crime.* Washington: NAS.

Pfohl, S. 1985. "Towards a Sociological Deconstruction of Social Problems." *Social Problems* 32:228–32.

Piaget, J. [1935] 1963. *The Origins of Intelligence in Children.* New York: Norton.

Polanyi, M. 1958. *Personal Knowledge.* Chicago: University of Chicago Press.

Pollner, M. 1978. "Constitutive and Mundane Versions of Labeling Theory." *Human Studies* 1:269–88.

Propp, V. 1975. *Morphology of the Folktale.* Austin: University of Texas Press.

Quinney, R. 1977. *Class, State, and Crime.* New York: D. McKay.

Rabkin, J., and E. L. Struening. 1976. "Life Events, Stress, and Illness." *Science* 194 (4269): 1013–20.

Rafter, N. H. 1990. "The Social Construction of Crime and Crime Control." *Journal of Research in Crime and Delinquency* 27:376–389

Ragin, C. 1987. *The Comparative Method.* Berkeley and Los Angeles: University of California Press.

Reiss, A. J. 1961. *Occupations and Social Status.* New York: Free Press.

———. 1967. "Measurement of the Amount of Crime." U.S. President's Commission on Law Enforcement and the Administration of Justice, Survey #3. Chicago: National Opinion Research Center.

Reiter, J. B. 1993. "A Gentleman's B." *Harvard Crimson,* 15 March 1993.

Repplier, A. 1910. "The Nervous Strain." *Atlantic Monthly* 106:198–201.

Reskin, B., and P. Roos. 1990. *Job Queues, Gender Queues.* Philadelphia: Temple University Press.

Reskin, B., and T. Steiger. 1990. "Baking and Baking Off." In B. Reskin and P. Roos 1990, 257–74.

Richards, E., and J. Schuster. 1989. "The Feminine Method as Myth and Accounting Resource." *Social Studies of Science* 19:697–720.

Ricoeur, P. 1984–85. *Time and Narrative.* 3 vols. Chicago: University of Chicago Press.

Roos, P. A., and C. Jones. 1993. "Shifting Gender Boundaries." *Work and Occupations* 20:395–428.

Rosen, G. 1959. "Social Stress and Mental Disease from the 18th Century to the Present." *Milbank Memorial Fund Quarterly* 37:5–32.

Rosenberg, C. E. 1962. "The Place of George M. Beard in 19th Century Psychiatry." *Bulletin of the History of Medicine* 36:245–259.

Rosenberg, H. 1959. *The Tradition of the New.* New York: Horizon Press.

Ross, C. E., and J. Mirowsky. 1979. "A Comparison of Life-Event Weighting Schemes." *Journal of Health and Social Behavior* 20:166–177.

Ross, D. 1991. *The Origins of American Social Science.* Cambridge: Cambridge University Press.

Rothblatt, S. 1968. *The Revolution of the Dons.* New York: Basic.

Roy, W. G. 1987a. *Comparative Historical Sociology: Teaching Materials and Bibliography.* Washington: American Sociological Association.

———. 1987b. "Time, Place, and People in History and Sociology." *Social Science History* 11:53–62.

Sahlins, M. 1976. *Culture and Practical Reason.* Chicago: University of Chicago Press.

Samuel, R. 1980. "On the Methods of the History Workshop." *History Workshop Journal,* no. 9: 162–76.

Sandefur, R. L. 2000. "Prestige and the Division of Labor." Unpublished ms., University of Chicago, Department of Sociology.

Saussure, F. [1915] 1966. *Course in General Linguistics.* Trans. W. Baskin. New York: McGraw Hill.

Schäfer, W., ed. 1983. *Finalization in Science.* Dordrecht: D. Reidel.

Scheff, T. J. 1966. *Being Mentally Ill.* Chicago: Aldine.

————. 1974. "The Labelling Theory of Mental Illness." *American Sociological Review* 39:444–52.

Schivelbusch, W. 1979. *The Railway Journey.* Trans. A. Hollo. New York: Urizen.

Schneider, J. W. 1985. "Social Problems Theory." *Annual Review of Sociology* 11:209–29.

Scholes, R., and R. Kellogg. 1966. *The Nature of Narrative.* London: Oxford.

Schwartz, M. A. 1987. "Historical Sociology in the History of American Sociology." *Social Science History* 11:1–16.

Scull, A. 1988. "Deviance and Social Control." In *Handbook of Sociology.* Ed. N.J. Smelser, 667–94. Beverly Hills: Sage.

Selbourne, D. 1980. "On the Methods of the History Workshop." *History Workshop Journal,* no. 9: 150–61.

Sellin, T., and M. E. Wolfgang. 1964. *The Measurement of Delinquency.* New York: Wiley.

Selye, H. 1946. "The General Adaptation Syndrome and the Diseases of Adaptation." *Journal of Clinical Endocrinology* 6:117–230.

————. 1976. *Stress in Health and Disease.* Boston: Butterworth.

Sewell, W. H., Jr. 1992. "A Theory of Structure." *American Journal of Sociology* 98:1–29.

Shapin, S. 1994. *A Social History of Truth.* Chicago: University of Chicago Press.

Sherif, M., and C. W. Sherif. 1969. *Interdisciplinary Relationships in the Social Sciences.* Chicago: Aldine.

Skocpol, T. 1979. *States and Social Revolutions.* Cambridge: Cambridge University Press.

————, ed. 1984a. *Vision and Method in Historical Sociology.* Cambridge: Cambridge University Press.

————. 1984b. "Emerging Agendas and Recurrent Strategies in Historical Sociology." In Skocpol 1984a, 356–91.

————. 1987. "Social History and Historical Sociology." *Social Science History* 11:17–30.

————. 1988. "An Uppity Generation and the Revitalization of Macroscopic Sociology." *Theory and Society* 17:627–43.

Skura, B. 1976. "Constraints on a Reform Movement." *Social Problems* 24:15–36.

Slezak, P. 1989. "Scientific Discovery by Computer as Empirical Refutation of the Strong Programme." *Social Studies of Science* 19:563–600.

Small, A. W. 1911. "Socialism in the Light of Social Science." *American Journal of Sociology* 17:804–19.

Smith, K. R. 1985. "Work Life and Health as Competing Careers." In *Life Course Dynamics.* Ed. G. Elder, 156–87. Ithaca: Cornell.

Social Science Research Council. 1934. *Decennial Report, 1923–1933.* New York: SSRC.

Somers, M. R. 1996. "Where Is Sociology after the Historic Turn?" In MacDonald 1996a, 53–89.

Sorokin, P. A. 1956. *Fads and Foibles in Modern Sociology and Related Sciences.* Chicago: Henry Regnery.

Spector, M., and J. I. Kitsuse. 1987. *Constructing Social Problems.* New York: Aldine de Gruyter.

Sprague, D. N. 1978. "A Quantitative Assessment of the Quantitative Revolution." *Canadian Journal of History* 13:177–92.

Stark, W. 1958. *The Sociology of Knowledge.* London: Routledge.

Stedman Jones, G. 1976. "From Historical Sociology to Sociological History." *British Journal of Sociology* 27:295–305.

Stinchcombe, A. L. 1968. *Constructing Social Theories.* New York: Harcourt, Brace and World.

Stokesbury, J. L. 1995. *A Short History of the Civil War.* New York: William Morrow.

Suleiman, E. N. 1978. *Elites in French Society.* Princeton: Princeton University Press.

Suttles, G. D. 1968. *The Social Order of the Slum.* Chicago: University of Chicago Press.

———. 1972. *The Social Construction of Communities.* Chicago: University of Chicago Press.

Swierenga, R. 1970, ed. *Quantification in American History.* New York: Atheneum.

Szasz, T. 1961. *The Myth of Mental Illness.* New York: Harper.

Szreter, S. 1993. "The Official Representation of Social Classes in Britain, the United States, and France." *Comparative Studies in Society and History* 35:285–317.

Sztompka, P. 1986. "The Renaissance of Historical Orientation in Sociology." *International Sociology* 1:321–37.

Tannenbaum, F. 1938. *Crime and the Community.* Boston: Ginn.

Taylor, I., P. Walton, and J. Young. 1973. *The New Criminology.* New York: Harper.

Teilhard de Chardin, P. 1961. *The Phenomenon of Man.* New York: Harper.

Tennant, C., P. Langelud, and D. Byrne. 1985. "The Concept of Stress." *Australia and New Zealand Journal of Psychiatry* 19:113–18.

Thernstrom, S. 1964. *Poverty and Progress.* Cambridge: Harvard University Press.

Thoits, P. A. 1982. "Conceptual, Methodological, and Theoretical Problems in Studying Social Support as a Buffering System for Stress." *Journal of Health and Social Behavior* 23:145–59.

———. 1995. "Stress, Coping, and Social Support Processes." *Journal of Health and Social Behavior.* Extra issue:53–79.

Thomas, W. I., and F. Znaniecki. 1918–20. *The Polish Peasant in Europe and America.* 5 vols. Chicago: University of Chicago Press (vols. 1–2); Boston: R. G. Badger (vols. 3–5).

Thompson, E. P. 1966. *The Making of the English Working Class.* New York: Vintage.

Tilly, C. 1981. *As Sociology Meets History.* New York: Academic.

———. 1984. *Big Structures, Large Processes, Huge Comparisons.* New York: Russell Sage.

Todorov, T. 1969. *Grammaire du Décameron.* The Hague: Mouton.

———. 1977. *Poetics of Prose.* Ithaca: Cornell University Press.

Trollope, A. [1874] 1983. *Phineas Redux.* Oxford: Oxford University Press.

Turner, S., and R. A. Factor. 1994. *Max Weber.* London: Routledge.

Veysey, L. R. 1965. *The Emergence of the American University.* Chicago: University of Chicago Press.

Vico, G. [1744] 1961. *The New Science.* Trans. T. G. Bergin and M. H. Fisch. New York: Doubleday.

Vine, I. 1981. "Crowding and Stress." *Current Psychological Reviews* 1: 305–23.

Vogel, L. Forthcoming. "Telling Tales." *Journal of Women's History.*

Wagner, P., and B. Wittrock. 1990. "States, Institutions, and Discourses." In *Discourses on Society.* Vol. 15. Ed. P. Wagner, B. Wittrock, and R. Whitley, 331–57. Dordrecht: Kluwer.

Walzer, M. 1965. *The Revolution of the Saints.* Cambridge: Harvard University Press.

Warner, W. L., and P. S. Lunt. 1941. *The Social Life of a Modern Community.* New Haven: Yale University Press.

Weber, M. [1922] 1978. *Economy and Society.* Ed. G. Roth and C. Wittich. Berkeley and Los Angeles: University of California Press.

Wedel, J. 1986. *The Private Poland.* New York: Facts on File.

Weisz, G. 1983. *The Emergence of Modern Universities in France.* Princeton: Princeton University Press.

Whewell, W. 1989. *Theory of Scientific Method.* Indianapolis: Hackett.

White, H. 1973. *Metahistory.* Baltimore: Johns Hopkins University Press.

White, H. C. 1970. *Chains of Opportunity.* Cambridge: Harvard University Press.

White, H. C., S. A. Boorman, and R. L. Breiger. 1976. "Social Structure from Multiple Networks." *American Journal of Sociology* 81:730–80.

Whitehead, A. N. 1925. *Science and the Modern World.* New York: NAL.

Whitley, R. 1984. *The Intellectual and Social Organization of the Sciences.* Oxford: Clarendon Press.

Whitman, D. 1996. "I'm OK, You're Not." *U.S. News and World Report,* 16 December, 24–30.

Wiener, J. 1989. "Radical History and the Crisis in American History." *Journal of American History* 76:399–434.

Wilson, K. G. 1979. "Problems in Physics with Many Scales of Length." *Scientific American* 241 (August):158–79.

Wirth, L. 1937. "Report on the History, Activities, and Policies of the Social Science Research Council." Prepared for the Committee on Review of Council Policy. Typescript, Joseph Regenstein Library, University of Chicago.

———. 1940. *Eleven Twenty-Six.* Chicago: University of Chicago Press.

Woolgar, S. 1981. "Interests and Explanation in the Social Study of Science." *Social Studies of Science* 11:365–94.

————. 1989. "A Coffeehouse Conversation on the Possibility of Mechanizing Discovery and its Sociological Analysis." *Social Studies of Science* 19:658–67.

Woolgar, S., and D. Pawluch. 1985. "Ontological Gerrymandering." *Social Problems* 32:214–27.

Zablocki, B. D. 1971. *The Joyful Community.* Chicago: University of Chicago Press.

Index

This book contains glancing mention of many people and examples. I have limited the index to examples and people who make a substantial appearance. All definitions of special terms appear at the heading "concept of." I thank Jim Anderson of Rutgers for teaching me how to index.